AN ASTROLOGICAL MANDALA The Cycle of Transformations and Its 360 Symbolic Phases

Dane Rudhyar
AN ASTROLOGICAL MANDALA The Cycle of Transformations and Its 360 Symbolic Phases

 Vintage Books

A Division of Random House
New York

Library of Congress Cataloging in Publication Data
Rudhyar, Dane, 1895–
   An astrological mandala.
   1.   Astrology.   I.   Title.
[BF1708.1.R835 1974]   133.5   73–14736
ISBN 0–394–71992–1

Manufactured in the United States of America
0123456789B

To Sam Bercholz
in grateful appreciation
and friendship

D.R.

Contents

AN ASTROLOGICAL MANDALA The Cycle of Transformations and Its 360 Symbolic Phases

Introduction

AFTER I MET MARC EDMUND JONES IN LOS ANGELES IN 1930, he was generous enough to mail me copies of the mimeographed courses on astrology he was then sending to the members of the Sabian Assembly which he had founded.* "Symbolical Astrology" was written in 1931, and it listed and interpreted symbols for each degree of the zodiac. I became very much interested in these symbols which, for various reasons that I will presently state, I found far superior to previously published sets of degree symbols; and when urged by my friend Alice Bailey, I decided to write my book *The Astrology of Personality* (summer 1934 to spring 1936) I asked Marc Jones for permission to include in it a condensed version of the symbols and their interpretations. This permission was readily granted.

While I saw the original index cards on which brief descriptions of the symbols were written as received in 1925 through the intermediary of Elsie Wheeler—under circumstances

*In order to answer questions which have occasionally been asked of me, may I state that I never have been a member of the Sabian Assembly, nor have I enrolled in any of Marc Jones's classes.

which I shall describe in Chapter 2—I had not sufficiently studied and meditated upon these original descriptions to realize
how different they were from what was written in the mimeographed course, which came some six years later. Thus I was
content to follow the statements and interpretations of the
course. I had, however, to condense them; and I introduced
here and there remarks which had reference to depth psychology, for in 1933 I had become deeply interested in Carl Jung's
writing. I had first studied astrology in 1920, but at that time I
was mainly occupied with musical composition and the study of
Hindu philosophy and theosophy. It took the combination of
Marc Jones's approach and of Jung's psychology, and of various
personal changes and opportunities, to make me realize the
possibility of using astrology as a practical application of a cosmic, holistic and cyclic philosophy of existence.

As I came more and more to use the 360 Sabian symbols I
grew dissatisfied with many of their formulations and interpretations, even though I was ever more amazed by the inner
structure of the entire series, especially considering the totally
aleatory manner in which the symbols were obtained. As a result I started to write a long series of articles, entitled *The Wheel
of Significance,* which were published serially in *American Astrology* magazine between October 1944 and December 1945.

In 1953 Marc Jones published his book *The Sabian Symbols
in Astrology,* in which he used the brief original descriptions of
the symbols obtained in 1925 in San Diego. He added to these
descriptions completely new and different interpretations
which were conditioned by his special social psychology and
abstract philosophy, and which pointed to a relationship between opposite zodiacal degrees. And in 1954 and 1955 *American Astrology* printed four articles I had written presenting
some new ideas about the symbols and particularly about the
possibility of making them serve a purpose similar to that which
people today seek to satisfy through the use of the symbols of
the I Ching.

I shall discuss the validity and the limits of such a use of the
Sabian symbols in the last chapter of this book. Part Two, the
largest section of this volume, is consecrated to a reformulation

and complete reinterpretation of the entire series of symbols, considered as a cyclic and structured series which formalizes and reveals the archetypal meaning of 360 basic phases of human experience. Part One introduces the whole subject and discusses the meaning of symbols when used in such a cyclic frame of reference and in relation to a structured process of growth in consciousness. Part Three discusses in greater detail the different ways in which this factor of structured unfoldment can be analyzed and the quite extraordinary results which can be produced by such an analysis.

The book ends with considerations of the use to which this series of Sabian symbols can be put for what might be called, somewhat inaccurately, the purpose of "divination." The study of what is involved in divinatory practices in itself could take up an entire volume, especially as it challenges Western man's concept of time. Here I can only touch upon a few basic points and present a simple way in which the Sabian symbols can be used to answer basic questions which baffle the ordinary conscious mind.

In Marc Jones's version of the symbolic series, particularly in the book published in 1953, the fact that each symbol refers to one degree of the zodiac has been emphasized. It should be clear, however, that the concept of symbolization of a cyclic series of basic individual experiences within the context of our modern society is not to be limited to the study of the meaning of zodiacal degrees. The concept includes, but also transcends, astrology.

While this text is most likely to be used mainly by people interested in astrology and desirous of discovering, as it were, a "new dimension" of astrological interpretation, its validity reaches beyond such a use. The symbols can be applied to any cycle of experience that can be conveniently divided into 360 phases. For instance, it could be used to interpret the cycle of precession of the equinoxes, if one were absolutely sure when this cycle began. It can be used with reference to the cycle of daily motion of the Mid Heaven and Ascendant. Nevertheless, the cycle of the year—the tropical zodiac—is the most natural field for its application.

It is hardly necessary to add that this book leaves many things unsaid concerning both the theory of symbolic series and the interpretation of each of the 360 symbols. But to extend the size of the volume would have been impractical and would defeat the essential purpose of my writing. I can only hope that in these pages the attentive reader and user of the symbols will find, distilled into significant statements and consciousness-expanding vistas, much of the harvest of a long and complex life span of experience in many fields of creative and philosophical activity—a life concerned with significance and understanding.

This is not a book for cursory reading, no more than is Richard Wilhelm's translation of the texts and commentaries of the I Ching. The material in it is to be *used*, to serve as a catalyst to deepen thinking about individual experiences and their essential meaning. It is a book about MEANING. And a life without meaning is hardly worth living. The worth of an individual indeed depends upon the meaning and the structural, archetypal character with which he endows all his acts, and as well his feelings and his thoughts.

Part One

THE INTERPRETATION OF LIFE CYCLES AS A CLOSED SERIES OF ARCHETYPAL PHASES

1. Symbols and the Cyclic Character of Human Experience

◉

THERE HAS PROBABLY BEEN NO TIME IN THE HISTORY OF human civilization when the word symbol or its equivalent in any language has been as much used or given so many varied meanings as it is today. Some philosophers and psychologists have coined new words in an attempt to make these meanings more precise. The words "symbol" and "sign" have been differentiated, and the distinction is useful provided no strict boundaries are established between the two sets of meaning. Roughly speaking, a sign is a deliberately shaped indication revealing that certain conditions or circumstances are to be expected at a certain place or time. For instance, road signs tell the motorist that a dangerous turn or crossing lies ahead, or that certain roads lead to specific places. A sign, if precise and accurate, is strictly factual. It is a conventional and socially understandable way of presenting facts.

Facts, however, are strange entities, and different human beings respond to them differently according to their temperament, expectations, or emotional states. A "mere fact" can differ considerably from an "expected fact." The rationalist and the scientist may think they deal with mere facts, but these facts can arouse many varied emotions. If they reach a collectivity of men at special times their meaning can be magnified or distorted and can radiate into many unforeseen directions. Einstein's formula, $e = mc^2$, refers to a mere fact of the atomic realm, but after Hiroshima it became far more than a sign or a factual indication of the objective relationship of energy to mass. It stood as a symbol of the possible fate which the Western scientific mind and technology had foisted upon mankind, incorporating an immense variety of direct or indirect consequences, a constellation of emotions, such as pride, greed and fear. Indeed, a basic question about the end value and moral implications of a certain type of knowledge and of its unprotected and possibly premature dissemination became implied in the fact-defining equation. Einstein's objective discovery and the purely factual statement of it has become an extremely potent symbol of the state of existence which mankind has reached today—and it is a crucial and potentially frightening as well as perhaps inspiring and challenging state. As I stated in my recent book *The Planetarization of Consciousness**:

A fact is what it is *particularly and exclusively* as a fact; it can be described and recorded in such a manner that, at least theoretically speaking, its precise character is not open to doubt. We might also say that "facts" belong to the category of rational entities: these entities can be precisely defined inasmuch as the definition implies all that they *are not*, i.e. the definition essentially excludes other conceptual entities. On the other hand when one deals with a symbol one is in the presence of something that goes beyond the rational and the factual, something *that is more than it is*, because the symbol describes not only what it appears to be rationally and objectively, but also the relationship between a specific human need and the possibility of satisfying this need.

A symbol is formulated when there is a human need for it. It may be a strictly personal need. The psychological or prophetic dreams of a particular person belong to this category; they bring to the individual an *intimation* of a particular condi-

*Cf. Chapter IX, "Symbols and Values," p. 256.

tion of existence, be it physiological, psychological or social. They may suggest an answer to a problem, perhaps until then but superficially understood. Likewise when a clairvoyant to whom a client has come with an unsolved problem "sees" in front of him or in his mind a symbolic shape or a scene with several actors, this should theoretically be an answer to the client's need, although the need may as yet be only subconscious or half conscious. The symbol is "person-centered."

Similarly, for the humanistic astrologer, a birth chart is a person-centered symbol.* That is to say, it carries a "message" —the symbolic formulation of the individual's dharma. It *suggests* how he can best actualize the innate potentialities of his particular and unique selfhood. It is a symbol, a mandala, or logos, a word of power. Astrology, seen from this point of view, is a language of symbols. Because it is a language, it implies a process of unfoldment of an idea of feeling-response. A birth chart is static, yet it can be "progressed" and related to the continuing movements of the planets after birth ("transits"). In the same sense, a true mandala is more than a static geometrical figure; it suggests a process of unfoldment or, as Carl Jung might have said, of "individuation."

The entire zodiac constitutes a mandala. There are time mandalas as well as space mandalas. The cycle of transformations studied in this book is a time mandala. It has rhythm as well as form. Any language, particularly any poem, also has rhythm and form. The 360 Sabian symbols are words in a vast cosmic poem whose meaning transcends the often banal images visualized by the clairvoyant.†

All words are symbols. They answer the basic human need of *communication*. At first they seem to have often been onomatopoeia, i.e. vocal imitations of actually heard sounds, sounds which the collective experience of the men of a tribe associated with a particular animal or natural phenomenon. A

*Cf. My *Humanistic Astrology* series of booklets, particularly No. 1: "Astrology for New Minds."

†For a thorough study of the mandala, the reader is referred to the beautifully illustrated book *Mandala* (Shambala Publications, Berkeley, California, 1972) by José and Miriam Argüelles.

developed language is a collection of symbols; some of its words go beyond merely representing entities, to expressing the character of the relationship between entities, or the quality of an activity (past, present, or future) and often its biological polarity or gender. Algebra is a symbolic language which answers the need for precise yet abstract and universal statements of relationships; its formulas are actually more than mere statements of fact, for they imply the existence of universal order and the belief in permanent laws of nature and "constants."

All cultures depend on the use of symbols which are accepted more or less consciously by the total community. Cultural institutions, and the arts and sciences of a fully developed community, whether "primitive" or modern, constitute essentially complex and systematized organizations of symbols which *structure* the behavior, basic feelings and thinking of the human beings belonging to this culture. As the culture develops, matures and decays, so do the symbols on which it rests and from which its cohesive strength and vitality emerge.

SYMBOLS INTEGRATE THE SEPARATE EXPERIENCES OF A VAST number of men. They take events from the realm of the fortuitous, the unprecedented, the unique and the incomprehensible to the realm of "universals." The logical sequence of symbols which one finds in all languages, in all scientific theories, in all traditional art forms and in all religious rituals creates from the seemingly chaotic, unpredictable and senseless facts of life patterns of order and meaning. A thousand events or personal situations come to be seen as mere variations on a central theme. The symbol depicts for us this one significant theme. And the theme is part of a coherent sequence of similar challenges, which acquire purpose through their interrelationship. Expressed through symbols, life becomes condensed into a relatively few *interrelated* units of experience. Each unit is a concentrate of the experiences of millions of people.

Today, we who have been molded by the Western tradition usually think that there is for each of us an infinite variety of possible experiences. What we experience is strictly our own;

every moment is new; no event is ever repeated. However, while it is true that human experience is unlimited, the normal experience of man is finite insofar as the number of *characteristic and significant* types of experiences is concerned. If a man could be moving, regardless of physical obstacles, on the surface of the globe along the equator, he could go on endlessly. His motion would be "unlimited." Yet his experiences of conditions and scenes along the route would be finite. After having completed a whole turn around the globe he would begin to encounter the same geographical features again. His experiences would *basically* repeat themselves, *even though he might respond to them differently at each new encounter*. In the same way, man's basic life experiences constitute a closed series. By "basic" I mean typical and characteristic underneath surface variations.

We find the same principle of *repeated series of experiences* in relation to time. Time is cyclic. Everything that lives begins, reaches a climax and ends—*but only to begin again*. The universal illustration of this is the cycle of the seasons in temperate climates.

That there is a yearly cycle of the seasons does not mean, however, that we can expect an exact and literal repetition of actual events or facts each year. What recur are, for the living plant, basic challenges of growth. Each spring the seeds of wheat are new seeds, the weather differs somewhat, and other facts may vary. But the overall, basic spring challenge for the species of wheat is that there should be germination and growth. The *facts* may vary, but the meaning remains, year after year.

In other words, human experience is essentially cyclic and it unfolds according to structural principles. However varied men's experiences may appear to be, they nevertheless fall within the limits of a series of what might also be called "archetypal" meanings. Such a series has a recurring character insofar as its structure is concerned; it constitutes a *whole of meanings*. But I cannot repeat enough that "structure" and "contents" belong, as it were, to two different realms, even if these realms interpenetrate at every point.

I have discussed these ideas in *The Planetarization of Consciousness*, but they have to be restated briefly here because if they are not understood and at least accepted as significant hypotheses, the logical and philosophical foundation for the use of cyclic series of symbols—as, for example, the I Ching and the Sabian series—loses all solidity. Indeed, the whole of astrology rests philosophically on the basic idea that it is possible to refer *all* the essential functions implied in the existence of an *organized field of activity*, and especially of a living organism, to ten variables represented by the ten "planets" of modern astrology (including the Sun and Moon). Astrology also claims that the twelve Houses constitute archetypal classes of experiences necessary for the development of a mature individual person, and that the twelve *signs* of the zodiac refer to twelve basic modes of "energy," or archetypal *qualities of being*, which essentially color any functional activity (i.e. planet) operating in their fields. In these and related instances the basic idea is always that we are living in an ordered and structured universe which constitutes a "cyclocosmic" whole, which is finite. All structured fields of activity are *finite*, yet the existential events and the possibilities of interrelationships are *indefinite*—which does not mean infinite!

We have been more or less accustomed to the idea that the internal activities of any organism are limited and periodical. We speak of the cycle of food metabolism, of blood circulation, and in a broader sense of the cycle of activity of the endocrine glands throughout a complete life cycle, from birth to death. But we are usually unready to assume that the experiences of the person as a whole are also limited and periodical; or, to put it differently, to admit that there are only *a certain number of basic meanings* to be gathered by a human being in his lifetime, and that these meanings can be seen in terms of structural and cyclic sequence.

Again, this does not mean that a person cannot experience a great variety of events. He may have many thoughts and experiences. But to experience events is one thing; to release from them vital and creative meanings is another. What counts, spiritually speaking, is the *harvest of meanings* a person is able to gather from these many and varied experiences. For this reason a life crowded with events is not necessarily the richest in meanings.

Hindu yogis claim that the number of breaths an individual can take during a lifetime is limited and set; this might apply to heartbeats as well. All natural organic functions are limited or finite in their schedule of operation, but what sets the boundaries is *generic human nature*. The amount of vitality wound up in the germ cell is probably limited. An individual, however, *acting as an individual and having succeeded in becoming free from collective patterns*, may break through the circle of limitations and tap a deeper source of life and consciousness; this indeed is what true occultism is about.

Generically man is organically bounded; as a creative and free individual, however, he can break through nature's "Ring-Pass-Not" (to use an occult term) and become a functioning part within a greater organism, thus becoming vitalized by the power of this greater life. Generically speaking, collectively speaking, culturally speaking, a person has a certain *range of meanings* open to him for him to incorporate into his actual experience. It is to this "range of meanings"—conditioned by collective factors and controlled by the images of the collective Unconscious of his race and culture—that the series of picture symbols of the Chinese I Ching as well as the series of 360 Sabian symbols refer.

Even though a normal cultured person meets all the facts of experience that can possibly be crowded into the few decades of life, only those experiences from which meaning has been extracted count spiritually, and are remembered. These meanings, finite in terms of their archetypal characteristics, constitute an organic whole because they are creative products of the person's total personality, which is an "organism" in the broader sense of the term. In their sequence and unfoldment they display an organic and cyclic quality; and the structural factor in this process of extraction of meanings from experience can be derived from simple numerical principles, such as those of the I Ching or the Sabain cycle of symbols.

In the Chinese system, the basic mathematical principle of

structuring is fundamentally dualistic. There are two life principles operating in and through all human experiences: Yang and Yin—light and darkness, positive and negative, Day-force and Night-force, masculine and feminine, "essence" and "life," "Logos" and "Eros," etcetera. These two polarities, combined in a three-fold and six-fold pattern of interaction (or at three and six "levels" of being) produce the eight permutations represented by the trigrams of the I Ching, and the sixty-four hexagrams ($8 = 2^3$, and $64 = 2^6$. The next increase, 2^{12}, would be 4096).

In the Sabian system, the cyclic structure is more complex: it is founded upon a pattern derived from the relationship between the day and the year—periods which constitute the two most basic factors in the structuring of human experience. It is true that the year contains more than 360 days, which means that the earth rotates more than 360 times around its polar axis during a complete revolution around its orbit; but an intriguing feature common to all celestial periods is that they can never be measured in whole numbers and no planetary cycle is an exact multiple of another.

This means that one has to distinguish between archetypal and existential cycles and relationships. *Rationally* we divide the circle into 4 or 6, or 360 parts; but the *facts of existence* present us with a little over 365 days of the year-cycle. The 360-degree zodiac is *a formula of archetypal relationships;* but our human experience presents to our consciousness a slightly larger sequence of days and nights. The 360-degree cycle refers to *the meaning* of experience; the days-and-nights sequence to *the facts* of experience.

We shall see how this 360-degree pattern subdivides itself geometrically through a two-fold, three-fold, four-fold, five-fold and six-fold rational segmentation. Such interior processes of subdivision of the *organic* series of 360 degrees define various patterns of relationships and subseries of degrees which, considered in their entirety, constitute the structure of a cycle of meanings. *No cyclic series of symbols can be considered significant which does not reveal some definite kind of internal structuring, however interesting and apt isolated symbols may be.*

This is why, in my opinion, out of the few sets of 360 degree symbols which have been recorded in Western astrology only the Sabian symbols should be considered truly valid. Other sets might reveal an equally significant internal structure if carefully studied and reformulated, but I have not seen any work done in that direction. The issue here reaches much deeper than a superficial evaluation of this or that set of 360 symbols. It deals with the difference between a holistic and an atomistic approach to human experience and to life or knowledge in general.

When we deal with *any* cyclic series of factors or phases, merely to consider the character, quality and value of the symbolic representation of *any one* of these factors as a separate entity without an essential (or structural) relationship to all the others makes no sense to the holistic mind. Every phase no doubt has a character of its own which can be described in one way or another, but this character should be given some kind of functional or "organic" meaning in terms of the cyclic process as a whole. If one looks at the process of growth of an organism every phase of that process has a functional meaning in relation to the preceding and succeeding phases. It does not represent an isolated occurrence. In the same way, if one studies the 22 Tarot cards or the 64 symbols of the I Ching, one is dealing with a succession of phases referring to a whole process; the 12 signs of the tropical zodiac—which as a whole refer to the annual cyclic relationship of the Earth to the Sun—likewise have meaning according to their position in the complete cycle of the year.

In my book *The Pulse of Life* (published in 1943, but originally written as a series of articles a few years earlier)* I stressed the fact that every zodiacal sign represents a specific combination of two interacting and interdependent forces, the Day-force and the Night-force (Yang and Yin). It is the relative intensities of these two forces and their polarization which determines fundamentally or structurally the dynamic nature and function of each sign.

*Present edition: Shambala Publications, Berkeley, California, 1970.

The zodiac as a whole refers to a vitalistic process of transformation of energy; but when we deal with the series of 360 degree symbols we see the relationship of the Earth to the Sun operating at a different level. It is a level at which literally every day-and-night period (every rotation of the globe) acquires a symbolic and structural meaning. The twelve-fold zodiac deals essentially with varying modalities of solar energy, as the waves of this energy strike the Earth. It deals with *life*. The series of 360 degrees deals with *meaning*. It represents, I repeat, a finite cyclic series of meanings which an individual *may* extract from experiences related to these degrees and their symbols; while he may, the individual surely does not *need* to discover, assimilate and consciously become aware of these meanings.

The potentiality of meaning depends basically on the stage of development of mankind and especially of any particular culture out of whose collective Unconscious (or archetypal Mind) the symbols have emerged, becoming formed into images, scenes and words. The Chinese hexagrams and symbols recorded in the I Ching were not based on degrees of the zodiacal cycle, since they took shape out of a simple, uncomplicated, agricultural culture at the "vitalistic" stage of human society—a stage basically related to the male-female polarities of the life force. Yet the 64 symbols formulate profound meanings deeply rooted in the universal experience of man when in close relationship to the energies of Earth-nature, and of his own generic nature as well. The symbols use an imagery that is close to the foundations of the natural life—and these foundations are still very real and active in the immense majority of human beings.

Today we live in a much more complex and highly individualistic society, and it is logical to find the need for a much greater number of symbols. In the Sabain set some of these symbols deal with rather trivial scenes depicting phases of American life; others are far more fundamental in their philosophical implications. Taken together they present a characteristic motley picture of American society at the beginning of the second quarter of the twentieth century. As our entire globe is "Americanized" and technologized, it could be that these Sabian symbols will have a long life. The formulations can be altered, and Marc Jones himself has modified them greatly several times. In this book I have kept the pictures as originally recorded, but I have rephrased obscure statements and tried to clarify the contents of the symbols through their relationship to preceding and following images.

What is important is that the series of symbols should bring order and meaning to what very often seems a chaotic and confused sequence of life events, by revealing the meaning, quality, direction and purpose of any puzzling situation which the inquirer seems unable successfully to cope with by means of rational judgments. Chaotic as events may be, one can nevertheless state that a person has the experiences he is entitled to, or has asked for, consciously or not—and no others. Events occur in relation to the process of actualization of his innate potential of being, i.e. his individual self. Each basic event *conditions* the manner in which the person is to take a step ahead in his structural development. Whether or not the individual takes this step, and the quality of his advance—which can also appear to be a temporary regression—depends on the meaning he gives to the event. He may not be truly aware of giving it a particular meaning, but in some manner his organism and/or his ego responds as a result of past sociocultural and personal conditioning.

Conflicts arise because various parts of the personality very often give different value to events; especially in periods of deep-seated cultural and social confusion when collectively accepted traditional values are breaking down, *conflicts of meaning* are frequently experienced. Values and meanings are always conditioned by certain "frames of reference." When old sociocultural and religious-ethical frames of reference have become unreliable and can no longer convincingly structure the series of experiences and the responses of individuals, the urge to discover some new frame of reference becomes urgently necessary. And it is for this reason that today's disenchanted adults and restless, disbelieving youth—once they thoroughly weary of practices and groups which seek to "de-condition" them by freeing them from binding patterns and old "hang-ups," yet offer no convincing and secure foundation for a new conception of order—are searching for some kind of "revelation" with a superhuman and even superrational and supermental origin.

This is obviously the deepest reason for the present popularity of astrology; for in the order of the cosmos the uprooted consciousness hopes to find a solid frame of reference from which new meanings—new to him—can be derived. These new meanings in turn can provide him with the yearned-for inner security.

In this sense, astrology constitutes a cosmic type of oracle, at least insofar as it is person-centered, referring to the problems and the search for meaning of individual persons. The "solar astrology" of popular magazines and newspaper columns is oracular in that it is meant to convey to human beings, categorized according to the twelve Sun signs, general value judgments concerning the character of those responses to everyday circumstances which would be most suited to their basic temperaments. The position of the planets in zodiacal signs and their mutual relationships are believed to establish such value judgments. That is to say, the state of the solar system at any time is said to provide an oracular message to human beings according to their Sun-sign relationship to the solar system.

Obviously such an oracle can at best be very general, and unless it is formulated in very abstract terms—which then are susceptible of an infinite variety of interpretations—it can be ludicrous and meaningless for the individual. On the other hand, the oracular potentiality of astrology becomes precisely focused in what is called "horary astrology," for there a particular individual at a precise moment demands the solution to a particular problem. The pattern of the sky for that precise moment requires a very complex type of interpretation, but traditional rules are available to at least guide the interpretation.

We find the same type of situation whenever the I Ching is asked for oracular pronouncements. The Sabian symbols can serve the same function, even though so far the astrologers who have made use of them have applied them almost exclusively to giving a new dimension of meaning to the exact positions of the planets and the angles in the charts erected for the birth moment of an individual, or for some spectacular event.

What is to be stressed, as we begin the study of the Sabian symbols, is that their character should be considered at two levels, one purely abstract, the other existential (i.e. the image or scene depicted in the symbol). A degree symbol has archetypal meaning because it is, let us say, the eleventh in a series of 360 symbols, and because the number 360 is the result of *the abstracted relationship* between the daily axial rotation and the yearly orbital revolution of the Earth. It has an existential meaning because it carries a "revealed" pictorial symbol; in this case *The ruler of a nation* (cf. p. 57).

The revealed image could theoretically be dispensed with. But how then would we interpret the meaning of the eleventh phase in a cyclic process numbering 360 phases? Astrology could help us by saying that the year's cyclic process archetypally begins at the spring equinox, and therefore that the eleventh phase of the process (Aries 11°) refers to the eleventh day after the equinox. But one could hardly base a significant value judgment dealing with either the position of Jupiter in a birth chart or the answer to what could be expected of a new relationship just entered into, on the assumed character of the eleventh day of spring. One has to obtain a more definitive existential situation or image from which the value judgment can be extracted, a situation or image *truly full of potentiality of meaning*.

But here again we have to return to the point that what is "full potentiality of meaning" for the man of one culture may not have this same character for a man of another culture. Many of the Sabian symbols would have meant nothing whatsoever to a Chinese of the early Dynasties. In the same way, some of the symbols of the I Ching need to be given modernized interpretations to fit the search for meaning of an American faced with the intricate and artificial problems of our complex families or professional existence within chaotic cities.

The difficult question is why the symbols of the Sabian series should be significant. For the empirically minded person this question would immediately be rephrased: *Are* they significant? Do they really work?

We shall deal with these questions in the next chapter. But in closing this discussion it seems necessary to state that the symbolic and holistic characterization of the 360 degrees of the zodiac has nothing to do with the analytical and statistical attempts, which a number of astrologers have been making for some time, to relate at least some degrees of the zodiac to specific bio-psychological characteristics or tendencies and to particular faculties or diseases. In these attempts the analytical and would-be scientific astrologer is not concerned with meaning, but only with definite and standardized traits of human nature, unusual or outstanding circumstances, or telluric events. The entire procedure is existential and statistical, and fundamentally it should not interest the individual person. Its results can actually be most detrimental to the individual: for instance, if in the degree characteristics of his Sun or Mars or Ascendant he sees a degree of "suicide" or "insanity" or "consumption" or one showing "homicidal tendencies" or even "homosexuality."

It should be evident to any psychologically alert and intelligent astrologer that such negative and, in several instances, appalling characterizations might easily throw an insecure personality off balance. Making them available to the average person surely has psychologically destructive potentialities. In fact, such statistics should be altogether disregarded in any type of person-centered astrology, for they cannot be taken as a basis for an answer to any problem which an *individual* person may seek to solve by way of astrology, *including the fundamental problems of "Who am I?" and "What am I here for?"* If statistics seem to show that many people dying of tuberculosis have "malefic" planets, or even the Sun and Moon on a particular degree of the zodiac, it does not indicate in any way that a person with Mars, Saturn or the Ascendant on that degree will contract tuberculosis. Perhaps 65 percent of the persons having such a natal configuration can be said to have developed TB; but even if this were so, it tells nothing to an individual with this configuration, for he can just as well belong to the 35 percent who are totally free from the disease.

The modern mind hypnotized by quantitative values and

statistics will claim that if a person knows about the 65 percent possibility he will naturally be "more careful" to avoid causes of the disease or be more alert to early symptoms. But actually this is at best to be blind to the opposite and far more likely probability—that the very fear of being marked for the illness will bring it about.

Man should not seek tensely and self-protectively to avoid or control events. Events do not happen to an individual person; *he happens to them*. He meets them and imparts to them his own meaning. It is only when an individual is placed in complex situations involving unknowable factors—unknowable to his normal perceptions and his rational mind—that he may, and indeed should, seek to broaden his perspective by trying to see the events or the prospects facing him *sub specie aeternitatis*, that is, in their relationship to a cosmic whole of meaning. Carl Jung would probably have said that in such a case an individual mind opens itself to the vast collective Unconscious; I would call it the One Mind of Humanity.

The mind of the human being whose process of individualization has been conditioned by the collective mentality and the traditions of his culture should seek to forget such socioculturalethical factors and to reach a state of "planetary consciousness." He will then come to realize that however baffling and unpredictable his present situation may seem to his analytical and rational mind—which is loaded with precedents, anticipations, doubts and anxieties—this development is part of a universal process. It is a very, very small phase in the evolution of mankind and of the planet Earth and the solar system; seen as a phase within the frame of reference of the whole process, *it makes sense*.

Symbols help man to do this—to make sense of his existence, to see each personal event as a focalized and particularized manifestation of one phase of the whole cosmic process of existence. He can see the most tragic event—tragic by ordinary sociocultural standards—as a phase of growth. At the precise moment when he asks a question from the oracle, the entire universe comes down, as it were, to give him the necessary answer. It is necessary because all truly constructive, creative or redeeming acts are performed *through* the individual person by a focalization of the whole universe. This is the "transpersonal way" of which I have spoken for many years.* It is the way of the symbolic life, which is not merely a life lived in "the presence of God," but a life *lived by* the Divine within the individual person as well as within the entire universe.

The mystic states: "I do not live. God lives me." But if this is actually what takes place, he has become the Avatar of his own Divinity, which is one with the divine Meaning of all existence.

* *Modern Man's Conflicts* (1945–46) and my previous articles in *The Glass Hive* magazine (1930–31) on "The Philosophy of Operative Wholeness"; also more recent volumes like *The Planetarization of Consciousness.*

2. The Sabian Symbols: Their Origin and Internal Structure

⊙

IT IS ESSENTIAL TO KNOW HOW THE SABIAN SYMBOLS WERE obtained in order to understand the intrinsic validity of the entire set, for it reveals a quite startling combination of random selection and subsequent structural order. While the facts surrounding the procedure followed in the visualization of the symbols by a clairvoyant woman, Miss Elsie Wheeler, and their recording by Marc Edmund Jones are not mentioned in the book *The Sabian Symbols in Astrology*, they have been given some publicity for many years and are indeed most relevant in this study.*

I do not know the exact date on which the event occurred, but it was in 1925 and the locale was the large park in the center of San Diego, California. Miss Wheeler and Marc Jones were the two actors, at least as far as physical realities are concerned. During 1936 I visited Miss Wheeler twice at her home in San

*After writing this chapter I came across a published long letter by Marc Edmund Jones in which he explains what led to the production of the Sabian symbols, and describes the manner in which they were obtained. This letter is reproduced in the Appendix (p. 387).

Diego. She was a lovely woman, crippled by arthritis and confined to a wheelchair when I saw her. She was a clairvoyant medium and had a remarkable ability to "see" symbols, a talent which made it possible to help clients who came to see her. This is true of many clairvoyants of this type, but she proved to have the ability to a spectacular degree.

In the morning of a certain day, Marc Jones took Miss Wheeler in his car to the San Diego park and stopped in a quiet place. He had with him a pack of 360 small index cards; each card was blank except for a very small, hardly visible marking at the extreme top right corner indicating a zodiacal sign and degree: for example, Aries 1, Aries 2, Aries 3, etcetera. Marc Jones then began to shuffle the cards thoroughly, and kept shuffling them throughout the operation. He then took one card at random, and without looking at the small marking, so that neither he nor Miss Wheeler could know which zodiacal degree was noted on it, asked her what she saw. Apparently a scene flashed to her inner vision; she described it quickly and Marc Jones made a brief pen notation of what she said. These notations are reproduced exactly in Marc Jones's book. I saw the original pack of 360 cards in 1936 when I was working on the chapter on Sabian symbols for my book *The Astrology of Personality*.

Not only was the procedure entirely aleatory as far as the normal consciousness of the two participants was concerned, but the amazing thing is that the 360 symbols were obtained during a few hours in the morning, and a few hours during the afternoon. I am not certain of the exact number of hours involved, but even if it were four hours in the morning and four in the afternoon, this would mean that on the average 45 symbols were visualized per hour, or one every minute and a half.

What makes this whole production almost incredible is that while it operated purely at random and at a fantastic speed, the result was a series of symbols which, when carefully studied, are shown to possess a definite and very complex internal structure. Some kind of "consciousness" was undoubtedly at work; the question is what type of consciousness—which is likely to mean *whose* consciousness, that of an individual or a collectivity of minds. Marc Jones has related it to the type of occult Brotherhood which apparently existed in ancient Mesopotamia (whence the name "Sabian" that he has used for the group of students he has been directing and teaching for nearly half a century).

But whatever the exact manner in which the Sabian set of symbols was produced, it is not enough merely to say that "they work." What has to be clearly understood is the nature of their validity and what is really implied in their existence and character. One may speak of inspiration from some ancient Brotherhood or the presence of an occult partner in the work, but it is obvious that the scenes and images visualized by Elsie Wheeler are entirely modern and, what is more, in many instances strictly American in character. They contain references which even a European, especially one living in 1925, would have some difficulty understanding. They belong to the collective consciousness of the average educated American.

Thus we have a significant antinomy: randomness versus internal structure, and a purely American mentality (or mentalities, if we include that of Marc Jones) versus a postulated archaic occult source of inspiration. Such a dualistic situation is not unusual in occult or spiritual training, for there the extremes meet and interact to produce a total transformation of the consciousness. In this sense, the polarization of the highly intellectual and abstract mind of Marc Jones, many of whose concepts link him with the medieval scholastics, and of the mediumistic middle-class mentality of Elsie Wheeler also implies a kind of dialectical process. The occult and the commonplace are synthesized in the symbols, which is another way of saying that they should be understood at two levels: the archetypal-structural and the existential. The symbolic images or scenes are existential and relatable to the mostly ordinary experience or dream fantasy of the collective American consciousness; *through* the commonplace and the collective, one may reach the archetypal level at which a cyclic sequence of phases occurs, each phase meant to actualize a specific quality of being and endowed with a structural meaning because of its rank and function within the cycle-as-a-whole, the Eon.

An eonic consciousness is a consciousness able to perceive, at once and as a whole, a complete cycle of existence in which each phase of the structural process is in its own place of destiny (dharma) for the actualization of one of a great number of innate potentialities. The Eon is the cycle-as-a-whole in terms of integrating power and consciousness. The Eon of a particular human life extending from birth to death is, in terms of *consciousness,* the "Soul" of that person. Considered as a source of *power* — as a rhythmic vibration or "tone" which keeps on unchanged from the alpha to the omega states of the life cycle—the Eon is what I have called the "self" of the individual person.

A set of symbols like the Sabian symbols, or the I Ching or the Tarot, confronts us with the challenge of integrating the archetypal and the existential through a symbolic image, scene or statement in which these two realms are in a state of confluence and interpenetration. Ideally, therefore, the production of a valid set of symbols should *enact* this interpenetration and confluence; and it is just what the actors in the car in the San Diego park—the two visible, and the invisible Presences—did. In this sense, the performance was highly ritualistic. It focused Meaning of an archetypal and cyclic character through polarized contemporary minds.

There remains, however, the problem of interpretation of the products of the ritualistic focusing. An ideal interpretation should reveal the existence of all the factors implied in the symbol and should formulate their implications in such a way that they are susceptible of as general as possible applications to situations encountered at our present stage of human evolution and history. This is a nearly impossible task to perform, for there are as many levels of possible interpretation as there are levels at which the consciousness of human beings can operate, particularly today in our chaotic and individualistic society. One can only try to present formulations which are inherently able to branch into various byways of significance. The essential requirement, however, is that the interpretation should include the structural and the existential approaches.

The symbol has meaning because it is a complex interweaving of factors, each of which is potentially significant as to its revelatory purpose and function. The symbol is a whole of meaning, yet this meaning is what it is only in relationship to the meanings of all other images—particularly the preceding and following, the opposing and the squaring symbols. The approach should be holistic, yet based on a keen analysis of all the significant features within the symbol. Moreover, it ideally should not be biased by a too-specialized philosophical, cultural or social outlook. Above all, it should not be conditioned by an emotional reaction or an ethical response to what is pictured.

As Marc Jones himself pointed out, there are in the Sabian set quite a few ambiguous symbols. But if these symbols are considered as *phases of a cyclic process rather than as isolated images*—that is, when the possible interpretations are considered in the light of preceding and following phases in a characteristic five-fold sequence, and in terms of wider relationships —the ambiguity usually disappears.

It certainly is not for me to judge the interpretations of the Sabian symbols that are now publicly available. I feel none are quite adequate and many of them seem to me at least partially biased by considerations that are extraneous to the symbols themselves; I am sure, however, that a similar criticism will be leveled at the approach and the interpretations which this book presents. There is room for many approaches and for several levels of interpretation. My main purpose in writing is to point out what is actually implied in such a set of symbols, involved in its interpretation, and possible in terms of its use at the oracular level. I also want to show in what sense the Sabian set can be compared to the I Ching and other cyclic series of symbols.

THE INTERNAL STRUCTURE OF THE SABIAN SET WILL BE DIScussed in Part Three, after the reader has had time to familiarize himself with the actual images. In order to avoid a superficial and atomistic interpretation, however, the reader must have at least a general understanding of the structural relationships between the individual symbols and of the underlying process of subdivision of the 360-degree circle into various patterns. This process follows the usual astrological practice in many ways, but it has really quite a different meaning and purpose. As already stated, the Sabian symbols do not deal exclusively with the degrees of the zodiac. They refer to the division of any cyclic life process into 360 phases; for this reason I have stressed *the phase number* of the symbol as much as the zodiacal degree to which it refers. The essential point to remember is that we are dealing with a life process; we might say a cosmic process, but in any case it is a gradual process of actualization of a set of new potentialities. It is a gradual process, i.e. it proceeds by "degrees." But the progression is not to be considered unidirectional; it is rather multidirectional and in a sense multidimensional, as it involves the actualization of potentiality on at least three levels. We should not expect that the sequence of symbols will reveal a straight line of progress. There is progression, but only within a number of definite structural fields of activity.

First, it should be clear that any life cycle divides itself essentially into two hemicycles, just as the soli-lunar cycle is divided into waxing and waning halves. One may use different names to characterize these two halves. In the soli-lunar cycle —which deals *not* with the Moon itself but with *the changing relationship* of the Moon to the Sun, as this relationship is perceived by human observers on this Earth—one can speak of the hemicycle of "action" and of that of "consciousness."* During the first period concrete forms of the energy released at New Moon are being progressively built (unless the entire cycle proves to be negative and the energy release ineffectual); during the second period the capacity for action tends to gradually wane while, on the other hand, energy is focused (after Full Moon) at the consciousness level and becomes productive of, or subservient to, mental forms (including ideological systems and sociocultural institutions).

In the cycle of the year, the period between the spring and the fall equinoxes represents an effort toward the formation of life organisms or of individualized persons at the human level. The One Life becomes differentiated into and through many

*Cf. Dane Rudhyar, *The Lunation Cycle* (Shambala Publications, Berkeley, California, 1970).

living organisms, each of which constitutes a whole—i.e. a structured field of interrelated and interdependent activities. The
One seeks to become the Many—the many little "ones" which
nevertheless at least reflect the fundamental wholeness of the
universal Whole.

After a transition period of readjustment the Many tend to
gather together for the purpose of establishing a larger whole,
a vaster organism. The phase of Integration succeeds that of
Differentiation. The spring-summer half of the year cycle is one
marked by an *individualizing* trend, while the fall-winter half
witnesses the opposite, that of *collectivization*. Each of the annual hemicycles displays a moment of triumph, or of maximal
intensity at the solstices. Thus the great ritual drama of the year
can be characteristically divided into four Acts. I have used four
Keywords: Differentiation, Stabilization, Group-Integration,
Capitalization. We are dealing here not merely with the four
seasons—spring, summer, fall and winter—but more generally
with the four basic periods of any cycle of cosmic manifestation,
whether micro- or macrocosmic, because all concrete physical
manifestations answer to the rhythm of the four. We will see
therefore that the Sabian symbols for the phases 1, 91, 181 and 271
(i.e. Aries 1°, Cancer 1°, Libra 1° and Capricorn 1°) form a very
characteristic and significant sequence.

Next in importance is the six-fold pattern of cyclic unfoldment, and indeed the numbers 6 and 60 have figured significantly in ancient astrology, particularly in Chaldea. The fact
that one can inscribe six contiguous circles of the same size
within a circumference, plus a seventh one at the center, has
been given great prominence in geometrical symbolism. It can
be considered at least one of the main reasons for the division
of the circumference (and thus in astrology of the zodiac) into
360 degrees, i.e. 6 times 60, and for the numerological emphasis
placed upon the number 7, the latter defining the fulfillment of
a process, and thus the "seed" of it; that is, both a conclusion and
the prenatal foundation of a new cycle.*

*Cf. Dane Rudhyar, *The Astrology of Personality* (original edition, Lucis
Publications, New York, 1936), p. 230. Also available in paperback from Doubleday & Company, Inc.

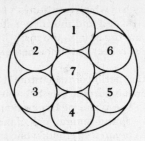

By dividing the zodiacal belt—which is actually the orbit of the Earth—into six sections, we characterize six basic types or polarizations of the one central power of the Sun, source of all energies operating on the planets. Each polarization produces a male/female couple (or zyzygy); and the zodiac is thus divided into alternatively "masculine" and "feminine" signs: Aries/-Taurus, Gemini/Cancer, Leo/Virgo, etc. We shall see in Part Three how these pairs can be correlated with the six great forces (or *shakti*) of Hindu occult philosophy.

Number 5 occupies a highly significant place not only in symbolism, but in the structure of living organisms in contrast to that of nonliving material systems. In terms of the subdividing of cyclic processes one may use this number 5 in two ways: the whole process can be divided into five sections, each of 72 phases, thus inscribing a five-pointed star in the circle; or, even more significant in terms of the scheme of interpretation, by studying the successive sequences of five degrees it can be seen that such sequences all have a broadly similar structure. That is to say, each sequence (for instance Aries 1°, 2°, 3°, 4°, 5°) represents *archetypally* five steps, or five stages of development.

Moreover, these five stages can be seen to take place successively at the three basic levels of human activity and experience. These levels can be defined very broadly, yet characteristically, as the *actional*, the *cultural-emotional* and the *individual-mental* levels. What we have is a kind of dialectical process, but one which does not operate as the ordinary sequence of thesis, antithesis and synthesis broadly used in Western philosophy since Hegel and Marx, but rather according to a five-fold rhythm. This five-beat dialectical sequence has been studied in some Oriental systems, particularly in Zen philosophy*; but it came to my mind some forty-five years ago when I attempted to outline what I then called "a pentarhythmic system of social organization"—an attempt which at that time I did not carry to completion.

Such a "pentarhythmic" (five-beat) process, operating at three levels, produces unit sequences of 15 phases. There are 24 such sequences in a complete cycle; and here the 24 hours of the day period at once comes to mind. The day can be divided into four periods—from sunrise to noon, from noon to sunset, from sunset to midnight, and from midnight to sunrise. In a series of articles entitled *The Wheel of Significance* which I wrote in 1944–45 for *American Astrology* magazine, I spoke of these four periods as "Watches." According to Cyril Fagan, however, the term was apparently used to refer to an archaic division of the astrological day into eight parts (Watches) corresponding to what we now call the twelve Houses of a chart, but operating in the opposite (i.e. clockwise) direction. This is partly why here I have instead used the term "four Acts."

Each Act has six Scenes, or Hours; thus the number 24 is obtained. Sacred scriptures have spoken of the 24 Elders surrounding the Deity. Marc Jones used the term "Span" in his mimeographed course on symbolical astrology, and I kept it in my initial condensation of that course in *The Astrology of Personality*. The term one uses is not of great importance, provided it can be referred to a single frame of reference. As I now stress the concept of cosmic process, this whole process can most significantly be considered a ritual drama in four Acts and twenty-four Scenes. However one may wish to subdivide it, this cosmic process, when apprehended in its essential structure, is a ritual; indeed, all life is a ritual—a symbolic performance—for the individual who intuitively "sees" himself as a participant in the universal process of actualization of the potentialities in-

---

*I heard it mentioned in Paris a few years ago, by the eminent philosopher-psychologist Karlfried von Durckheim, author of the well-known book *Hara*.

herent in the Creative Word "in the Beginning," the Logos.

I used the word "actor," but at a certain stage of human development the actor becomes an "agent," for he has come to realize that *through* him the purpose of the universe is indeed focused according to the time and place of his life performance. The ego in him has become a crystalline lens through which the "Will of God" is concentrated into individualized acts. He does not think; the One Mind thinks him. His life has become "sacred" because it is no longer "his" life, but the Whole performing within and through the space of his total organism, and at the time determined by the rhythm of the planetary process, whatever act is *necessary*.

3. The Positive and Negative Approaches to Individual Experience

◉

ONE BASIC FACT DOMINATES MAN'S EXPERIENCE: WHENEVER a new way of releasing power is made possible, implying a fundamental reorganization of either the human person or society in general, this possibility can be, and indeed is bound to be, actualized to some extent in both an essentially constructive and an inherently destructive manner. A generalization of this fact of human experience has to be the foundation of any cosmology or world-view, at least as far as *our* universe is concerned. It is a universe in which the principle of duality is to be observed everywhere. One can postulate beyond and/or through this dualistic universe a condition of essential unity, and the reflection of this unitarian state is found in the fact that all existence is perceived by us in terms of "wholes of existence," i.e. of units that are born, grow and decay. The very fact that there is birth, development of generic or individual potentialities, and eventual disintegration implies a dualistic process. It implies the interplay of two polarized forces, symbolized by Chinese philosophers in the dynamic interaction of Yin and Yang.

To live is to consume energy. There are two basic ways in which this consumption of energy can be said to take place: the *purposeful use of power* or the *automatic operation of forces*. In either case energy is consumed, but the meanings given to this consumption differ; that is, the type of consciousness arising from the living and experiencing of life is positive in the first instance and negative in the second.

The distinction between "powers" and "forces" should be clear when we consider even briefly the cosmological approach taken by traditional philosophies and the contrasting world-view implied in the average scientific mentality of the present, at least in the West. To the ancient philosopher as well as to his modern heirs, "the building of the universe" was the result of the purposeful and supremely intelligent (though not "conscious" in the human sense of the term) work of Creative Hierarchies of spiritual Beings, themselves the seed-products of previous cosmic evolutions or the direct Emanations of the creative God—Freemasonry's "Great Architect of the Universe." On the other hand, most modern scientists (with notable exceptions) regard the universe as the product of the interplay of "forces" which somehow exist of themselves and operate without reference to an intelligent or purposeful Source. The real scientist, it is true, refuses to commit himself in regard to metaphysical principles and a Cause of causes; nevertheless, the scientific training and the concentration upon analysis of material facts tend to build into modern men a belief in "forces" rather than in "powers"; human consciousness and personality tend to be seen as the end products of the long evolutionary interplay of these immutable and nonpurposeful forces of nature.

To another type of human mind, however, consciousness and personality, culture and civilization, are the results of the constant use by human individuals of "powers" which are latent in every human being as well as expressed in the activities of the universe. Every human being is understood to be a microcosm in whom all the creative powers of the great universe (macrocosm) are to be found in a state of potentiality. Human evolution—whether it is that of the race at large, or of a particular individual—is thus interpreted as a process of unfoldment of creative powers and faculties. This process is directed from within and is purposeful, at least to the extent that given a number of seed-potentialities "in the beginning" of the cycle of human evolution, the end of that cycle should find these potentialities (or in individual cases, some of them) expressed in actuality. Such an expression culminates in a creative activity (or a karma), which in turn generates or conditions the beginning of a new cycle.

The philosopher who holds such views thinks of the universe as ruled by laws, but it is also the expression and incorporation of universal consciousness. The events presenting themselves to human experience not only display a sequential order which permits inferences as to what future events will be, but these events fit into the pattern of unfoldment of a cosmic whole and of a cyclic sequence, and as such they have meaning. Both the scientist and the philosopher believe in universal order and predictability; but in considering any group of events the scientist is satisfied if he discovers how they came about and how they will cause new events, while the philosopher asks the question: "What does it mean?"

To the scientist-astronomer, the zodiac is merely a way of tabulating and classifying sequences of celestial events and periodical changes. To the true philosopher-astrologer, the zodiac is a structural framework within which man can shape his unceasing search for more inclusive and vital meanings. Needless to say, in this book I am taking the point of view of the philosopher exclusively, for I am dealing with a series of symbolic pictures that are meant to arouse in the student a realization of the power of his own creative Spirit. The purpose of this work is to develop a profound understanding of the nature, character, sequence of unfoldment, and the overall scope and significance of those powers that are the mark of the spirit in man—those powers man must use as he faces his own experience and extracts from it meaning, direction and purpose. As man does this (as an individual or as a race, nation or group) he becomes truly "human"; that is, he lives up to the capacities inherent in the human kingdom, capacities which actually are as yet very little developed. He lives his life, instead of being lived by events. He uses powers, instead of being swayed by natural forces. He lives *from* the creative Spirit in him. And this is positive living, spiritual living.

One should add that this type of positive living can be demonstrated as well by the materialistic scientist as by the philosopher who believes in universal creative intelligence. Indeed *on the surface* modern Western man displays a far more "positive" approach to everyday living than does archaic man, or the followers of Zen and similar philosophies who believes in "letting" things happen. This is superficially a more passive attitude; yet we must go beneath surface orientations if we want to reach the vital creative meaning of human behavior. The modern individual imbued with scientific and materialistic concepts may make a most positive and purposeful use of natural forces; but so does any man who handles machines, tanks, explosives. Count Keyserling once referred to modern man as characterized by the "chauffeur type." Today we would speak of the technologist or the technocrat. However, the man who deliberately uses machines and the forces operating them acts fundamentally in a way not too different from the powerful warrior of old who dominated his surroundings by sheer force and an instinct for quick and sound decisions in battle.

Let me take an extreme example from the recent past: Nazi Germany nearly succeeded in dominating mankind by using natural "forces" (physical and psychological) with great positiveness; however, Nazism failed to use the creative powers of the Spirit within Man. It achieved spectacular successes for a while through the ruthless use of technology, but it was defeated, not only by superior forces but by the very power of human evolution. The Roman empire some sixteen centuries ago suffered much the same fate, in spite of excellent administrators and its masses of slaves. And the Vietnam war should have shown us how "superior forces" can be successfully met by the power of the collective human will when focused by an unyielding desire for self-determination and autonomy, a desire based on the deeper realities represented by the phase in human evolution which mankind has reached.

Because by the very logic of planetary evolution a phase of

global organization and integration of mankind is now ahead of us, what is today loosely called "imperialism" has become obsolete—just as dinosaurs became obsolete. The Nazi or Fascist type of technocracy—and I must add the Pentagon type—constitute a throwback to a period of the vast cycle of human evolution which is now definitely past. This behavior has therefore lost its positive spiritual meaning. It represents the negative actualization of the new set of human potentialities which has been released during the last centuries of our Western civilization. It is based on the use of "superior force" in an attempt to overwhelm any manifestation of the deep-seated, planet-wide urge for human—personal and social—transformation.

He who lives from the creative Spirit in him lives not only in a determined, active and positive manner; he lives in terms of the need of the particular, present moment in the cycle of his individual evolution, and in the cycle of collective human evolution as well. He acts within the framework of an evolutionary whole, each moment of which has a particular meaning *in terms of* the timely use of particular powers. Timeliness and the accurate focalization of action upon the point of space which fits this action are essential factors in *significant living*. Essential also is adequacy in terms of the overall cyclic purpose of the life of the one who acts.

The modern engineer, it is true, also considers these three factors—timeliness, spatial accuracy and fitness to purpose—but he considers them in relation to his machines rather than in relation to his life as a creative participant in the organic wholeness of humanity and, ultimately, of the universe. Thus many of his machines turn destructive. They do so because they are produced and put to use by a society that chooses to be forceful, rather than purposeful; that, by seeking above all to control the automatic operation of forces, has come to consider human beings merely as products of such an automatic operation of meaningless and purposeless forces of nature.

To be force-full is not to be purpose-full. Modern society today functions for no really significant purpose except perhaps that of generating more material comfort and abundance for an ever-increasing mass of human bodies, thus making our planet increasingly uninhabitable. Modern society demonstrates in the main a *negative* type of consciousness, because any consciousness without a universal frame of reference within which action can be seen in its timeliness, spatial accuracy and fitness to cyclic purpose is a negative type of consciousness. It is consciousness devoid of creative significance and therefore spiritually empty, however great the intellectual and engineering capacities stemming from it.

IF ONE UNDERSTANDS WHAT I HAVE JUST SAID, IT SHOULD BE clear that any symbol can be interpreted in a positive and a negative manner. The symbol is *the key to the adjustment between the individual act, problem or situation and a universal frame of reference*—relative as this universality may be. In this present study, which is derived from a symbolization of the 360 degrees of the zodiacal cycle, the constantly changing annual relationship of the Earth to its basic source of energy, the Sun, provides us with the basic frame of reference. It is a frame of reference for the release of energy within the total field of activity of the Earth-as-a-whole, and more particularly the biosphere. The adjustment to such a year-long release of solar energy can take place on the basis of either the "purposeful use of power" or the "automatic operation of forces"—depending upon the positive or negative character of the consciousness confronted with the need for adjustment.

In most cases, obviously the adjustment will be made by the individual person without any *deliberate* reference to symbolism. Yet, in actual fact, a *subconscious* reference to collective "images" is always present; that is to say, the individual will act in a personal situation by unconsciously identifying himself with the "image" of what a father, a husband, a faithful citizen, a devoted son, etcetera, is supposed to do according to some kind of a social or religious tradition; or he will act by associating the new situation with previously experienced ones which hurt or exalted him (i.e. according to a "complex"). In any case, the present behavior will be conditioned by the mental-emotional memories of the individual or his race and family—such memories having crystallized into an "image" or symbol.

The Sabian series of picture symbols (or any similarly valid series, ancient or modern) intends to help the individual make such images *conscious*, and to establish them within a universal frame of reference. The ability to do this is latent in every human being, but it needs to be trained and developed, and the deeper purpose of the series of symbols is to stimulate it by actual and consistent use. What is at stake here is the development of *the power* to relate every particular activity to a universal meaning and every individual consciousness to its spiritual source in the universal Mind. This source is fundamentally to be understood as *the moment* in cyclic Time, *the place* in spheroidal Space, and *the purpose* in the Harmony of the Whole (or "God") that the individual occupies and fulfills.

If this power of symbolic relatedness between the acts of the individual self and the rhythm of the universal Whole is used positively, every situation of the individual's life becomes an opportunity for growth and for the creative expression of the Spirit within man. If it is used negatively, then—as Marc Jones writes in the Introduction to "Symbolical Astrology"—"all things are engaged in what to him is a very real conspiracy against him; while his satisfactions are elements of destruction, transformed by his own symbolizing of them in desirable factors."

In his book *The Sabian Symbols in Astrology*, as well as in his earlier mimeographed course, Marc Jones offers positive and negative interpretations of each of the 360 degree symbols of the zodiac. Partly because I feel that such either-or polarized interpretations can be quite confusing at the psychological level, and partly because I have been trying here to go beyond a strict relationship between this set of symbols and the zodiac so that they can be referred to any basic cycle of actualization of new potentialities of existence and human unfoldment, I have omitted such clear-cut positive-negative characterizations. I find some of Marc Jones's interpretations very significant, others much less so or hardly even justifiable; and they are completely different in two versions that have been made public. In *The Astrology of Personality*, as I had to condense the material in "Symbolical Astrology," I only introduced the positive-negative characterizations in a few instances and in a short-ened form.

As I see it, the interpretation of the symbols should be based on two sets of factors: (1) An objective analysis of the most signifi-cant features in the symbolic image, and (2) the relationship of the symbol to other symbols *within the framework of the entire cyclic process.* We find the same situation as we deal with any cyclic set of symbols or images from which meaning is to be derived. This is particularly true of the images characterizing the twelve signs of the zodiac—which have little apparent resemblance to the group of stars they were supposed to repre-sent when constellations and signs coincided, presumably to-ward the close of the Greek period (around 100 B.C.).

In the same way, if we consider the ten original Rorschach cards used in clinical psychology, it seems most evident that the cards constitute a definite sequence beginning with simple shapes and ending with a complex picture in which several colors add to the meaning. The appearance of color in one of these cards at a characteristic stage of the sequence should be significant to anyone who thinks at all holistically and in terms of structured process. Yet I am told that the people to whom this test has been given, including Carl Jung, have not been aware of the significance of there being ten cards in a clearly—even if perhaps unconsciously—structured series. Thus, I feel con-strained to repeat that no experience can be understood in its total meaning unless it is related to the whole process in which it occurs, at the very place and the very moment that conditions and reveals its function. No *isolated* occurrence has any basic meaning *of itself.* It only acquires meaning as it is related to the larger whole or process of which it is a part. The relating may be entirely unconscious, yet it is the foundation of the meaning.

Moreover, it is *not* the function which should be considered positive or negative; no action *of itself* is positive or negative, good or evil. It is the *response* of the individual-as-a-whole to the performance of the function when the time has come for it to be performed, and in the particular environment in which it has to be performed, which determines the positive or negative character of the act. We acclaim the soldier who has killed five enemies in hand-to-hand combat, but we send to the electric chair the person who has been crazed by frustrations and social conditioning and has killed policemen who tried to beat him after he perhaps stole food from a store. The function of the acids and enzymes of the digestive tract breaking down food into chemicals is as positive as that of brain cells transforming sense input into a beautiful painting or an inspiring concept.

No doubt one can define in principle at an abstract or archetypal level the basic positive and negative meanings of a symbol or of an interpersonal confrontation. But the very suggestion of a negatively polarized archetype introduces into the situation a negative undertone of meaning which can easily influence an oversusceptible person. This person may appreciate the positive meaning; but if he feels unable or is reluctant to embody such a meaning in his own response, he is likely to read the negative meaning in a mood that conditions him to accept it as what "fate" has in store for him, or as the evident result of his being a failure or a weak person.

No symbol should be considered inherently negative. Even if the image or scene presented seems full of negative implications, these should be considered as a form of teaching and thus perhaps as the *via negativa* which leads man to spiritual heights by forcing him to experience a violent revulsion from the depths of human misery and even degradation. *Nothing* in astrology indicates "This is so as a fact" or "This *will* occur." Astrology shows us the best—because natural—way of facing any situation in terms of *our own* individual nature. There are easier as well as much harder ways, considering what man is today and how he has been conditioned by Western society and a materialized Christianity; but the "culture-of-making-things-too-easy" (as Keyserling wrote) leads men to a loss of inner vitality, character and mental acuity.

IN ORDER TO SHOW HOW THE STATEMENTS MADE IN THE preceding paragraph can be applied to definite cases, I shall take what is perhaps the most "negative" symbol in the Sabian series:

the symbol for Cancer 5°.* In his book *The Sabian Symbols in Astrology* Marc Jones states the symbol as follows: *An automobile wrecked by a train.* Then in order to remove some of the negativity from the picture, he interprets it as follows:

This is a symbol of the irresistible power of completion inherent in the very make-up of man's world whenever a sequence of events once is set in motion, as is evident continually on the objective side of things. Implicit in the reverse symbolism is the concept of control, or the assurance that it is not necessary to continue any given action to the point of self-cancellation. The ultimate obligation of the individual is to himself and not to the narrow and momentary direction of circumstances. The keyword is DISPERSION. When positive, the degree is a special genius for a creative reorganization of all experiences, and when negative, an insensitive recklessness.

I cannot help feeling that this interpretation is not based strictly on an analysis of the elements in the picture, but centers on the emotional implications of the word "wrecked." I do not know, of course, how Miss Wheeler described the image she "saw," but let us analyze it carefully. There is practically no way an automobile can be wrecked by a train except when the road on which the automobile is driven *crosses* a railroad track. We must therefore consider three factors involved in the image: the automobile, the train and the crossing of their paths.

An automobile is a *private* means of transportation; a train a *public* one. Obviously therefore the symbol relates in a certain way—a tragic or destructive way—the private or individual and the public or collective spheres in a technologically developed society. These two spheres or realms of activity usually exist more or less parallel with each other; a person may give his allegiance to, or at least prefer to operate in, one or the other realm. But there are times when these realms "cross"; that is to say, their directions become roughly perpendicular, and a mo-

*I should make it clear here that, if the symbol is referred to the position of a planet in an astrological chart, Cancer 5° *begins* at 4°1″ (four degrees and one second or minute) and ends with Cancer 4°59′59″; just as the first year (year number 1) of a life begins at birth and ends with the first birthday. We are dealing *with a process*, and "Phase One" starts the very moment the process begins.

ment of potential tension arises. They work at cross-purposes. When this happens, the symbol tells us that there is a potential of destruction involved for the person who does not stop to consider the possible results of his "rugged individualism." Society should make it impossible or very difficult for the individual to be so careless; but even though society may build safeguards or red-light signals, the individual may senselessly or carelessly ignore them. Then the automobile may be wrecked. This does not necessarily imply that the driver is killed—he could jump out at the last moment—yet his *consciousness,* i.e. what his ego rides in, his set of values and his approach to life, may experience a more or less total breakdown.

As I see it, this is what the symbolic image presents; it presents it *not* as a fact, but as a "message," a teaching or warning. If a person has one of his planets on that fifth degree of Cancer he is warned that if he insists on allowing the function or psychological drive represented by that planet to operate carelessly or recklessly in a strictly individualistic manner at times when his own and society's purposes cross, then he will presumably experience a crucial defeat, and this function or drive is likely to be invalidated, perhaps beyond repair.

There is nothing inherently negative or frightening about this symbol *in itself;* it is simply a warning. I do not see why it should mean an "irresistible power of completion inherent in the very make-up of man's world," etcetera. It simply tells us that if at a certain time the ways of the individual and those of society are at cross-purposes, it is to be expected that society will win—or, colloquially speaking, "crime does not pay."

But we must go a step further and see how and where the symbol fits into the process to which the entire set of symbols belongs. If the reader refers to the seventh scene of the ritual drama of the year (cf. pp. 110–20) he will see that his Cancer 5° symbol constitutes the fifth stage of a five-fold sequence which began with Cancer 1°, i.e. the degree of the summer solstice. The symbol for this Cancer 1° is said to refer to a phase of activity implying "A radical change in the allegiance exteriorized in a symbolical act: a point of no return."

Thus we have in the last symbol of this pentarhythmic

sequence a warning of what the first symbol might lead to—i.e. of how at critical times society might react to the "radical change of allegiance." If the symbols had been visualized today we might have had the image of a policeman beating a youthful protester during an antiwar demonstration! If we consider carefully the sequence of the first five degree symbols of the sign Cancer, we can see the possibilities which the "radical change of allegiance" opens up in terms of action. The entire sequence has to be considered and understood; and much more still should be considered, for the whole seventh scene refers to "Decision." For instance, this seventh scene in Act Two of the entire ritual can be related to the corresponding nineteenth scene of Act Four, whose Keyword is "Crystallization."

The whole series of 360 phases is structured in a manner quite clear to anyone able to consider it in the light of a holistic, if not eonic, consciousness. We are dealing here with a significant process of gradual and purposeful transformation. The symbols enable us to get a new perspective on the interrelated phases of this vast process of existence, the keynote of which is indeed transformation.

After becoming acquainted with each of the symbols we can return to the study of their interrelationship and to the two basic ways they can be used.

Part Two
A REFORMULATION
IN DEPTH OF THE
SABIAN SYMBOLS

First Hemicycle:
The Process
Of Individualization

ACT I: DIFFERENTIATION

SCENE ONE: *DESIRE*
(Aries 1° to Aries 15°)

FIRST LEVEL: ACTIONAL

PHASE 1 (ARIES 1°): A WOMAN JUST RISEN FROM THE SEA. A SEAL IS EMBRACING HER.

KEYNOTE: *Emergence of new forms and of the potentiality of consciousness.*

This is the first of the 360 phases of a universal and multi-level cyclic process which aims at the actualization of a particular set of potentialities. These potentialities, in the Sabian symbols, refer to the development of man's individualized consciousness—the consciousness of being an individual person with a place and function (a "destiny") in the planetary organism of the Earth, and in a particular type of human society and culture.

To be individually conscious means to emerge out of the sea of generic and collective consciousness—which to the emerged mind appears to be unconsciousness. Such an emergence is the primary event. It is the result of some basic action: a leaving behind, an emerging from a womb or matrix, here symbolized by the sea.

Such an action is not to be considered a powerful, positive statement of individual being. In the beginning is the Act; but it is often an imperceptible, insecure act. The small tender germ out of the seed does not loudly proclaim its existence. It has to pierce through the crust of the soil still covered with the remains of the past. It is all potentiality and a minimum of actual presence.

In the symbol, therefore, the emergent entity is a Woman; symbolically speaking, a form of existence still close to the unconscious depths of generic biological nature, filled with the desire to be rather than self-assertion. The woman is seen embraced by a seal because the seal is a mammal which once had experienced a biological, evolutionary but relatively unconscious emergence, yet which retraced its steps and "returned to the womb" of the sea. The seal, therefore, represents a regressive step. It embraces the Woman who *has* emerged, because every emergent process at first is susceptible to failure. This process is indeed surrounded by the memory, the ghosts of past failures during previous cycles. The impulse upward is held back by regressive fear or insecurity; the issue of the conflict depends on the relative strength of the future-ward and the past-ward forces.

The possibility of success and that of failure is implied throughout the entire process of actualization. Every release of potentiality contains this two-fold possibility. It inevitably opens up two paths: one leads to "perfection" in consciousness, the other to "disintegration"—the return to the *undifferentiated state* (the state of humus, manure, cosmic dust—i.e. to the symbolic "great Waters of space," to chaos).

This symbol characterizes the first of five stages which are repeated at three levels. This stage represents the initial statement, or theme, of the five-fold series which refers to the first level: IMPULSE TO BE.

PHASE 2 (ARIES 2°): A COMEDIAN REVEALS HUMAN NATURE.

KEYNOTE: *The capacity to look objectively at oneself and at others.*

While the first phase of the process of emergence is essentially in terms of subjective impulse and the desire to act, the second phase represents the attempt to evolve an objective awareness of existence. Through a sense of contrast, consciousness is gradually being built. It is what Teilhard de Chardin calls "reflective consciousness": the ability to see oneself reflected as in a mirror, and eventually to laugh at the inadequacy of the form one sees; thus "humor," the triumph of objective consciousness over subjective feeling or moods, or involvement in self.

This symbol characterizes the second stage in the first five-fold sequence of phases: the stage of OBJECTIVATION OF CONSCIOUSNESS. This second phase complements and polarizes the first, which stresses the subjective desire to become individually conscious.

PHASE 3 (ARIES 3°): THE CAMEO PROFILE OF A MAN, SUGGESTING THE SHAPE OF HIS COUNTRY.

KEYNOTE: *The sustaining power of the Whole, as the individual identifies himself with Its life.*

Having become objectively aware of his nature and his basic humanity, the individualizing person finds power and inner security in realizing his essential identity with the section of the universe in which he operates. He and it seem to his consciousness united in a cosmic-planetary process—in a "participation mystique." Metaphysically expressed, this is the concept of the identity of Atman and Brahman. In another sense, through his ability to identify himself with the complex of life activities surrounding him, the individual person can become truly, not only an image and representation of the Whole of his natal environment (local, planetary and perhaps eventually cosmic), but an agent *through whom* the Whole may express itself in an act of creative resonance and outpouring. This is the avatar ideal—the ideal of a "transpersonal" life and consciousness totally consecrated to and directed by a divine Power. This Power can also be conceived as the archetypal Self, the Christ-principle as it operates in and through an individual person and destiny who have become its outward manifestation in order to meet a collective human need.

The concept of the formal-structural identity of the universal macrocosm and the human microcosm is a very important one, as it manifests itself at many levels. It provided an inner sense of security and harmonic strength to archaic man. To the modern individual assailed by surface evidence of meaninglessness and futility it gives a feeling of participation in the vast tide of evolution. It is the answer to the tragic sense of alienation so prevalent today.

This symbol characterizes the third stage of the first five-fold sequence of phases: the stage of PARTICIPATION IN A GREATER LIFE.

PHASE 4 (ARIES 4°): TWO LOVERS STROLLING ON A SE-CLUDED WALK.

KEYNOTE: *The progressive polarization of energies needed for fulfilling one's life function.*

In order to respond fully to the potentialities released by a sense of identification with a greater Whole, the human being should be himself whole. An interplay of bipolar energies is needed to provide a sustained and dynamic "resonance" to any superior and encompassing form of life. This may imply a temporary withdrawal from routine activity, i.e. a "secluded" process. It is not, however, a *closed* process. The positive and negative polarities do not meet in a closed circuit, reconstituting a neutral state of potentiality. They operate in dynamic, open, un-resolved togetherness in contact with the surrounding energies of nature.

This symbol characterizes the fourth stage of the first five-fold sequence of phases: the stage of dynamic and unresolved POLARIZA-TION. It introduces the basic means—one might say, the technique—to establish consciousness in the world of duality.

PHASE 5 (ARIES 5°): A TRIANGLE WITH WINGS.

KEYNOTE: *The capacity for self-transcending.*

This is the symbol of the desire to reach a higher level of existence, of pure aspiration or devotion, of bhakti. What has emerged in the first phase of the process of differentiation is becoming aware of the possibility of further up-reachings. The principle of "levitation" is seen as one of the two essential factors in evolution. The emergent being glorifies and deifies it, but it is still only an ideal. At this stage, nevertheless, the whole being experiences a childlike longing for its eventual realization.

At this point the last and synthesizing stage of the first five-fold unit in the cyclic process is reached. A NEW DIMENSION of being is envisioned mobilizing creative endeavors.

SECOND LEVEL: EMOTIONAL–CULTURAL

PHASE 6 (ARIES 6°): A SQUARE, WITH ONE OF ITS SIDES BRIGHTLY ILLUMINED.

KEYNOTE: *The emotional desire for concrete and stabilized existence as a person.*

This desire for individualization operates at first as a one-pointed or one-sided drive focusing itself upon an exclusive goal. All emotions are at first possessive, and all cultural manifestations operate on the principle of exclusion. All that does not belong to the tribal sphere (one blood, one land, one folk) is the potential enemy. This is a necessary phase, for—as in the case of "the woman emerging from the sea"—the first attempt at building an inner realization of integral being may be defeated at any time by the regressive pull toward undifferentiation and the prenatal state of nonindividualization within the vast womb of nature or within unformed cosmic space.

This first stage of the second five-fold sequence of symbols presents the theme which will be dialectically developed—a five-phase dialectical process: A ONE-SIDED URGE FOR INNER STABILITY.

PHASE 7 (ARIES 7°): A MAN SUCCEEDS IN EXPRESSING HIM-SELF SIMULTANEOUSLY IN TWO REALMS.

KEYNOTE: *The first realization of the dual nature of man and of the possibilities it implies.*

This symbol represents the antithesis of the thesis pictured in Phase 6, yet in such a five-fold sequence what we see is contrast rather than opposition. The primordial one-sidedness of emotional and cultural manifestation actually calls for the compensatory ability to operate at two levels. Thus the primary dualism of Sky and Earth, of the divine and the human, of spirit and matter. The vision and the emotions are focused within sharply defined boundaries, but within these boundaries they express themselves at two levels. This is the foundation of religion as well as of magic.

A situation which has become characterized by this symbol can be successfully faced if its spiritual and material implications are understood and actualized.

At this second stage of the second five-fold sequence of symbols we see at work man's capacity for LIVING TWO SEPARATE LIVES—and finding fulfillment and happiness in both. On this capacity are founded many of the complexities of human nature.

PHASE 8 (ARIES 8°): A LARGE WOMAN'S HAT WITH STREAM-
ERS BLOWN BY AN EAST WIND.

KEYNOTE: *Protection and spiritual guidance in the development of consciousness.*

This somewhat strange image can be understood if every stated
feature in it is clearly analyzed without preconceptions. Here
again we see a woman; but now her head is covered with a large
hat—a protection against the forces of nature, i.e. cold and/or
the penetrating rays of the sun. At this emotional-cultural level
(Phases 6 through 10) the mental processes are still largely un-
developed; thus they need protection from the elemental forces
of life. A too great openness to the Sky-energies and the
"spiritual" level could lead to obsessions of one kind or another.

The symbolic image implies a rather strong wind, thus the
activity of some more-than-material, and especially psychic,
forces. These originated in the East, traditionally the seat
of spiritualizing and creative-transforming influences. The
woman's hat has streamers, which enable it not only to respond
to the wind but to indicate its source. In other words, the image
symbolizes a stage of development of consciousness in which
the nascent powers of the mind are both protected and influenced by energies of a spiritual origin. This suggests a probationary stage in the process of individualization. Under protective guidance a still most receptive person (a woman) is being
influenced by spiritual forces.

This is a third stage symbol in which we see the first and second stages
of this second five-fold sequence producing results which require PRO-
TECTIVE FORMS (which is what a culture and ethical precepts provide)
and SENSITIVITY to spiritual energies.

PHASE 9 (ARIES 9°): A CRYSTAL GAZER.

KEYNOTE: *The development of an inner realization of organic wholeness.*

The crystal sphere symbolizes wholeness. Within the sphere images take form. These images may reveal future events, but more significantly they picture "the situation as a whole"—the situation which the clairvoyant is meant to interpret. The nascent mental faculties operating through still dominant emotions (or collective cultural incentives) act as a centralizing and whole-making power. What the intelligence perceives in its concentration is the function of every inner impulse and outer events in the open field of a "personality" still unclouded by egoism.

At this fourth stage of the five-fold sequence the new technique required for the development of individualized consciousness is revealed: CONCENTRATED ATTENTION.

PHASE 10 (ARIES 10°): A TEACHER GIVES NEW SYMBOLIC FORMS TO TRADITIONAL IMAGES.

KEYNOTE: *Revision of attitude at the beginning of a new cycle of experience.*

This phase is the fifth of the second five-fold sequence, and in it we find expressed the capacity to restate the problem inherent in the first phase, i.e. the problem of focusing one's energies upon emotional drives and cultural values which exclude far more than they include. The subsequent stages of development taken together have added considerably to this attitude; as a result, there arises in the consciousness a desire to reformulate at a new level much that had been taken for granted because it indeed originally had been an evolutionary necessity. The very concrete emotion-arousing images of the past can now be reinterpreted as "symbols" with a wider scope of meaning.

At this fifth stage a new dimension of consciousness is discovered, revealing higher possibilities of experience and mental development. This is a phase of ABSTRACTION and of emotional allegiance.

THIRD LEVEL: INDIVIDUAL–MENTAL

PHASE 11 (ARIES 11°): THE RULER OF A NATION.

KEYNOTE: *The power resulting from the formal integration of the collective desire for order.*

At this stage of the cyclic process this symbol refers to the appearance of the (personal) ego as the central manifestation of a type of "order" which transcends and seeks to rule the emotional and instinctual drives of the individual person. Actually the ruler at this social-political and mental level of integration is often the one who is being ruled by collective pressures. Nevertheless, a desire for a larger type of integration has now emerged. It is no longer biological-impulsive (Aries 1°) or emotional-personal (Aries 6°), but social-collective and institutional. At this ego level, laws and the restrictive power of a police force are dominant features. Psychologically speaking, this means that the integrative principle is the limited, more or less narrow "I am" realization. It manifests itself as the personal ego exerting its will to control the reactions of the bio-psychic organism.

This is the first stage of the third five-fold sequence of the cyclic process. It indicates a CENTRALIZATION OF POWER at the level of a rigidly structured consciousness.

PHASE 12 (ARIES 12°): A TRIANGULARLY SHAPED FLIGHT OF WILD GEESE.

KEYNOTE: *An idealistic reliance upon a mental image of universal order.*

The wild goose is the mystical bird, *hamsa,* of Hindu tradition. This word, which has recurred in various cultures (the *Hansa*

League of Germanic cities in the late Middle Ages, and *El Hanza*, the founder of the occult Brotherhood of the Druzes in Lebanon, during the era of the Crusades), has always had at least an undertone of integration at an expansionistic level, spiritual or economic. The Hindu *hamsa* was the symbol of man's transcendent soul. What previous interpretations of this Sabian symbol have failed to grasp is that the flight of geese presents not only a remarkably geometrical V-shape moving through the sky, but also that this flight is seasonal and therefore attuned to planetary rhythms. Thus, it symbolizes *cosmic order,* in contrast with the social-political order within a nation which is represented by its ruler. It is order made visual on the background of the clear sky. It is a "celestial" type of order, even though it is earth-born birds which reveal it by their ability to keep their flight structured. The symbol therefore refers to the Soul-consciousness as visualized by the heaven-oriented mind. Yet this soul-consciousness can be called transcendent because it has not yet become "incarnated."

Because this is a second stage in the third five-fold sequence begun with Phase 11, we have to consider what it pictures *in contrast to* the preceding symbol. A basic dualism of consciousness is thus suggested. We see arising a potential conflict between cosmic and social principles of order. The principle of COSMIC ORDER polarizes the all-too-human reliance on the social concept of law and order.

PHASE 13 (ARIES 13°): AN UNEXPLODED BOMB REVEALS AN UNSUCCESSFUL SOCIAL PROTEST.

KEYNOTE: *An immature evaluation of the possibility of transforming suddenly the status quo.*

The symbol pictures the result of a particular attempt to resolve the conflict between two concept-feelings of order. Resolution by violence fails because the ego-power at this stage of the process of individualization is far too strong. "The State" thwarts attempts at popular revolution, because these are premature expressions of a consciousness which is not free, but can only react "wildly" to constraint and to a central ruling power. It is thus a symbol of immature refusal to conform, in the name of an overidealistic desire for harmony and peace.

This is the third stage of the third five-fold sequence. A negative attempt at reconciling the spiritual ideal and the very earthly reality, denying the validity of the latter. It suggests ADOLESCENT FRUSTRATION.

PHASE 14 (ARIES 14°): A SERPENT COILING NEAR A MAN AND A WOMAN.

KEYNOTE: *Identification in bipolar relationship with the impersonal rhythm of natural energy.*

The symbol for Phase 4 pictures a man and a woman in love walking together. At this new and more mentally stimulated level of experience and consciousness, a third factor appears: the serpent, whose coiling represents the spiral-like process of evolution—not merely "sex" according to the maker of cathartic symbols, Sigmund Freud. We can understand this "triangular" image—man, woman and the serpent—if we relate it to the preceding one in the series, the unexploded bomb of the anarchist or activist. The urge to blow up some structure which somehow has become in the activist's mind a symbol of the Establishment—the ruling elite—is usually the protest of an alienated and often immature mind that *refuses relationship,* because in the relationship he would occupy a subservient position. In this symbol, the serpent represents the *acceptance of relationship* by the two polarized human beings.

There must be a polarization before there can be fulfillment. The tragedy of so many contemporary lives is that, having become sharply individualized, the men and women cannot find their truly matching polar-opposite. Because they are not fulfilled at the root level of human emotions and vitalistic forces, they pass their lives seeking the ideal complement, often glamorized as the "soul mate." This search can find its expression at several levels. At the mystical level we have the examples of the "spiritual marriage" of Saint Francis of Assisi and Santa Clara, or recently of Sri Aurobindo and Mother Mira.

The Adam and Eve story (in Hebrew, *Ish* and *Isha*—much more significant names!) refers to this principle of polarization, although the story has been turned upside down by priestly intellects to serve their purposes. Adam and Eve accepted the Presence, not of the Tempter, but of the Individualizer, who sought to have them born out of the womb of unconscious passivity to Nature's God. But the result of the experience frightened them. They "hid"; they failed in the great test of individualization, and *in this sense* the archetype of that failure is deeply imbedded in man's *generic* unconscious. It is repeated time after time.

Modern "individuals" are confronted with another test, but they do not understand its meaning. It is the test of polarized conscious participation in the evolutionary process—a polarization that could dissolve alienation, isolation and egocentricity. In a sense at least, this was the old Tantric concept in India; but today many young people accept the concept only superficially and miss its real essence. They cannot understand the meaning of *entering into* the serpent, i.e. of developing eonic consciousness and that transpersonal living which once was characterized by the words: Not I live, but Christ lives me—Christ, whose symbolic number in Gnosticism is 888.

At this fourth stage of the third five-fold sequence, we are confronted with an image suggesting the transpersonal way to the "cosmification" of desire and the conscious acceptance of polarization as the solution of the problems generated by individualization. But this need not mean what is currently meant by "sex" and the glorification of the orgasm. It implies rather the RITUALIZATION OF RELATIONSHIP.

PHASE 15 (ARIES 15°): AN INDIAN WEAVING A CEREMONIAL BLANKET.

KEYNOTE: *Projecting into everyday living the realization of wholeness and fulfillment.*

In Christian tradition one hears of Jesus' "seamless robe." In Asia one is told of the "spiritual vesture" of the Perfect Ones. The man who has attained the spiritual state is figuratively robed in the universe—and more precisely, in the Milky Way, the Great White Robe of interwoven stars. This is the ultimate kind of weaving. There was also Penelope's weaving and un-weaving, waiting for the return of her polarizing mate. The mind of the American woman in which these symbols took concrete form could think only of "Indian weavers." For the white man who is hungering for symbols of a state of living in total harmony with the universe, the traditional Indian can be glamorized as the answer to the inner emptiness of the city-dweller surfeited with artificial values. At any rate, we may thus *prefigure* a future state of fulfillment in conscious harmony and unpossessive love.

If this symbol comes to the consciousness of the inquirer after meaning, deliberately or through an aleatory act of revela-tion (like the act of throwing sticks to obtain an I Ching symbol), implied is the profound fact that every individual has as his ultimate conscious task the weaving of his "immortal body," his Gnostic Robe of Glory. It may sound very mystical and "far out," but there is a moment in every cycle when, in however small a degree, every individual may be confronted with the potentiality of a fulfilling act of self-realization and may, ever so relatively, find himself "clothed in light" for an instant.

This fifth stage of the third five-fold sequence of symbols ends the first of the twenty-four "scenes." We are told by it that the FULFILLMENT OF DESIRE is a possibility, at whatever level and in however incom-plete a manner it may be experienced.

SCENE TWO: *POTENCY*
(Aries 16° to Aries 30°)

FIRST LEVEL: ACTIONAL

PHASE 16 (ARIES 16°): NATURE SPIRITS ARE SEEN AT WORK IN THE LIGHT OF SUNSET.

KEYNOTE: *Attunement to the potency of invisible forces of nature.*

In the light of personal fulfillment (symbol of sunset and wisdom) man may be able to establish a life-giving contact with natural forces. These are active any time growth processes take place, but man's individualized mind is usually too focused on working for consciously set goals to be able to realize concretely the presence of invisible (or "occult") forces in operation. These forces constitute a specific realm of any planetary life. They are inherent in all "biospheres," on whatever planet. They are nonindividualized and unfree energies forming in the substratum of all life processes—thus of the process of integration at the level of the planet-as-a-whole, i.e. the planet *as an organism* with its automatic systems of growth, maintenance and organic multiplication. In this planetary organism those nature forces act as guiding and balancing-harmonizing factors—somewhat as the endocrine system does in a human body, and behind this system the more occult web of chakra energies related to prana—the solar energy. It is when this energy becomes less dominant—thus symbolically at sunset—or when the body energy is weakened by illness, fasting or sensory deprivation, that it becomes easier to perceive these "nature spirits" and to give them forms that symbolize the character of their activities. These forms differ with the cultural imagery of each human collectivity, retaining nevertheless some basically similar characteristics.

When this Sabian symbol reaches into the consciousness of a man seeking meaning, it should be seen as an invitation to open his mind to the possibility of approaching life in a holistic and nonrational, intuitive manner.

This is the first stage of the fourth five-fold sequence of cyclic phases. It implies a call to REPOTENTIALIZATION. What this means also is the process of "becoming like a little child."

PHASE 17 (ARIES 17°): TWO DIGNIFIED SPINSTERS SITTING IN SILENCE.

KEYNOTE: *The ability to transform a natural lack of potency into poise and inner serenity.*

Here we have a symbol which contrasts with the preceding one. In our culture, the "spinster" represents the woman who has been unable to meet or accept the vitalizing power of love and organic fulfillment through biological polarization. Yet the symbol depicts *two* spinsters, emphasizing that refusing the natural expression of bipolar love has produced a special kind of dualism of experience. The two women are silent because this dualism has a narcissistic character. Life has turned inward seeing itself in a self-created mirroring. We have here the result of a negative inward approach to potency. The ascetic or saint also turns inward, but he accepts a higher nonbiological type of polarization: man and God. Just as the activity of nature has a compulsive character, so the resistance of the spinster to biological fulfillment is also compulsive.

This is the second stage of the fourth five-fold sequence. Like all second stages it reveals a contrasting potentiality of experience which can also be seen to complement or polarize the symbol of the first stage. It refers to the value of a dignified INWARD WITHDRAWAL.

PHASE 18 (ARIES 18°): AN EMPTY HAMMOCK STRETCHED BETWEEN TWO TREES.

KEYNOTE: *A constructive alternation of activity and rest.*

The symbol refers to the ability to balance outer vitalistic activity and withdrawal from such activity and relaxation. The owner of the hammock is active, but in his consciousness he can hold the image of rest in the midst of reenergizing nature. The concept of following the rat race of business therefore has no hold. Potency may be preserved and extremes avoided. Time is found for recuperation.

This is a third stage symbol which suggests a middle path between total involvement in instinctual or social drives, and withdrawal in impotent silence and narcissism—thus LIVING RHYTHMICALLY.

PHASE 19 (ARIES 19°): THE "MAGIC CARPET" OF ORIENTAL IMAGERY.

KEYNOTE: *The use of creative imagination.*

A way of life refusing a hectic involvement in social competition and waste-producing overproduction allows for the development of unattached and transcendent understanding. The static floor (carpet) on which man's feet (symbols of understanding) rest can become transformed into the means for great flights of imagination and super-physical perception. The period of rest from outwardly directed activity bound to collective normality presents the creative mind with the possibility of surveying in dreams the totality of the present-day social situation, thus "to see whole."

The fourth stage of the fourth five-fold sequence of symbols invokes the possibility of developing a new technique of perception, A STRIFE-TRANSCENDING AND UNATTACHED OUTLOOK UPON EVERYDAY REALITY.

PHASE 20 (ARIES 20°): A YOUNG GIRL FEEDING BIRDS IN WINTER.

KEYNOTE: *Overcoming crises through compassion.*

Nature's seasonal rhythms imply an oscillation between living and dying. Through creative imagination man can "fly over" the cycle, and discover means not only to escape from the fatality of seasonal decay or deprivation, but to assist other living entities to survive through crises. Migrating birds fly south (cf. symbol of Aries 12°), but by establishing a partnership with other creatures unable to escape wintry deprivation or death, man can maintain the life of the spirit (symbolized by birds) steady through all crises *if*, like a "young girl," he is widely open to the promptings of love and sympathy.

At this fifth stage of the symbolic sequence we witness human activity motivated by sympathy overcoming the seasonal phase of impotence. Life potency in nature spirits reaches a higher level in the human being. The theme is THE TRANSMUTATION OF LIFE INTO LOVE.

SECOND LEVEL: EMOTIONAL–CULTURAL

PHASE 21 (ARIES 21°): A PUGILIST ENTERS THE RING.

KEYNOTE: *The release and glorification of social aggressiveness.*

Here we find potency glorified as muscular strength and will-to-power. Because it is potency operating at a harshly competitive level, it can and often does imply the possibility of defeat or disfiguration. In one sense the symbol translates into social terms the primordial struggle for survival of the fittest, adding to it an eagerness for social fame and social power (i.e. money). In another sense, the ring with two fighters in it can be referred to the Tai Chi symbol and the interplay between Yang and Yin. Each of the two types of energy wins in turn. Victory is always temporary in a dualistic world.

This is the first stage of the fifth five-fold sequence of cyclic phases. Potency and the two-fold possibilities inherent in any release of power are seen operating at the sociocultural and emotional level. The symbol reveals man's deeply rooted feeling of admiration and envy for whoever can generate OVERWHELMING POWER.

PHASE 22 (ARIES 22°): THE GATE TO THE GARDEN OF ALL FULFILLED DESIRES.

KEYNOTE: *Abundance made possible by human togetherness and cooperation.*

In contrast to the crude and cruel road to fame and power symbolized by the prize fighter, we now see a symbol of apparently wide-open and effortless fulfillment. Alone, a human being can barely survive in nature's great life drama; in organized groups men can in due time fulfill their desires. The abundant life is in theory open to all. At least this is the ideal, the great dream. This symbol can also be given an erotic meaning, referring to womanhood.

At the second stage of this series of symbols, the goal of happiness dominates the consciousness of cultural man, the more validly so the more modest his desires. Religious philosophies, like American New Thought, glorify this social feeling of abundance, glamorizing it into an avid COSMIC OPTIMISM and a cult of success.

PHASE 23 (ARIES 23°): A PREGNANT WOMAN IN LIGHT SUMMER DRESS.

KEYNOTE: *Fecundity.*

Masculine aggressiveness and the woman's desire for fulfillment (Phases 21 and 22) are integrated and realized in the expected child. This three-fold sequence can be seen operating at several levels, and the third term, the child, can take various emotional and cultural forms. The basic meaning remains the same. Summer is the period of fruition. Man—at the receptive "woman" level—reaps the fruits of his dynamic activity.

This is the third stage of the fifth five-fold sequence of cyclic phases. It combines the two preceding ones and suggests INNER FULFILLMENT.

PHASE 24 (ARIES 24°): BLOWN INWARD BY THE WIND, THE CURTAINS OF AN OPEN WINDOW TAKE THE SHAPE OF A CORNUCOPIA.

KEYNOTE: *Openness to the influx of spiritual energies.*

The principle of abundance is brought to a further stage in this rather cryptic symbol. Physical fruition is shown operating at a more subtle and spiritual level. The wind (*pneuma*, spirit) blows through the open mind-window and brings into the house of personality a promise of more-than-material potency. Wind blows from a region of high pressure to one of low pressure. As the window curtains are blown inward, the individual consciousness represented by the house is receiving a more concentrated influx of spiritual energies, enabling this consciousness to extend the scope of its awareness and creative expression.

This message applying to this fourth stage of the five-fold sequence is that inner growth demands not just an open mind but one able to provide a container for a spiritual harvest. The cornucopian shape of the window's curtains suggests that the subtler translucent aspect of the mind (the curtains) has acquired a plastic quality enabling it to be MOLDED BY TRANSPERSONAL FORCES.

PHASE 25 (ARIES 25°): THE POSSIBILITY FOR MAN TO GAIN EXPERIENCE AT TWO LEVELS OF BEING.

KEYNOTE: *The revelation of new potentialities.*

In some unspecified way the symbol is a guarantee that man can operate successfully at two levels of consciousness, if he has previously met the condition mentioned in the preceding symbol. "Be open. Be able and willing to shape your translucent mind in the form revealing spiritual fulfillment. And you will be able to experience life and power on inner as well as outer planes." The implied message is one of *faith*. Man can only truly experience what he deeply believes he can experience.

This is the last stage of this fifth five-fold sequence of cyclic phases. It announces the possibility of a new step in evolution, but it is still only a possibility, a promise. The individual is truly ON PROBATION.

THIRD LEVEL: INDIVIDUAL–MENTAL

PHASE 26 (ARIES 26°): A MAN POSSESSED OF MORE GIFTS THAN HE CAN HOLD.

KEYNOTE: *Obsession by potentiality.*

The mind which finds itself confronted with a totally unfamiliar and as yet unexperienced type of potency finds it difficult at first to adjust to its new world of perception and possibilities of action. He may rush ahead excitedly and lose his bearings. He should try to reach a state of calm watchfulness, and to learn that at this level too there are limits and restrictions, i.e. laws expressing this new type of "order."

This is the first stage of the sixth five-fold sequence of cyclic phases. This entire sequence of symbols shows us that man at this evolutionary station has to move carefully in his new realm, for his consciousness is not yet fully able to operate in it, except with closely defined limits. It is a symbol of WARNING—a warning against undertaking more than it is as yet safe and sound to attempt.

PHASE 27 (ARIES 27°): THROUGH IMAGINATION A LOST OPPORTUNITY IS REGAINED.

KEYNOTE: *Revision of attitude and inner revaluation.*

The second stage of a five-fold sequence of phases always reveals a contrast to the first, but not necessarily an opposition. This symbol makes it clear that the mind that has become overstimulated and obsessed by all it appears to be able to accomplish in some new realm of experience *may* easily fail. The disciple fails in his test, or at least it seems to him that he has failed. Actually the "failure" may have been meant by his guru to be a challenge to the emergence of a new capacity; generally speaking, this capacity is what one calls "creative imagination." The mind must first "imagine" that which he will then be able sooner or later to actually experience.

At this stage it may be difficult to distinguish success from failure. Nothing may fail like success, people say. What counts is the development of UNDAUNTED FAITH in the pursuit of one's ideals.

> **PHASE 28 (ARIES 28°):** A LARGE AUDIENCE CONFRONTS THE PERFORMER WHO DISAPPOINTED ITS EXPECTATIONS.
>
> **KEYNOTE:** *The necessity for mature preparation and self-criticism.*

We see here the tangible results of the situation evoked by the two preceding symbols. Great hopes, excited expectations cannot be sustained. The last symbol reveals the performer's state of consciousness; in this one he is actually made fully aware of having promised—to the many elements of his own personality as well as perhaps to other human beings—more than he was able to deliver. The issue is *how to handle this situation*. In one form or another, it is an often recurring situation in the life of an individual person. The manner in which it is met determines the individual's future possibilities of development and achievement.

This is the third stage of this five-fold sequence. What is implied here is the need to be more than "obsessed by potentiality" and *subjectively involved* in the use of the new powers. The objective results have to be considered, i.e. what this use will do. The individual is not alone concerned, for in a sense mankind as a whole will be affected. What is required, therefore, is an objective inclusiveness of the whole environment; thus a sense of RESPONSIBILITY for what one's actions will produce in people who have been made to expect significant results.

PHASE 29 (ARIES 29°): THE MUSIC OF THE SPHERES.

KEYNOTE: *Attunement to cosmic order.*

At the fourth stage of a five-fold sequence a technique is often presented. It is based on the experiences implied in the preceding symbols. In this case, what the individual who has entered into a new realm of possibilities of action should learn is the harmonic principles operating in this realm. The music of the spheres is the celestial embodiment of principles of polyphonic interplay. The individual advancing "on the Path" should seek to understand and realize his place in the vast scheme of mankind's evolution, in the immense Chord of the harmony of the universe.

The message to the seeker for meaning which is implied in this symbol is TO LISTEN TO THE INNER VOICE; to listen without personalizing this Voice in a glamor-producing manner. It is the Voice of the Whole, of which one begins to realize that one is a tiny little part—yet a significant part, for every note of the universal Chord has its place and its ineradicable meaning.

PHASE 30 (ARIES 30°): A DUCK POND AND ITS BROOD.

KEYNOTE: *The realization of natural boundaries.*

After the preceding symbol this may seem anticlimactic. What is shown here is that every form of activity has its limits, and that even the consciousness that has been able to get a glimpse of universal order has to bring down to its own "karmic" field of operation the message of harmony it has heard inwardly. Peace and inner contentment with one's essential destiny (dharma) is required to meet the everyday world. The mystic may experience flights of imagination and transcendent vision, but he must return to the concrete earth and to his task in his social environment. Extensive as the latter may seem it is still very small compared to the galactic field; it is indeed a duck pond compared to the ocean. But it is *there* that the substance for concrete action has to be found, and every effective activity has to be focused; thus the boundaries imposed by the very nature of this activity have to be consciously accepted.

This is the last stage in the last five-fold sequence related to the second scene, characterized by "Potency." It leads to the third scene, whose Keyword is "Substantiation." Potency has to become substantiated—it has to mate with substance—in order to be effective power. Power must accept the principle of FOCALIZATION.

SCENE THREE: *SUBSTANTIATION*
(Taurus 1° to Taurus 15°)

FIRST LEVEL: ACTIONAL

PHASE 31 (TAURUS 1°): A CLEAR MOUNTAIN STREAM.

KEYNOTE: *The pure, uncontaminated and spontaneous manifestation of one's own nature.*

Here we see life substance in its original dynamic form and as it emerged from its spiritual source. This is true whatever the nature of the source may be. In a sense the mountain stream is conditioned by the nature of the soil and by all the forces which in the past have formed the mountain's rock strata: that is to say, by past history. Yet out of this past a new, pure (i.e. unadulterated) release of potentiality has emerged. It is ready to perform whatever work its dharma is to accomplish.

This is the first stage of the seventh five-fold sequence of phases. Matter is still imbued with great potential energy, energy being matter at its source. It is flowing irresistibly toward its own destiny. It is simply ITS OWN NATURE.

PHASE 32 (TAURUS 2°): AN ELECTRICAL STORM.

KEYNOTE: *The cosmic power able to transform all the implications of natural existence.*

At this second stage of the five-fold sequence we see a picture which contrasts with the one for the first stage: thus, a celestial display of power *versus* a clear, lovely-sounding little stream. Back of every natural self-expression stands the tremendous power of the "Soul-field," itself but one of the myriad aspects of the Creative Word that is the origin of this universe. At certain times, this power compels the natural earth-conditioned personality to accept, perhaps in awe, the spiritual potentialities of its "higher" celestial destiny. This experience of power can both illumine and shatter. The next symbol reveals its positive possibilities.

This is a stage of existence in which "revelation" is implied, at least as a potentiality. The *consciousness* may be deeply disturbed by THE VISITATION, but the *substance* of the individual being can be fecundated by the experience.

PHASE 33 (TAURUS 3°): NATURAL STEPS LEAD TO A LAWN OF CLOVER IN BLOOM.

KEYNOTE: *The gradual expansion of the individual consciousness after a fecundating experience.*

Having been "activated" by electrical energy, the pure water of the mountain stream is able to fertilize the soil which covers itself with small blossoms. "Clover" however, is normally a symbol of the Triad ("Trinity"), and thus of the often-mentioned "three natures" in man. To reach the flowering garden of mind, the consciousness must proceed by steps. Effort is needed. What is reached is a flowering display of the simple, quite humble kind, yet bees are after it for honey. There is sweetness and energy latent in the blossoms.

This is the third stage of the seventh five-fold sequence of phases. It is a stage at which one should seek with diligence and determination, but in humility and faith, to reach NATURAL FULFILLMENT.

PHASE 34 (TAURUS 4°): THE POT OF GOLD AT THE END OF THE RAINBOW.

KEYNOTE: *Riches that come from linking the celestial and the earthly nature.*

In Genesis, the rainbow is the symbol of the Covenant of God with Noah. In all mythologies it expresses, in one way or another, a linking process—or the bridge used by divine beings to communicate with mortals. What the linking process brings to the individual consciousness is elusive, as the rainbow never ends where you are, yet it is the source of symbolic, universally valid wealth. All wealth, in a very real sense, comes from "commerce"; i.e. from the commingling of minds and from contracts, and thus is based on faith in the validity of a promise.

At this fourth stage of the five-fold process we are given a mode of operation, which reminds us of the symbol for the second stage, "an electrical storm." Man need not be overawed by the celestial display of power, for it leads to a fruitful contact with beings of light. This is a natural kind of COMMUNION, involving a transubstantiation of matter.

PHASE 35 (TAURUS 5°): A WIDOW AT AN OPEN GRAVE.

KEYNOTE: *The impermanence of all material and social bonds.*

"All natural compounds decay," said the Buddha. The most beautiful and most enjoyed substance loses its potential energy through continuous actualization and the principle of integration and form is withdrawn, leaving the Void—"the open grave" that ends all attachments. The Void is the great challenge: What next? One must begin anew, and if possible at a "higher," i.e. more inclusive and universal, less egocentric, level.

This fifth conclusive stage of the sequence which deals with root elements and basic actions and responses may seem negative, yet it opens the door to self-renewal. Beyond the personal attachment rises the possibility of participating in a larger sphere of existence. This possibility rarely manifests itself except as one is ready to DISCARD THE PAST.

SECOND LEVEL: EMOTIONAL–CULTURAL

PHASE 36 (TAURUS 6°): CANTILEVER BRIDGE ACROSS A DEEP GORGE.

KEYNOTE: *The conquest of separativeness through group-cooperation.*

The person who has suffered deprivation and loneliness can give new substance to his or her emotional life by participating in a collective project. All great evolutionary challenges imply the overcoming of basic difficulties. A step ahead must be taken, yet an abyss confronts evolving man. It is no longer a personal Void—an "open grave"—but a chasm that is an integral part of the "land" upon which man's evolution must proceed. A link must be built through the power of the collective mind of the group or of the community at large, on the basis of the legacy of the past, to make a bridge over the canyon.

This is the first stage of the eighth five-fold process of "Substantiation." The man-made bridge built with collective skill gives substance to and demonstrates man's capacity to CONQUER OBSTACLES and to achieve evolutionary continuity as well as expansion in space.

PHASE 37 (TAURUS 7°): THE WOMAN OF SAMARIA AT THE ANCESTRAL WELL.

KEYNOTE: *The meeting of the traditional past and of the creative spirit pointing to the future.*

The symbol refers to a most important, but usually narrowly interpreted (or interpreted away!) episode of the Christ *mythos.**
Early in his ministry, Jesus meets a Samaritan woman at an ancestral well. This woman belongs to a tribe despised by the

*See discussion of *mythos* on p. 382.

Jews; moreover, she is unmarried and therefore on the fringe of even her own society. It is to just that kind of woman that Jesus reveals that he is the Messiah: "I am He," a revelation that he apparently will not bestow even upon his disciples, at least not *in words*. (Words in occultism are the creative factor.)

What does this mean? Jesus, as the Avatar incorporating the Christ-Impulse, came to replace the old tribal order with a new order based on universal Love. It is not to representatives of, or even to men still attached to, the old order that Jesus could reveal his spiritual, evolutionary and society-transforming status; they had instead to reach a point where *they could discover his avatar-ship*—as did Peter just before the Transfiguration scene. But to the woman of Samaria—who, in her openness to love's urgings, had already repudiated any narrow subservience to the old order—Jesus could reveal his function. The highest meets the lowest when this lowest is free from traditional bonds and open to love. The creative future descends first to that which has become chaos. An old order is never open to a new Revelation until it has accepted disorder in the name of that Power which subsumes all forms of order, i.e. Love.

In this second stage of the five-fold sequence, a contrasting element enters upon the scene. It is no longer a collective-cultural effort based on past knowledge—as in the preceding symbol—but a "meeting" that introduces into the collective situation a totally new factor which transcends it. A NEW QUALITY OF BEING is revealed which renders the old patterns obsolete.

PHASE 38 (TAURUS 8°): A SLEIGH ON LAND UNCOVERED BY SNOW.

KEYNOTE: *The value of anticipating and preparing for expectable conditions.*

Here we have a combination of two factors: "the sleigh," which is a product of traditional skill (cf. Taurus 6° symbol) and the ability man has to foresee and thus to prepare for a future situation. This ability relates this symbol to the one for Taurus 7°, because the woman from Samaria had the capacity to receive a revelation of the future state of human evolution, though in a different and subconscious sense. Man should be ready to use past knowledge and skill to meet the demands of a stage yet to come.

At this third stage of the eighth five-fold sequence we should realize the value of FUTURE-ORIENTED IMAGINATION but also of relying upon the natural order of unfoldment of all life processes.

PHASE 39 (TAURUS 9°): A FULLY DECORATED CHRISTMAS TREE.

KEYNOTE: *The ability to create inner happiness in dark hours.*

In northern or mountainous countries where the Christmas tree symbol took form, we find a contrast between the tree *outside* —bare and normally covered with snow—and the tree *inside* the home—loaded with decorations and gifts for the family. If we follow up the meaning of the preceding symbol, we see that snow has come outside; but the prepared and closely united group has created abundance, beauty and happiness *within*, overcoming the cold barrenness of the outside world—just as man had overcome, in a previous symbol (Phase 35), the natural obstacle to his progress. The Christ symbol is also included in the background—that is, the vivid faith in a transformed future.

This fourth stage symbol suggests the ever-present possibility open to man to transfigure the darkness and deprivation of the low point of a life cycle by incarnating in it an antiphonic response celebrating the ever remembered and always expected high moments of life. It evokes man's undying FAITH IN CYCLIC RENEWAL.

PHASE 40 (TAURUS 10°): A RED CROSS NURSE.

KEYNOTE: *The compassionate linking of all men.*

This symbol reveals the feeling of human cooperation at the stage of pure altruism and service to the social Whole. On that foundation of Christ love (*agape*, or true companionship), man can reach a still higher level of experience made possible by the refinement of the substance of his being, his consciousness and his will. This goes beyond imagination and faith in the future—beyond Christmas tree celebrations—for it implies going into the dark to bring life and love to the tormented and the deprived.

At this final stage of the five-fold sequence we see what is finally open as new potentiality to the "widow before an open grave"—the closing symbol of the preceding sequence. Personal attachment in love to a husband or wife has changed level becoming a CONSECRATION TO HUMANITY.

THIRD LEVEL: INDIVIDUAL–MENTAL

PHASE 41: (TAURUS 11°): A WOMAN WATERING FLOWERS IN HER GARDEN.

KEYNOTE: *Development of the powers of the mind on which ego-consciousness is based.*

The psycho-mental nature of a human being takes form out of the fulfillment and transcendence of biological functions and drives, much as the bud appears as the sap rises, and bursts forth into bloom. "As the roots, so the flowers" is an old axiom. The consciousness attaches itself to this wondrous efflorescence; it lavishes its attention upon it, its love—alas, usually a possessive kind of love ("This is *my* garden!"). Thus the ego develops. It may develop in a negative, resentful way if a belated frost destroys the buds.

This is the first stage of the ninth sequence of phases, a sequence that basically refers to the overall situation related to the development of the ego. The Keyword here is CULTIVATION.

PHASE 42 (TAURUS 12°): A YOUNG COUPLE WINDOW–SHOPPING.

KEYNOTE: *The fascination of the youthful ego with the products of its culture.*

The woman waters flowers in her garden: this is the *inward-turned* attention of the mind reveling in its own flowering. But now we have a scene symbolizing the *outward* longing of the ego, which has polarized itself and become "man-woman." The "man" aspect is that part of the ego which craves direct participation with society and the world of other egos. Fully to participate requires a special kind of substantiation—and we are still in this third scene, the Keyword of which is "Substantiation." Clothes, goods of various types, adornment, and working tools are needed. The consciousness surveys possibilities; they are defined by organic nature (personal abilities) and by the ambition to succeed in society.

This second stage is defined in contrast to the first. The ego becomes aware of what society has to offer. Its attention is turned outward. An interplay takes place between the individual and his culture. He is being molded by what he sees and by prospects for growth in social prestige. It is a phase of SOCIALIZATION OF DESIRES.

PHASE 43 (TAURUS 13°): A PORTER CARRYING HEAVY BAGGAGE.

KEYNOTE: *Self-mobilization for social advantage.*

The "man" spoken of in the preceding symbol is now integrated in a social pattern. He has to carry a load—perhaps a load of debts following an ambitious buying spree, or some other social burden. He is the strong man, the man of ambition who has to take care of the inward-turned "woman" aspect of his consciousness, the aspect that seeks to grow a beautiful "garden" of individual selfhood.

At this third stage of the ninth five-fold sequence we see the outcome of the first two. The relationship of ego-man and society has taken the aspect of COMPULSION FOR GAIN.

PHASE 44 (TAURUS 14°): ON THE BEACH, CHILDREN PLAY WHILE SHELLFISH GROPE AT THE EDGE OF THE WATER.

KEYNOTE: *Returning to simpler joys for revitalization.*

This somewhat ambiguous picture suggests the way in which simultaneous activities of different natures can fill the individualizing mind. The consciousness of socialized man operates at two levels, in close parallelism with what goes on in the unconscious parts of the mind (i.e. the sea). Natural urges are half conscious, half unconscious. They exist in a borderland—the wet sands still partly covered by small waves. The children play a little further away, learning imaginative yet sociocultural games. The hardworking porter loaded with baggage should remain a little child at times and allow himself to be close to subconscious but natural urges. At least he should do so for a while until he feels surer of himself.

This symbol suggests that it is better not to attempt at once more than one can achieve through conscious and ego-driven ambition. It refers to the value, at this stage, of close contact with natural energies and simple pleasures, of a LIVE AND LET LIVE attitude.

PHASE 45 (TAURUS 15°): HEAD COVERED WITH A RAKISH SILK HAT, MUFFLED AGAINST THE COLD, A MAN BRAVES A STORM.

KEYNOTE: *The courage needed to meet the crises precipitated by social ambition.*

The man with the silk hat has seen some of his ambitious efforts bring him social success; but he learns that often "nothing fails like success." The storm may be within him, or it may attack his social status. He is ready to face it daringly. This shows a willingness to accept crises and to go through them—and therefore great character, the soil upon which a higher kind of consciousness may develop.

This is the fifth and final stage of this ninth five-fold sequence of symbols. It implies a transition to a new level at which the individual who has learned from experience demonstrates a truly mature mind. What is revealed here is CHARACTER under adverse circumstances.

SCENE FOUR: *CONFIRMATION*
(Taurus 16° to Taurus 30°)

FIRST LEVEL: ACTIONAL

PHASE 46: (TAURUS 16°): AN OLD TEACHER FAILS TO INTEREST HIS PUPILS IN TRADITIONAL KNOWLEDGE.

KEYNOTE: *The inadequacy of past knowledge in time of crisis.*

During this Act One of the cyclic process the emergence of new developments is emphasized. In time of crisis—as, for example, the "storm" being braved by the man of the last symbol (Phase 45)—the type of wisdom learned from this past remains in the background to be revived later on in new forms; what is emphasized is change. Traditional concepts are not adequate to *confirm* the new conditions of existence. Thus whenever this symbol comes to a seeker's attention it indicates that even the most consecrated tradition does not have the real answer to the problem.

At this first stage of the tenth five-fold sequence of phases of the cyclic process a seemingly negative picture is shown. From the Zen point of view the mind facing trouble should not depend on past concepts but should repeat: "Not this! Not that!"—until the pure Void is reached. We might speak here of the principle of CREATIVE FRUSTRATION.

PHASE 47 (TAURUS 17°): A SYMBOLICAL BATTLE BETWEEN "SWORDS" AND "TORCHES."

KEYNOTE: *Refusing to depend upon the past, the seeker turns warrior, fighting anew the eternal "Great War."*

When Gautama, having sought in vain for the answers to his questions among the teachers of tradition, sat under the Bodhi Tree, he had to fight his own battle in his own way, even though it is an eternal fight. The spiritual light within the greater Soul must struggle against the ego-will that only knows how to use the powers of this material and intellectual world. There is no possibility of escape; it is the energy that arises out of the present moment—the inescapable NOW—that the daring individual has to use in the struggle.

This second stage symbol suggests that salvation is attained through the emergent individual's readiness to face all issues as if there were only two opposed sides. So teaches the Bhagavad-Gita. This is the dharma of this stage of human evolution: a stage of POLARIZATION OF VALUES.

PHASE 48 (TAURUS 18°): A WOMAN AIRING AN OLD BAG THROUGH THE OPEN WINDOW OF HER ROOM.

KEYNOTE: *The cleansing of the ego-consciousness.*

In this third stage of the present sequence the first two stages should be considered background. The traditional teachings concerning man's nature are somehow reconciled with the youthful enthusiasm that sees in every problem of growth an issue between the "good" and the "bad." The symbol suggests that the real enemy is within the mind; it is the ego and its attachment to possessions. The mind is shown in the likeness of a "bag," now empty and needing to be aired in the sunlight. But the "window" must first be opened and the bag emptied.

The phrase "cleansing the doors of perception" has become well known of late. But even more to be cleansed is the container of perceptual images—i.e. the ego mind. The Keyword is PURIFICATION.

PHASE 49 (TAURUS 19°): A NEW CONTINENT RISING OUT OF THE OCEAN.

KEYNOTE: *The surge of new potentiality after the crisis.*

The symbol need hardly be commented upon. When the mind has been emptied and light has been called upon to purify the consciousness freed from its attachment and contaminations, a new release of life can emerge out of the infinite Ocean of potentiality, the Virgin SPACE. What will it be used for?

Because this is a fourth stage symbol we find in it a suggestion of how to approach whatever new phase of life has been not only hoped for, but actually confirmed. The "technique" is simply *to allow* the infinite Potential to operate in unconstrained SPONTANEITY. This means to have reached a state in which the conscious, rational ego is no longer a controlling factor.

PHASE 50 (TAURUS 20°): WISPS OF WINGLIKE CLOUDS STREAMING ACROSS THE SKY.

KEYNOTE: *The awareness of spiritual forces at work.*

Any emergence of life potentialities from the depth of the vast Unconscious is answered by the spiritual activity of superconscious forces in a cosmic kind of antiphony. The individual who has taken a new step in his evolution should look for the "Signature" of divine Powers confirming his progress. It may reveal the meaning of what is to come next. The "winglike clouds" may also symbolize the presence of celestial beings (devas, angels) blessing and subtly revealing the direction to take, the direction of "the wind" of destiny.

This is the fifth stage of the tenth five-fold sequence. It concludes a process, having experienced which the individual should find himself more securely established in his own original nature, receiving the BLESSINGS of super-natural forces.

SECOND LEVEL: EMOTIONAL–CULTURAL

PHASE 51 (TAURUS 21°): A FINGER POINTING TO A LINE IN AN OPEN BOOK.

KEYNOTE: *Learning to discern what in your culture and religion is meaningful to you personally.*

This symbol evokes the traditional practice, when one is in need of guidance, of opening at random a Sacred Book (for Christians, the Bible) and spontaneously placing one's finger on a paragraph. We are parts of a cultural-religious whole, and every whole has a message for its many parts, if these are willing to submit their little wills to the great meaning and destiny of the whole. In an even broader sense, the open mind can learn to detect "signatures" in many events which he has allowed to occur. The too great reliance on repeated symbolizations can lead to a schizoid state of over-subjective dependence upon signs and omens.

This is the first stage of the eleventh five-fold sequence of symbolic phases in the general process of "Differentiation" (Act One). By relying on cultural guidance a person identifies himself with a differentiated type of collective response to a particular environment. It is a state of SUBSERVIENCE TO COLLECTIVE VALUES.

PHASE 52 (TAURUS 22°): WHITE DOVE FLYING OVER TROUBLED WATERS.

KEYNOTE: *The spiritual inspiration that comes to the individual in the overcoming of crisis.*

Here also we are confronted with a symbol of guidance, and the dove flying over troubled waters reminds one of the story of Noah and the Ark. Noah met his and mankind's crisis courageously and in complete obedience to God's promptings. The test completed, he received the dove's message. It is a message from the Holy Spirit announcing a new Dispensation. This symbolic scene can be applied to personal crises resulting from emotional upheavals or from the irruption of unconscious forces and impulses into the consciousness—if the crisis has been faced in the right spirit.

This second stage symbol is in contrast to the preceding one because here it is not the product of a culture, a "book," but instead the rhythm of cosmic, God-ordained cycles that reveals its conclusive beat through a living and concretely significant sign—a REWARD TO THE FAITHFUL.

PHASE 53 (TAURUS 23°): A JEWELRY SHOP FILLED WITH VALUABLE GEMS.

KEYNOTE: *The social confirmation of natural excellence.*

Two elements should be distinguished in this symbolic picture: the gems that result from natural processes, often induced by extreme volcanic heat and pressure, and the finished products of refined craftsmen. Both the gems themselves and the artistry are highly prized and bring prestige to the owner of the jewels.

The symbol applies to any product in which culturally acquired skill has embellished or transformed the end results of a lengthy and demanding natural process.

This is the third stage of the eleventh five-fold sequence of phases. At this stage we are concerned with the social process which brings about a CERTIFICATION OF PERSONAL WORTH.

PHASE 54 (TAURUS 24°): AN INDIAN WARRIOR RIDING FIERCELY, HUMAN SCALPS HANGING FROM HIS BELT.

KEYNOTE: *The aggressiveness of human instincts when fighting for their earthly base of operation.*

In the mythology of early America, the Indian represents the "savage," close to nature and led by primordial instincts. Alas, our present century has revealed that under far less imperative circumstances so-called civilized man is capable of far more cruel tortures and extermination. This symbol related to a fourth stage seems to imply that violence and aggressiveness are basic components of human nature at the level of the emotions and of a deep-seated identification with a particular culture which insists on regarding men of other cultures as potential enemies.

What is being confirmed here is the value of a group of men's differences from other groups. We are still in the period of "Differentiation" (Act One of the cyclic process) and the need for a differentiation of human behavior and collective values is still very strong. At the emotional level man apparently still has to believe in VIOLENCE FOR SURVIVAL.

PHASE 55 (TAURUS 25°): A VAST PUBLIC PARK.

KEYNOTE: *The cultivation of natural energies for collective use and recreation.*

At this final stage of the sequence of symbols focusing on emotional-cultural values, we witness the positive and impressive results of man's collective endeavor to live in peace and to enjoy moments of relaxation. The public park is designed and kept for the enjoyment of all the people of the city.

This is a symbol of COLLECTIVE ENJOYMENT. The individual finds in the products of his culture an emotional enhancement born of the feeling of "belonging" to a large, organized, peaceful whole.

THIRD LEVEL: INDIVIDUAL–MENTAL

PHASE 56 (TAURUS 26°): A SPANISH GALLANT SERENADES HIS BELOVED.

KEYNOTE: *The ritualization of individual desires.*

At this level we see the play of collective values as they affect the individual person and indeed confirm his individuality by giving it a solid basis in a tradition. The individual is still attached to these group-values; he "belongs." Nevertheless, this state is necessary for a safe and secure sense of differentiation within an enfolding whole. Music and the culturally acceptable rituals of love are cultural products, yet each person can use them for the spontaneous fulfillment of his very own desires.

This is the first symbol in the twelfth five-fold series. It reveals the individual human being making use of his personal status to find fulfillment and a sense of social identity. This is ROLE-PLAYING in its most enjoyable form.

PHASE 57 (TAURUS 27°): AN OLD INDIAN WOMAN SELLING THE ARTIFACTS OF HER TRIBE TO PASSERS-BY.

KEYNOTE: *Peaceful adaptation to collective needs.*

In contrast to the impetuosity of the Spanish serenader, we now see the quiet and smiling face of an old Indian woman offering for sale the traditional products of her tribal culture. She too is functioning within the culture which has been sustaining her activity through a long life, bringing to her personal peace and inner contentment. In old age, the power of the collectivity once more reasserts itself, overcoming the perhaps wearying effort man makes to assert his uniqueness and individual character.

At this second stage of the twelfth five-fold sequence the aging mind of the individual peacefully reintegrates itself into the psychic matrix of his group and culture, in serene ADJUSTMENT to the vital needs of the whole of which he sees himself as a fleeting part.

PHASE 58 (TAURUS 28°): A WOMAN, PAST HER "CHANGE OF LIFE," EXPERIENCES A NEW LOVE.

KEYNOTE: *Man's capacity to rise in consciousness and feelings above biological limitations.*

After having stated the youthful and the aged approach of the human individual to the use of what his culture has brought to him, the symbolism stresses man's capacity to rise above the limitations which both biological nature and the "normal" social pattern of behavior have tried to impose on him. As in many of the preceding symbols, a "woman" is pictured, because at this early stage of the cyclic process the individual consciousness still has a receptive or "feminine" polarity—as was indicated in the very first symbol of the entire cycle (Aries 1°).

Whenever this third stage of the twelfth sequence is brought to a person's consciousness, the indication is that he or she should freely open his or her mind to the possibility of always new REBEGINNINGS. Ideally, the new beginning should imply a more mature response to the new possibility of experience.

PHASE 59 (TAURUS 29°): TWO COBBLERS WORKING AT A TABLE.

KEYNOTE: *The two-fold character of man's mature understanding.*

In symbolism the feet are the symbol of understanding. Understanding differs from mere knowledge because it implies at least some degree of identification in depth with what is being understood. Moreover it is impossible fully to understand anything except when its opposite is taken into consideration. The mental process of understanding—and therefore of appreciation—implies confrontation between two points of view. Thus the mind gains a sense of perspective. The way to dispel a shadow is to have the object illumined (on its own two-dimensional level) by two sources of light. True understanding dissipates any intellectual shadow. The "two cobblers" symbolize two contrasting ways of approaching the understanding of an experience—especially a new experience—and they provide concrete forms which may clothe and protect the understanding.

This is the fourth stage of this twelfth five-fold sequence. It reveals symbolically the way in which a mature individual mind works in an attempt to gain PERSPECTIVE; a true perspective becomes the foundation upon which to build a new approach to life.

PHASE 60 (TAURUS 30°): A PEACOCK PARADING ON THE TERRACE OF AN OLD CASTLE.

KEYNOTE: *The personal display of inherited gifts.*

A great person able to display a multitude of gifts is always, at one level or another, the consummation of a long past of efforts and victories. As a great occultist once wrote: "Adepts are the flowering of their races and cultures." The peacock is the bird consecrated to Venus; in occult tradition the Promethean Spirits who gave to animal mankind the divine gift of self-conscious intelligence had come from "Venus"—which may or may not refer to the *physical* planet we can observe in the sky.

This is the final symbol of the fourth scene, whose Keyword has been given as "Confirmation." This peacock symbol indeed confirms the social status of the owner of the ancestral estate. It indicates a CONSUMMATION of individual efforts; and it suggests that such a consummation is hardly possible except when a line of "ancestors"—biological or spiritual—forms its base.

SCENE FIVE: *DISCOVERY*
(Gemini 1° to Gemini 15°)

FIRST LEVEL: ACTIONAL

PHASE 61 (GEMINI 1°): A GLASS-BOTTOMED BOAT REVEALS UNDERSEA WONDERS.

KEYNOTE: *The revelation of unconscious energies and submerged psychic structures.*

Within the relative security of a "boat," an individual person can learn to be aware of the as yet hidden contents of man's collective Unconscious—provided this boat (that is to say, his ego that separates him from the collective planetary psyche of mankind) has been given a glass bottom. The conscious mind must have become, in part at least, translucent. This translucency is not direct openness. The window of the mind remains closed, but through it the individual can become aware of the outside—here "outside" means the psychic depths below the normal level of consciousness.

At this first stage of the "discovery" process one can only speak of vision, not identification. The feeling is one of wonder. "I did not know this could exist! How beautiful!" or "How exciting!" A NEW DIMENSION OF REALITY is perceived by the earnest inquirer.

PHASE 62 (GEMINI 2°): SANTA CLAUS FURTIVELY FILLING STOCKINGS HANGING IN FRONT OF THE FIREPLACE.

KEYNOTE: *A rewarded faith in spiritual blessings.*

The popular allegory refers to the spiritual blessings which come to the "pure in heart," whose consciousness is likened to that of a little child. Polarized by eager expectation and faith in the existence of celestial Powers, the pure consciousness as yet unsolidified by ego and rationalistic arguments experiences the concrete manifestation of what it had imagined. In this symbol, Santa Claus acts "furtively." The gifts from an imagined and intensely believed in spiritual world must not be examined closely or at length by the reasoning intellect. The would-be clairvoyant is told not to look straight and intently at what he begins to "see"; instead he should cast sideways glances at it, since the sharply focused mind would make the apparition vanish.

At this second stage of the thirteenth five-fold sequence we have once more a symbol in contrast to the one for the first stage. In order to discover the wonders of the normally unconscious depths of the collective psyche, the individual has to build the proper kind of vehicle (a glass-bottomed boat); but the reception of new blessings from the spiritual realm above (the superconscious) requires mostly faith and purity of heart, and a common type of understanding (stockings)—thus a state of INNOCENCE.

PHASE 63 (GEMINI 3°): THE GARDEN OF THE TUILERIES IN PARIS.

KEYNOTE: *The formalization of collective ideals through the application of reason and order to newly discovered aspects of nature.*

The gardens of the Tuileries and Versailles are typical representations of the classical spirit and its need for order and symmetry. The reign of the French king, Louis XIV, followed the Renaissance, which was filled with the excitement of a new spirit of discovery and a period of internal troubles. A reaction had to come to consolidate the gains made by the collective mind of European man. Such a consolidation usually leads to another extreme, i.e. formalism and often the narrow intellectual crystallization of dualistic concepts.

At this third stage of the thirteenth five-fold sequence of cyclic phases we see the contents of the first and second stages brought to the state of clear and lucid, but also formalized, conceptualization. The heavenly gift-bearing Santa Claus has become the paternalistic autocrat, king by "divine right." The warm family circle celebrating the birth of the Deliverer from wintry darkness is now the Court of the king ruled by rigid rituals. There is clarity, but there is also ego-centralization and the worship of FORMALISM.

PHASE 64 (GEMINI 4°): HOLLY AND MISTLETOE REAWAKEN OLD MEMORIES OF CHRISTMAS.

KEYNOTE: *A longing for the preintellectual state of consciousness.*

The intellect ruled by the ego has taken all that had been seen by the translucent mind (the "glass-bottomed boat") and has given it a logical, rational form. Yet old memories of childhood and its naïve faith sometimes make their way into the consciousness. They are aroused by what remains of the ancestral images that once had great vitality and power (mistletoe was sacred to the Druids). The holly with its brilliant contrast of red and green recalls a more primitive and magical sense of color, as exemplified in Tibetan art. A nostalgia for more natural and feeling-oriented values tends to lead to a movement of protest—thus, to the intensification of the emotions in the individual personality, or to the Romantic Movement after the post-classical and post-rationalistic European period.

This is the fourth stage in the thirteenth series. It recalls the fourth stage in the eighth sequence (Phase 39, Taurus 9°) symbolized by "a fully decorated Christmas tree." But the vivid experience of childhood now has become only an obsessive or nostalgic memory. It heralds a resurgence of deeper values and aspirations which had been forced back into the collective unconscious. What is stressed here is the value of tradition-based archetypes during the process of "discovery," a RETURN TO THE SOURCE. The contact with archetypes may nevertheless lead to explosive situations.

PHASE 65 (GEMINI 5°): A REVOLUTIONARY MAGAZINE ASKING FOR ACTION.

KEYNOTE: *The explosive tendency of repressed feelings and root emotions.*

Every movement overstressing one direction calls forth in time an equally extreme movement in the opposite direction. This is particularly true at the level of the dualistic mind symbolized in the zodiac by Gemini. What is rigidly bound in form and convention tends to explode into formlessness. It may do so violently if socially oppressed—through revolution—or at the psychological level in psychosis; or it may withdraw inwardly into the mystical state in which one identifies with an unformulatable Reality.

This fifth stage is related to the first, for it is the experience of a world of being so far unperceived by the everyday consciousness which starts the process. In the same sense a psychedelic experience may momentarily make the mind transparent to a non–ego-structured realm of consciousness, and may lead to a sustained attempt at understanding what has been revealed of a transcendent Reality. Whether the revolutionary action is violent or peaceful, bitterly resentful or loving, the one desire is TO REACH BEYOND ESTABLISHED FORMS.

SECOND LEVEL: EMOTIONAL–CULTURAL

PHASE 66 (GEMINI 6°): WORKMEN DRILLING FOR OIL.

KEYNOTE: *The avidity for that knowledge which ensures wealth and power.*

This symbol superficially considered can be referred to the insatiable drive of modern man for power and wealth, his readiness to accept the risk of failure. But it has a deeper meaning, especially if related to the next symbol. Oil is the end result of the decay of living materials. Drilling for oil may represent the attempt to penetrate to the deep layers of the collective Unconscious and to reawaken the powers of the archaic psyche which once flourished—for instance in the true ceremonial magic of the tribal world, perhaps among the adepts of the fabled Atlantis, or even among the shamans and witch doctors of more recent times. The archaic powers may be "refined" for modern situations, but the almost inevitable result is the release of noxious waste products, "pollution." And there is a pollution of consciousness as well as of the atmosphere man breathes.

The zodiacal sign Gemini has basically the meaning of insatiable curiosity and avidity for knowledge; it is logically a "human" sign (the Twins). One of the Twins tends to seek power and knowledge from the ancient past, the other to discover a living source of strength and wisdom which is forever being replenished by the celestial downpour of Spiritual Consciousness and love (cf. the next symbol). It is man's nature, alas, to begin with potentially negative emotions and desires.

This is the first stage of the fourteenth five-fold sequence of cyclic phases. It deals with the emotional and, at the present-day level of evolution, socially prized reaction of most human beings to the attainment of new forms of knowledge, i.e. AMBITION.

PHASE 67 (GEMINI 7°): A WELL WITH BUCKET AND ROPE UNDER THE SHADE OF MAJESTIC TREES.

KEYNOTE: *Man's primordial faith in the hidden sustaining power of life.*

In contrast with the ambitious drive of modern man for power and wealth we now have the image of the eternal search for that which is at the root of all living processes, i.e. water. This search also demands some effort—raising the water-filled bucket—but it is a simple natural effort under the shade of trees which attest to the presence of the life-giving fluid. This presence depends on the cooperation of sky (rain) and earth (the geological formation able to hold the water), and man must develop the intuitive sense which enables him to feel this presence and to make it effectual in his daily life. He must sense the hidden reality which preserves for the use of all living organisms this gift of the "sky," the bounteous rain.

At this second stage of the fourteenth five-fold sequence of symbols, the power of the collective and bio-spiritual energies which sustain all earth-rooted cultures is stressed, in contrast to whatever the technological mind of man can make available to increase his personal comfort and mastery over matter. The symbol implies A FUNDAMENTAL TRUST IN AND COOPERATION WITH LIFE.

PHASE 68 (GEMINI 8°): AROUSED STRIKERS SURROUND A FACTORY.

KEYNOTE: *The disruptive power of the ambitious mind upon the organic wholeness of human relationship.*

We are dealing in this sequence of symbols with man's discovery of the new powers residing in his special contribution to the total organism of this planet Earth—his consciousness and aggressive mind. The first stage (Phase 66) dealt with oil, the typical form of energy which the modern mind has made available. (These symbols were revealed before atomic energy was even thought of as a practical possibility.) Now we see in this new symbol a pictorial indication of what the use of this intellect-generated energy inevitably leads to: industrial unrest and violence. As man manages to rape the earth in order to demonstrate his power and intensify his pleasures and his sense of proud mastery, conflicts and disruptive processes are inevitably initiated.

The arousal is presented to us here in its collective social form because we have reached the emotional-cultural level. The type of power generated by the analytical intellectual faculties is essentially disruptive; it is based on the destruction of matter, and invites egocentric hoarding and spoliation—and, in general, privileges of one kind or another. This leads to a REVOLT AGAINST PRIVILEGES.

PHASE 69 (GEMINI 9°): A QUIVER FILLED WITH ARROWS.

KEYNOTE: *Man's aggressive relationship to natural life, as a basis for survival and conquest.*

The bow and arrows represent symbolically man's ability to extend the scope of his conquest of nature and to kill enemies in order to build a larger base for the collective development of a culture and an organized society. Implied in the symbol of the arrow is the piercing of a target. The mind of man is essentially a trans-piercing power; it goes *through* the object toward which it is aimed. It seeks to go through and beyond the obstacles on its path, and this usually implies the destruction of the obstacle. At a higher level—as in the Zen practice of archery—the obstacle is the ego.

At this fourth stage of the fourteenth five-fold sequence of phases in the cyclic process of human existence we are shown the archetypal symbol of Man, the Conqueror. It may be a conquest of outer nature, or that of instinctual drives and of the limiting power of the ego. It is always CONQUEST.

PHASE 70 (GEMINI 10°): AN AIRPLANE PERFORMING A NOSE DIVE.

KEYNOTE: *A superior ability to challenge nature and play with danger.*

Through the controlled use of mental powers man is able to challenge the most basic force in nature: gravitation. He enjoys playing with it as a lion tamer with his violent animals. But what he challenges is within himself as well as outside. Gravitation is the universal binding force of the material world. By challenging it man prepares himself to pierce beyond the physical and to reach higher realms of existence. He may lose the struggle, but that prospect makes the effort more exciting. He might gain "immortality."

This is the final stage of the fourteenth sequence. The symbol for it has a strong sense of finality. No possibility of half measures exist. Man is committed irrevocably to success or failure—at least as a conscious and self-reliant mind. The alternatives are clear-cut. One may describe it as MIND vs. MATTER, or as Man's will against the fate that gravitation so aptly symbolizes.

THIRD LEVEL: INDIVIDUAL–MENTAL

PHASE 71 (GEMINI 11°): NEWLY OPENED LANDS OFFER THE PIONEER NEW OPPORTUNITIES FOR EXPERIENCE.

KEYNOTE: *The power and joy of new beginnings.*

These "newly opened lands" can refer to any as yet unexperienced field of potential activity at any level—material, emotional, mental or supermental. We are now dealing with the third level of experience, at which individuality—or at least the ego character—operates more definitely. While in the preceding phases much was said concerning the powers of the mind, this mind was essentially based on the collective patterns of a culture and a society. Now, at this third level, we find the human being essentially engaged in his personal and particular struggle for full and effective individualization. And the initial realization he has to experience is that he has reached a potentially virgin field of consciousness and activity. He is facing the unfamiliar. Anything could happen.

This is the first stage of the fifteenth five-fold sequence of symbols. Having conquered, at least to some extent, the collective and material energies of nature and society, man has become relatively "separate" from the past. He faces the future. Every step ahead should show him RISING TO THE OCCASION.

PHASE 72 (GEMINI 12°): A NEGRO GIRL FIGHTS FOR HER INDEPENDENCE IN THE CITY.

KEYNOTE: *Liberation from the ghosts of the past.*

While "newly opened lands" theoretically offer virgin fields for experience, in fact those men and women who reach them find themselves conditioned by their own past. They carry the ghosts of their former lives and the memories of collective social patterns with which they had identified their egos. Every new beginning is surrounded with ghosts (or personal and social karma). The racial struggle for equality of opportunity must go on, even if this equality is officially guaranteed by the Law. The struggle is within and takes many forms. The Puritans brought to the theoretically "New World" the fears, the fanaticism and the aggressiveness of their European existence, and these often grew more virulent under the conditions found in the New World. But no field of activity is ever totally "virgin." It has its inhabitants, and they cling to their possessions or privileges. Whoever seeks to be truly an individual must be liberated from the past.

Here at this second stage we have the usual contrasting type of symbol. The new lands are opened, but they are filled with lives, and the pioneer's mind filled with ghosts, preconceptions, and prejudices or expectations. What is needed is a total LIQUIDATION of the past: virgin minds for virgin fields.

PHASE 73 (GEMINI 13°): A FAMOUS PIANIST GIVING A CONCERT PERFORMANCE.

KEYNOTE: *Individual fulfillment in the performing of a social function to which some prestige is attached.*

Having entered upon the path of individualized experience that brings him in touch with broader or higher realms of superpersonal inspiration, the individual person is able to become himself a source of inspiration, an agent for Man and the formative Powers guiding human evolution. His role is to mobilize emotions, to present to others an image of what for most people is beyond their mediocre and lukewarm responses to the challenge of becoming "more-than-man"—to experience more intensely and to see farther. This is the role of the true and ideal "virtuoso" (vir meaning strength, manliness; thus "virtue") and, in a far-reaching sense, of the Avatar whose example fascinates human beings, leading them to leave behind their past and to venture forth into new realms of experience.

At this third stage we see the meanings of the two preceding symbols, synthesized. One moves into new realms and successfully challenges the fears, the insecurity and the lack of self-confidence of the past *in oneself*—all negative attitudes which, while conditioned by the social environment, have become engraved upon the unconscious. Having achieved this liberation, one can bring to the environment the power generated by self-discipline, skill and self-confidence. One has become an at least potential SOURCE OF INSPIRATION.

PHASE 74 (GEMINI 14°): BRIDGING PHYSICAL SPACE AND SOCIAL DISTINCTIONS, TWO MEN COMMUNICATE TELEPATHICALLY.

KEYNOTE: *The capacity to transcend the limitations of bodily existence.*

In order to function in the world of material entities man needs to focus the energies of life in a limited organism and an ego-mind that is formed by the pressures of a particular culture and family background. Yet a time comes when the individual can still transcend the limiting boundaries of culture and ego. An effort should then be made to enter a realm of consciousness in which the communication from mind to mind can take a more direct form, *because* the minds then operate within the One Mind of humanity. It is then as if two cells in a human body were communicating to each other, perhaps through some kind of invisible nerve channels, or, as it were, from nucleus to nucleus by means of vibratory resonance.

At this fourth stage of the five-fold sequence we see the potentiality of a new technique to be used in the "newly opened lands" confronting the pioneers in human evolution. It is a TECHNIQUE OF TRANSCENDENCE. It evidently can also bring confusion and many failures, as well as illusory claims and self-deceit.

PHASE 75 (GEMINI 15°): TWO DUTCH CHILDREN TALKING TO EACH OTHER, EXCHANGING THEIR KNOWLEDGE.

KEYNOTE: *The need to clarify one's experiences through actual contacts with like-minded individuals.*

This symbol adds something vital to the preceding one. Transcendent experiences and supernormal faculties must be tested and clarified through the use of normal and collectively tested means of communication—which may mean through scientific procedures. The "Dutch children" seem to have been introduced by the subconscious mind of the formulator of the symbol because of an association with neatness and the open spirit of discussion which has prevailed in Holland. They are "children" because the new experiences are still very fresh and require certification; this demands a "clean" and open mind eager to test what is experienced in an exchange of views with one's peers.

This is the last stage of the fifteenth five-fold sequence of symbols. It closes the scene of "Discovery." All discoveries must be checked and their validity tested. In old tribal cultures a man's "great dreams" were accepted as valid and acted upon only if another tribesman also had a similar dream. The need for OBJECTIVITY has to be met; and this implies the confirmation of any subjective realization by some similar experience. It implies also the type of dualism inherent in all mental experiences as well as in mental concepts.

SCENE SIX: *EXTERIORIZATION*
(Gemini 16° to Gemini 30°)

FIRST LEVEL: ACTIONAL

**PHASE 76 (GEMINI 16°): A WOMAN ACTIVIST IN AN EMO-
TIONAL SPEECH DRAMATIZING HER CAUSE.**

KEYNOTE: *A passionate response to a deeply felt new experience.*

What has been "discovered" not only needs to be discussed and
tested through an intellectual exchange which permits its formulation, it also demands "exteriorization." This implies the act
of dealing with those who are still unaware of the new knowledge or realization. A public is needed, and it has to be convinced; its inertial resistance to change has to be overcome. This
usually requires an emotional dramatization of the issues at
stake. Here again, as at the very start of the cycle (Aries 1°), a
woman is depicted, which means a person depending upon
feelings and fiery images to sway the receptive public.

This is the first stage in the sixteenth five-fold sequence in the cyclic
process. We are dealing now with the exteriorization of the original
impulse—i.e. the emergence from the vast ocean of potentiality which
constitutes human nature at all levels. What is at stake is a process of
communication of new experiences. The mind is called upon to perform its work, but what comes first is the action of that mind which
is violently moved and which attempts to move other minds by violent
means, the PROSELYTIZING MIND.

PHASE 77 (GEMINI 17°): THE HEAD OF A ROBUST YOUTH
CHANGES INTO THAT OF A MATURE THINKER.

KEYNOTE: *The transformation of physical vitality into the
power to build concepts and intellectual formulations
through which knowledge can be transferred.*

While in the preceding symbol we see the explosive release of
impulses generated by a new realization of what is right and
wrong—the "woman" way controlled by feelings—now we
have a picture of a process of quiet and steady metamorphosis
of biological energy into mind-power, which can be seen symbolically as the "man" way. The symbolism may seem old-fashioned today, but the two contrasting approaches to communication of new experiences remain evident, however one wishes to
symbolize them.

This second stage of the sixteenth sequence, as is nearly always the
case, presents a contrast with the first stage. What we see pictured is
the transformation of emotions into mind, of instincts into thoughts—
a process of MENTAL METAMORPHOSIS.

PHASE 78 (GEMINI 18°): TWO CHINESE MEN CONVERSE IN
THEIR NATIVE TONGUE IN AN AMERICAN CITY.

KEYNOTE: *The need for the mind to retain its independence
from its physical environment in order to concentrate
on its special problems.*

Individuals who have entered into a new realm of activity usually find themselves alienated from their social environment. In
a sense they "live *in* the world" (the world of ordinary men still
bound to common earthly and biological pursuits) but "are not
of the world." They normally seek companions who can speak
their language. It may be an "old" language, that of wisdom
rather than that of knowledge. China's culture is far older than
that of the American masses swarming through greed-infested
cities.

This third stage of the process reveals what may occur when the individual has developed new capacities for experience that may enable him to tap the vast reservoir of the planetary mind of Man. To the common man he appears to speak a foreign tongue. He experiences a process of INSULATION; yet he is never really alone. Here and there he finds those who can understand him.

PHASE 79 (GEMINI 19°): A LARGE ARCHAIC VOLUME REVEALS A TRADITIONAL WISDOM.

KEYNOTE: *Contacting the all-human planetary Mind underlying any cultural and personal mentality.*

Occult tradition tells us that all cyclic manifestations of the human mind have had a primordial revelatory Source. It speaks of ancient books made of especially treated papyrus leaves and conveying through symbols the archetypal processes at the root of all earthly existence (see Blavatsky's *Secret Doctrine*). Such volumes, said to remain in the possession of certain Adepts, constitute the "exteriorization" of archetypal knowledge and wisdom. They contain the "seed-ideas" from which the human mind grows, cyclically producing cultures of various types.

This fourth stage symbol evokes for us the "technique" by means of which the human mind can uncover the foundations of its nature and acquire what might be called SEED–KNOWLEDGE, the knowledge of the structure of cyclic and cosmic manifestations of life on this planet.

PHASE 80 (GEMINI 20°): A MODERN CAFETERIA DISPLAYS AN ABUNDANCE OF FOOD, PRODUCTS OF VARIOUS REGIONS.

KEYNOTE: *The assimilation of multifarious knowledge through the synthesizing power of the mind.*

From the One, the Many arise in due time. The Original Source gives birth to the mountain stream which, gathering to itself the downflow of rain water, becomes the large river around which cities are built. These in turn pollute the river on its way to the vast ocean. This modern symbol expresses the fact that man, now at the close of a cultural cycle, is able to gather foodstuffs —mental as well as physical—from many regions of the globe. His diet has acquired a planet-wide foundation; history tells us that the search for salt and spices, then for commodities rare in local regions, provided the impetus for global trade and thus eventually for a planetary consciousness. The results may be satiety and indigestion, and mental confusion caused by lack of discrimination.

This is the last symbol of the sixteenth five-fold sequence. As is most often the case such a fifth stage implies a certain kind of synthesis or at least a preparation which leads to a new level. The keynote here is indeed ASSIMILATION; the negative potentiality of the symbol is WASTE.

SECOND LEVEL: EMOTIONAL–CULTURAL

PHASE 81 (GEMINI 21°): A TUMULTUOUS LABOR DEMON-STRATION.

KEYNOTE: *The revolutionary impact of mental concepts upon the collective emotions and desires of man.*

This symbol parallels the one which began the process of "ex-teriorization" (Gemini 16°), but the process is seen here operat-ing definitively at the level of collective responses. The mass of men have been aroused by mental images, slogans and an appe-tite for the abundance the "ruling class" enjoys. This also applies to the individual person in whom contrasting spheres of activity have taken shape as the result of the mind-based individualizing process. The organic functions make their collective demands upon the lordly intellect. The stage may be set for the kind of "revolution" we call psychoneurosis.

This begins the seventeenth five-fold sequence of symbols. It sets the stage for a tumultuous process, which may lead to a new approach to the problems resulting from individualization. The repressed or op-pressed instincts stage an EMOTIONAL OUTBURST, claiming their due.

PHASE 82 (GEMINI 22°): DANCING COUPLES IN A HARVEST FESTIVAL.

KEYNOTE: *The wholesome enjoyment of organic processes and emotional drives.*

Again we have an image in strong contrast to the first of this series. From the mind-built city, where workmen claim a larger sphere of social abundance, we find ourselves in the village, where men and women live in far greater harmony with natural and seasonal processes, giving free rein to their emotional instincts. The two poles of a wholesome society—the large industrial city and the agricultural village—should be included; likewise the two poles of a healthy personality—mind and natural emotions—should be active.

This is the contrasting second stage of the seventeenth sequence of five symbols. It stresses the value of rhythmic, healthful activity in a natural setup, for this leads to an often much needed process of BIO-ENERGETIC REBUILDING.

PHASE 83 (GEMINI 23°): THREE FLEDGLINGS IN A NEST HIGH IN A TREE.

KEYNOTE: *The growth of spiritually creative processes in an at least relatively integrated mind.*

In traditional symbolism birds usually refer to spiritual forces, or at least to the higher and freer aspects of the mind. Here we see only the very beginning of a process in what we might also call "the upper chamber" of the consciousness where the creative power of the spirit can be received and assimilated. Fecundated by the spirit and supported by a deeply rooted cultural and vitalistic tradition, man can gradually develop an integral personality. It is essentially three-fold, reflecting the Divine Trinity, in India expressed as Sat-Chit-Ananda.

This is the third stage of a process which should lead to a deeper and more natural understanding of human existence. It suggests that the ambitious mass protests of aroused and largely blind desires should be transmuted through harmonization with natural drives and in terms of spontaneous responses attuned to the phases of natural evolution. Stressed here is CREATIVE INTEGRATION.

PHASE 84 (GEMINI 24°): CHILDREN SKATING OVER A FROZEN VILLAGE POND.

KEYNOTE: *The use of inhibiting circumstances for the development of character and a transcendent approach to the environment.*

Winter symbolizes darkness and the restrictions imposed upon living things by cold. Natural life is in a state of hibernation or inward-turned activity. Yet the developing mind can learn to use restrictions and the disciplining power of "cold" external responses to rise above the outer "freeze" and to grow in strength and skill. Man is nature rising above the cyclic oscillation of natural polarities. His way is often the *via negativa*. He learns rhythmic freedom ("skating") by using the most binding situations ("ice") to demonstrate his transcendent capacity for pleasure and self-mobilization.

Here again the fourth stage symbol presents us with a special technique. It is a mental technique inasmuch as it is through mind that man can transcend the entropy of the universal process of existence. We see here indeed man's TRIUMPH OVER ENTROPY.

PHASE 85 (GEMINI 25°) A GARDENER TRIMMING LARGE PALM TREES.

KEYNOTE: *Bringing under control nature's power of expansion.*

The intellect of man is like a tropical plant in that it tends to expand "wildly" in many directions, seeking direct contact with the sun's rays. Like a palm tree it uses its dead leaves to protect itself against dry heat, the heat of the realm of mind when deprived of the complementary power of the feelings. A culture is characterized by specific "forms" and "prime symbols"; education's main object, at least in cultural and classical periods, has been to contain the imagination of individuals within these traditional forms. An entirely different approach to education is being attempted in our transitional age.

At this last stage of the seventeenth five-fold sequence we have reached the level of fulfillment of the impulses which began at the first stage (Gemini 21°) in a tumultuous upsurge of self-assertion and protest against the past. Now this upsurge has found its place in the evolution of mankind and society; and—symbolically speaking—"labor" has become not only unionized, but a strong force in the body politic. Yet the energies released seek constant expansion and therefore have to be controlled. There is need for repeated PRUNING.

THIRD LEVEL: INDIVIDUAL–MENTAL

PHASE 86 (GEMINI 25°): FROST-COVERED TREES AGAINST WINTER SKIES.

KEYNOTE: *The revelation of archetypal form and essential rhythm of existence.*

At this third level of "exteriorization" a contact with archetypes and pure forms of individual selfhood is to be sought—also with the characteristic images (Spengler's Ur-symbols) of the culture. Externals are left behind. This is a step beyond "pruning"; it is rather a process of removal of all superficialities of existence. Cyclically, nature helps us to reach this state of bare reality. It is not that we experience the Buddhist's void *(sunya)*, but rather that we reach the essence of our individual being, the form of pure selfhood which is the structuring power underneath all external features—all that belong to the "leaf" realm.

This is the first stage of the five-fold process, now in its eighteenth phase. In a sense we can speak of it as a stage of ascetic repudiation, but it is also one of ESSENTIALIZATION.

PHASE 87 (GEMINI 27°): A GYPSY EMERGING FROM THE FOREST WHEREIN HER TRIBE IS ENCAMPED.

KEYNOTE: *Reaching out toward participation in a larger whole of mind-structured existence.*

The contrast between this and the preceding symbol is significant. The first revealed the periodic opportunity nature offers man to penetrate beyond mere appearances and the glamour of existential abundance (the mass of green leaves); now we see at work another process which depends upon the individual— a conscious attempt to leave behind the tribal-instinctual stage of earthbound existence and to emerge into the realm of mind and complex, tense interpersonal relationships (i.e. the city). The "wild" drives of nature are reaching toward a situation in which they will be "tamed."

This is the second stage of the five-fold sequence. It reveals a period of transition, a more or less clear yearning for a new state of consciousness, and thus for inner transformation. It is a phase of REPOLARIZATION.

PHASE 88 (GEMINI 28°): THROUGH BANKRUPTCY, SOCIETY GIVES TO AN OVERBURDENED INDIVIDUAL THE OPPORTUNITY TO BEGIN AGAIN.

KEYNOTE: *A release from unbearable pressures, freeing one for new tasks.*

This symbol can easily be misinterpreted, for while it obviously has a connotation of failure, it nevertheless depicts a particular state of the complex relationship of an individual to his community. The bankruptcy proceedings mentioned here should not be construed as referring to a fraudulent type of bankruptcy. At least in the United States bankruptcy does not imply a moral condemnation; rather, it means that individual failure cannot be separated from the health of the community. The special nature of the whole is implied in the failure of the part to perform adequately under particularly harsh economic conditions. A society which enthrones the principle of ruthless *competition* must also develop mechanisms to exteriorize the principle of *compassion*. The latter was at first emphasized by Northern Buddhism, and soon after by Christianity. The concept of atonement is directly related to that of release from unbearable economic pressures in bankruptcy.

This is the third stage in the eighteenth sequence of cyclic phases. In the first two stages we have seen the emergence of a new consciousness based on leaving behind the externals of bio-psychic living in its at least relatively wild and exuberant aspect. Here we have another kind of "leaving behind," a LIBERATION FROM THE PAST.

PHASE 89 (GEMINI 29°): THE FIRST MOCKINGBIRD OF SPRING.

KEYNOTE: *The creative exuberance of the human soul in response to basic life experiences.*

The mockingbird is able to imitate sounds he hears, but actually he does more than imitate, for he weaves all these sounds into melodies which at times can have joyous amplitude and instinctively creative spontaneity. The symbol refers to the capacity which the talented individual has to take *collective material* and to transform it under the urge of biological productivity and instinctual love. The song rises, powered by these great natural drives, very much as so-called popular songs rise from the youthful soul in response to deep personal or social emotions.

At this fourth stage of the five-fold sequence, what is presented to us symbolically is the reaction of the individual who has become sensitive to many life currents in his environment and who is able to exteriorize this welling-up response as a gift to his society, displaying VIRTUOSITY.

PHASE 90 (GEMINI 30°): A PARADE OF BATHING BEAUTIES
BEFORE LARGE BEACH CROWDS.

KEYNOTE: *The setting of social standards through personal
excellence and competition.*

In this very American scene we see a very ancient and basic
process which can operate at several levels. Society sets certain
collectively acceptable cultural standards, and recompenses by
prestige and fame the persons who embody them, physically or
mentally. This generates emulation and the desire to bring the
social images to their most perfect and concrete manifestation.
The archetypal image or canon of proportion is thus incarnated
for all to behold and be fascinated by. The process of exteriorization is completed.

This is the last phase of the sixth scene. In the zodiac the spring season
has come to a close. It is summer solstice. Fulfillment leads to new
demands upon the individual human consciousness. The SHOW is over.
Now comes the hour of decision.

ACT II: STABILIZATION

SCENE SEVEN: *DECISION*
(Cancer 1° to Cancer 15°)

FIRST LEVEL: ACTIONAL

PHASE 91 (CANCER 1°): ON A SHIP THE SAILORS LOWER AN OLD FLAG AND RAISE A NEW ONE.

KEYNOTE: *A radical change of allegiance exteriorized in a symbolical act: a point of no return.*

We have now reached a square (90-degree angle) to the beginning of the cyclic process. This is a moment of crisis, a sharp turning point. In the zodiacal cycle, at the summer solstice the northward motion of the sun (in "declination") stops; the sun rises and sets as far north of exact east and west as it can during the year-cycle. Its motion is now reversed. Slowly the sunset points move southward on the western horizon, and the length of the day decreases. In the lunation cycle (from New Moon to New Moon) this is the First Quarter phase. On the "ship" which symbolizes the ego-consciousness floating, as it were, on the sea of the vast Unconscious, the individualized will makes a basic decision. The dominant Yang force allows the Yin force to begin its six-month long rise to power. The "collective" will gradually overcomes the "individual," and at the end the state will overpower the person. Now, however, the individual person enjoys his most glorious hour; he exults in his ability to make a "free decision"—i.e. to act as an individual who selects his life goal and his allegiance.

This is the first stage in the nineteenth five-fold series of degree symbols. In a decisive act heavy with consequences, the symbolic college-youth might realize that he should bring to an end his quest for the ideal companion and enter into matrimony. He assents to the possibility of progeny, of home responsibility. His consciousness accepts a process of fundamental REORIENTATION, implying the stabilization of his energies.

PHASE 92 (CANCER 2°): A MAN ON A MAGIC CARPET HOVERS OVER A LARGE AREA OF LAND.

KEYNOTE: *The ability to expand one's consciousness by stabilizing one's point of view at a higher level.*

This is the paradox which confuses so many minds. As long as the intellect restlessly searches for new horizons it is confused by its searching. Accepting a stable focus, the mind can raise its point of observation and see reality in a truer perspective. The individual becomes the whole focused at this particular point for a particular task and function. He can at least reflect the consciousness of the greater Whole, Humanity.

This second stage symbol establishes a contrast between a stabilizing new allegiance which limits the will, and the capacity to envision life from a wider perspective, thanks to which many lives are seen to converge upon the raised consciousness. At this stage one realizes that by giving up an indefinite search for two-dimensional extension, one gains ELEVATION in the third dimension of consciousness.

PHASE 93 (CANCER 3°): A MAN BUNDLED IN FUR LEADS A SHAGGY DEER.

KEYNOTE: *The need to overcome stagnation and "cold" during trial of endurance.*

This rather enigmatic symbol has suggested an exploration in arctic regions; but it seems more relevant to see in it simply the difficult phase imposed by the new allegiance upon the reoriented consciousness. In India the deer was the symbol of Brahma, the Creative God. The antlers represent the extension of the mind-power located in the head. The new path may lead to cold regions requiring insulation from harsh circumstances. There may even be a desire to escape from new responsibilities. The will leads the mind on toward the spiritual North of the soul.

This is the third stage in the nineteenth five-fold sequence. A period of trials is implied. The focalized mind may seek to escape its limits by venturing forth toward an idealized goal—the North Star, perhaps. This represents A TESTING OF THE WILL.

PHASE 94 (CANCER 4°): A CAT ARGUING WITH A MOUSE.

KEYNOTE: *An attempt at self-justification.*

We are still involved in the results of an act which brought about a radical reorientation of one's life. The drives of the bio-psychic organism are still not easily conquered. A multitude of lesser decisions inevitably follows the big and grand gestures of repudiation and realignment. The desires of the body still drown the voice of the "new man." One argues with oneself, hoping to convince oneself that the old impulses are still legitimate.

At this fourth stage of the five-fold sequence hesitancy and conflicting motives are still inevitable. The mind is very clever at not facing the consequences which follow from desires or even from restlessness. Attempts at RATIONALIZATION are experienced and should be understood.

PHASE 95 (CANCER 5°): AT A RAILROAD CROSSING, AN AU-
TOMOBILE IS WRECKED BY A TRAIN.

KEYNOTE: *The tragic results which are likely to occur when
the individual's will pits itself carelessly against the
power of the collective will of society.*

The automobile symbolizes the individualized consciousness eager to pursue its own course of action regardless of how it may
conflict with the collective consciousness of the community (the
train). The symbol implies that at this early stage of the new
process which began with this seventh scene, all such individual
and relatively anarchistic or law-defying attempts are bound to
fail. The driver may live, but his car will be wrecked.

Lest we consider this phase totally negative, we should realize that
most of the time man learns his lessons through relatively destructive
experiences—the *via negativa* of the mystic, or even the strange occult concept expounded in some sects of "salvation through sin." One
may speak here more generally of KARMIC READJUSTMENT. This will
become evident as the next five-fold sequence is considered.

SECOND LEVEL: EMOTIONAL–CULTURAL

PHASE 96 (CANCER 6°): GAME BIRDS FEATHERING THEIR
NESTS.

KEYNOTE: *An instinctual dedication of self to new forms
of life.*

The original symbol (which was subsequently altered) spoke
here of "game birds"; thus we deal with spiritual forces (birds)
placed within a social context. As in the symbol for Cancer 1° we
see here the beginning of a process; action is definitely oriented
toward the future. A new wave of life is starting and a concrete
—and no longer symbolical—preparation is made for it. At a
social level—we can speak of the pioneering efforts dedicated
to the building of a new culture, new institutions.

This is the first stage of the twentieth five-fold sequence of symbols. It reveals a preparation for rebirth, and a significant note is sounded by the mention of game birds. What is being built is instinctively—but not yet consciously—offered to a higher level of consciousness. The young-to-be are potential sacrifices to feed human beings, just as tribal men sacrificed virgins to satisfy the gods. Already the meaning of the second half of the cycle (the first degree of Libra, for instance) is implied, just as the entire social process is implied in the formalism of the marriage ceremony. An appropriate key would be SYMBIOSIS, i.e. a deep unconscious cooperation between different levels of existence, the "animal" level producing lives for the sake of the "human."

PHASE 97 (CANCER 7°): TWO NATURE SPIRITS DANCING UNDER THE MOONLIGHT.

KEYNOTE: *The play of invisible forces in all manifestations of life.*

To the clairvoyant who visualized these symbolic scenes, the nature spirits (or fairies) most likely were thought of as more or less imaginary or ideal creations. At least they were linked with hidden and mysterious processes in nature, and the "moonlight" emphasizes this otherworldly or elusive character. Thus a contrast is implied between this character and the concrete and material process of building a nest for a physical progeny. The basic concept is that behind all vital processes one can perceive occult forces at work. They operate within a realm often called "astral" or "etheric"; and the moon has a deep influence upon that realm, releasing special solar rays of occult potency.

This is the second stage of the twentieth sequence. It contrasts the invisible with the visible, the inner with the outer, the dream and the ideal with everyday reality. In a sense this refers to man's CREATIVE IMAGINATION.

PHASE 98 (CANCER 8°): A GROUP OF RABBITS DRESSED IN HUMAN CLOTHES WALK AS IF ON PARADE.

KEYNOTE: *The tendency in all forms of life to imitate higher forms as a stimulus to growth.*

This rather strange symbol points to what is essential in all first attempts at developing consciousness and furthering one's growth through association with those who have already reached a superior evolutionary or mental level. Every seeker looks for an "Exemplar." The religious mystic speaks of "the Imitation of Christ." In Japan the music student sits in front of his teacher playing an instrument, and carefully imitates his every gesture.

At this third stage of the five-fold sequence we see at work the basic features at the start of all LEARNING PROCESSES. At the next stage we will watch a more advanced, more typically human quest for knowledge.

PHASE 99 (CANCER 9°): A SMALL, NAKED GIRL BENDS OVER A POND TRYING TO CATCH A FISH.

KEYNOTE: *The first naïve quest for knowledge and for an ever-elusive understanding of life.*

The "small, naked girl" symbolizes the innocent and spontaneous mind, as yet unclothed in cultural patterns and unrestrained by *don't*'s, trying to satisfy its curiosity about what seems mysterious and fleeting. In a sense the "pond" is the infant's mind with a very limited scope of consciousness, yet eagerly reaching out to catch the swift and elusive first realizations of the meaning of life.

At this fourth stage we are confronted with the nascent curiosity about knowledge, a curiosity which makes the little mind reach out in spontaneity, rather than merely imitate the elders. Whenever a person is confronted with this symbol he or she should realize that there is much value indeed in simply reaching out with a pure and unconditioned mind to the most elementary experiences which natural life offers to us. The key here is PURITY IN UNDERSTANDING.

> PHASE 100 (CANCER 10°): A LARGE DIAMOND IN THE FIRST STAGES OF THE CUTTING PROCESS.
>
> KEYNOTE: *The arduous training for perfection in order to fully manifest an ideal.*

We are still dealing with the evolution of consciousness and of personality at a preliminary stage. The potentiality of a completely formed mind through which the light of understanding will shine brightly is already in evidence, but much work is still to be done. We may meditate upon the transformation of the "pond of water" (in the preceding symbol) into a diamond not yet completely cut. The conscious mind must acquire solidity so it can be worked upon by higher agencies—ideally by the teachers of the community. It no doubt must be a painful operation for the rough stone, but the goal is worth the suffering, the heat, the grinding noise . . . provided of course the diamond cutter is an expert craftsman—a rare case among teachers!

At this last stage of the five-fold sequence we once more deal with an operation which when completed will acquire a social value. When fully grown, the "game bird" (first stage) may satisfy a hungry stomach; once cut to perfection, the "diamond" may fill a woman with pride. As Keyword we suggest CRAFTSMANSHIP, here meaning especially the training for perfection.

> THIRD LEVEL: INDIVIDUAL–MENTAL
>
> PHASE 101 (CANCER 11°): A CLOWN CARICATURING WELL-KNOWN PERSONALITIES.
>
> KEYNOTE: *The value of humor in developing objectivity and independence of mind.*

Humor or irony is a powerful tool in assessing the value of sociocultural realities, and thereby in freeing oneself from glamor and prejudice. Laughter deconditions and often paves the way to a realization that we need not be unduly impressed by what our tradition has more or less forced upon our consciousness. The clown, of course, is the more popular manifestation of this urge to laugh, which seems to be such a basic characteristic of human nature. Caricature and satire are more intellectual forms of the same need for intellectual freedom.

In this twenty-first five-fold sequence we witness the development of true individuality in man. And the first step is a cathartic one—the ability to laugh, which includes the ability to laugh at one's petty habits and mannerisms—indeed, at one's own pomposity. It is a DECONDITIONING step.

PHASE 102 (CANCER 12°): A CHINESE WOMAN NURSING A BABY WHOSE AURA REVEALS HIM TO BE THE REINCARNATION OF A GREAT TEACHER.

KEYNOTE: *The revelation of latent worth in an experience once it is seen in its deeper meaning.*

In contrast to the "clown" symbol, which shows us man's capacity to criticize and laugh at his superficial mannerisms and automatic habits or gestures, we now have a symbol which demands that we look beyond common appearances and try to discover the "occult" (i.e. hidden) character of every person and every experience. This symbol has been unduly glamorized: there is no particular reference here to an avatar or messiah, except in the sense that every man is *potentially* the avatar or manifestation of a Soul that has a definite and relatively unique function in the vast field of activity we call the Earth. To discover this occult potential of being, one requires a deeper or higher "vision," a holistic perception—which is usually, but not always justifiably, called clairvoyance. The caricaturist also has to develop a special kind of "seeing" to enable him to extract the salient features of an *outer* personality or of a face. He picks out the most characteristic *parts* of a whole; the true clairvoyant perceives the essential meaning (or "message" and function) of the *whole*.

The contrast between the first and second symbols of this twenty-first five-fold sequence is indeed very significant. There may be no particular meaning in the fact that the nursing woman in this symbol is Chinese. Perhaps the psychic who visualized the scene may have mistaken a Tibetan for a Chinese woman, and unconsciously thought of the rather familiar process through which a new Dalai Lama, or other great Lamas, are searched for among newborn babies. The Keyword is REVELATION.

PHASE 103 (CANCER 13°): A HAND WITH A PROMINENT THUMB IS HELD OUT FOR STUDY.

KEYNOTE: *The power of the will in shaping character.*

Here again we see how a personal characteristic reveals what is behind it psychologically and spiritually. The thumb in palmistry signifies the will; a very rigid thumb shows an unbending will; a more flexible one, a more pliable individual. In the original formulation of the symbol the "hand" was said to be "slightly flexed" which may be taken to suggest a more flexible character. Nevertheless, the basic meaning is that individuality can only express itself through a strong character. Whenever this symbol confronts a person or a situation it is shown that a strong will is required to face the issue at stake.

This is the third stage in the twenty-first five-fold sequence, and the Keyword is CHARACTER.

PHASE 104 (CANCER 14°): A VERY OLD MAN FACING A VAST DARK SPACE TO THE NORTHEAST.

KEYNOTE: *Fulfillment in transcending and changeless wisdom.*

This symbol describes the Wise Old Man, an archetypal figure found in all systems of symbolism. In occult terminology the northeast is the direction from which spiritual-cosmic forces enter the Earth-sphere. This is probably because the polar axis of the Earth is inclined by some 23 degrees away from the exact perpendicular to the plane of its orbit. Thus the actual pole of our *globe* not only differs from the permanent pole of the Earth's *orbit*, but constantly changes its direction, successively pointing to several large "circumpolar" stars during the so-called precessional cycle (or "tropical year," or Great Polar Cycle), which lasts somewhat less than 26,000 years. Because of this inclination of the polar axis, we have the phenomenon of seasonal change. Supposedly during the early Golden Age no such change occurred; a "perpetual spring" reigned. This is the (traditionally) spiritual state. The Wise Old Man faces the Changeless Reality, the true North—which for us is located in a northeast direction. He faces the great Void, that apparent Darkness which is an intense Light invisible to our senses.

As this is a fourth stage symbol in the five-fold sequence, there is as usual a hint of technique. Implied is that by consistently and for a long time meditating on the changeless and spiritual reality at the very core of all experiences one can attain the supreme and age-old wisdom. We see in the symbol a way beyond appearances and toward PERMANENCE IN TRUTH.

PHASE 105 (CANCER 15°): IN A SUMPTUOUS DINING HALL GUESTS RELAX AFTER PARTAKING OF A HUGE BANQUET.

KEYNOTE: *The need that exists at an early stage of human growth to materialize the concept of fulfillment.*

This may be considered a curious symbolic scene following the preceding one, for it pictures a scene of fulfillment at the purely physical level of eating, if not overeating. Possibly the person who visualized the symbol could think of fulfillment—consciously or unconsciously—only in terms reminiscent of the Mohammedan picture of paradise, a place filled with all the good things earthly life provided, only most sparsely. It may also be that the symbol is a reference to the fact that what in European countries is seen rather broadly and spiritually as "plenitude of being" is usually related in the United States to the idea of "plenty." Thus when in books or articles I have used the word "plenitude," the printer in most instances wrote the nonexistent and barbaric word "plentitude." We are hypnotized today by the ideal of physical abundance. Perhaps physical abundance is less mind-haunting than deprivation, and there may at times be a need to "turn to superficial things for self-strengthening." This is the *via negativa* already mentioned. Through satiety man learns to appreciate and desire asceticism; after months of boredom the modern teenager in an ultramodern "progressive" school is often ready to accept disciplined work.

This is the last of the five symbols in the twenty-first sequence. It ends this part of the quest for individuality and the process of "decision"-making on a note which indicates a phase of only temporary fulfillment. The darkness in the northeast may have been too much for the consciousness at this stage of the great cycle. The mind yearns to translate what it has seen in purely physical terms. This is perhaps the keynote of American life: the MATERIALIZATION OF THE SPIRITUAL.

SCENE EIGHT: *CONSOLIDATION*
(Cancer 16° to Cancer 30°)

FIRST LEVEL: ACTIONAL

PHASE 106 (CANCER 16°): A MAN STUDYING A MANDALA IN FRONT OF HIM, WITH THE HELP OF A VERY ANCIENT BOOK.

KEYNOTE: *A deep concern with problems raised by the process of personality integration.*

After a person decides to follow a certain course of action, accepting a new allegiance, the results of this decision at the three basic levels of human experience (actional, emotional-cultural and individual-mental) have to be stabilized and consolidated.

This is what is meant by the process of personality integration. In Asia the great symbol of this process is the Mandala; in the Christian world we find, in various forms, the symbol of the Cross. The Christian design is often simple and bare; it is its reference to the crucifixion of a God-man that personalizes or emotionalizes it. The Oriental Mandala can take an infinite variety of forms and can encompass a vast multiplicity of contents; it is psychological and cosmic. The square—the foundation of the Mandala—potentially encloses diverse contents. The Cross, on the other hand, represents conflict in action; it is a symbol of tragic overcoming. The Mandala symbolizes integration of opposing trends and multiple bipolar energies.

This is the first stage of the twenty-second five-fold sequence. It reveals a deep effort on the part of the individualized consciousness to reach a solid basis of understanding that will allow it to perceive the structural relationship of every part of the personality to every other part. It is a mental process implying study and an inward-turning of the attention, CONCENTRATION; even more it is a symbol of what might at first be called CONFORMATION—that is, a profound and stabilizing sense of form, but of *one's own* individual form, not an external sociocultural pattern.

PHASE 107 (CANCER 17°): THE UNFOLDMENT OF MULTILEVEL POTENTIALITIES ISSUING FROM AN ORIGINAL GERM.

KEYNOTE: *The life urge to actualize one's birth potential.*

What is pictured here is simply the process of germination. As it unfolds from the sundered seed the plant pierces the crust of the soil and reaches up toward the light. This is a dynamic process turned outward, in contrast to the more static or introspective process of integration-through-understanding depicted in the preceding symbol. Germination is the crucifixion of the seed. The seed becomes the germ, just as the Tibetan student meditating silently and peacefully on the Mandala is followed by the Christian Crusader—and, at a materialistic level of productivity, by the engineer-technologist intent upon transforming the globe for the greatest possible enjoyment of the greatest possible number of human beings.

As usual, the second stage of the five-fold sequence establishes a contrast with the first. Action polarizes meditation. The expanding process of self-actualization—which may mean nothing more than ego-expansion through conquest—contrasts with the introspective study of the structural relationship between, and the meaning of, the various energies and potentialities of one's nature (*svarupa* in Sanskrit). The Keyword is GROWTH.

> PHASE 108 (CANCER 18°): A HEN SCRATCHING THE GROUND TO FIND NOURISHMENT FOR HER PROGENY.
>
> KEYNOTE: *The practical concern with everyday nourishment necessary to sustain one's outreaching activities.*

Every mother is originally responsible for the feeding of her progeny, and all the activities into which a person has poured his energy are his symbolic children. He has to feed them with social substance gathered from "the ground" of his community, and to watch with concern over their unfoldment. The tender stem consolidates into the tree trunk, the chicken into the hen, the infant into the theoretically self-reliant and socially wise adult.

This third stage of the twenty-second five-fold sequence shows the results of the two previous stages. Seed, germ and the growing plant requiring the chemicals of the soil for its daily growth form a clear sequence. What is at stake here is the FULFILLING OF LIFE'S RESPONSIBILITIES.

PHASE 109 (CANCER 19°): A PRIEST PERFORMING A MAR-
RIAGE CEREMONY.

KEYNOTE: *The ritualization of productive interpersonal re-*
lationships.

This scene symbolizes the profound need for referring the interplay and the relatively permanent and productive union of
all polarities to some third factor which either includes, or transcends and gives spiritual meaning to, the relationship. A conju-
gal union is essentially and traditionally the union of a man and
a woman for the sake of producing progeny able to perpetuate
the racial type, the family tradition and the way of life of a
particular culture (or "subculture"), including a set of religious
beliefs. The married couple is the basic productive unit in our
society—as it has been for millennia in all patriarchal societies.
The purpose of *any* established religion (including tribal cults)
is to glorify, sanction and bless with a superpersonal meaning
all personal and interpersonal activities. This occurs through
the "sacraments," and indeed through most religious rites.

At this fourth stage of the five-fold sequence we are given the basic
technique used in all processes of effectual social or group integration.
It is the technique which takes the form of sociocultural, and thus
business or religious, ritualization. Through this technique commonplace individual endeavors acquire SANCTION; that is, they are ritualized an indeed "sanctified."

PHASE 110 (CANCER 20°): VENETIAN GONDOLIERS GIVING A
SERENADE.

KEYNOTE: *Happiness as an overtone of social integration*
and conformity to custom.

Venice can be considered the symbol of a social consciousness
risen directly from the unconscious urges of human nature—
because the city emerged out of the sea, just as the lotus flower
floats on top of the lake, its roots implanted in the bottom mud.
The serenading gondoliers "float" over the water, their songs

raised to the balconies where the "flower" of consciousness, the beloved, may make her appearance. This play of basic human drives toward acceptance by the consciousness housed in the structures of the ego is performed according to social tradition. Everything plays its part, and man experiences social happiness and a sense of fulfillment.

This is the fifth of the twenty-second sequence of five symbols. The urge for individual integration represented in the first—integration through meditation on ancient traditional forms—is now reflected in the drive for social integration through the elegant and standardized play of acceptable emotions. The Keyword might be FESTIVITY.

SECOND LEVEL: EMOTIONAL–CULTURAL

PHASE 111 (CANCER 21°): A FAMOUS SINGER IS PROVING HER VIRTUOSITY DURING AN OPERATIC PERFORMANCE.

KEYNOTE: *The emotional reward accompanying cultural excellence.*

If anything represents the type of response that a well-developed society gives to the individual who successfully pours his energy into the skillful externalization of the great images of its culture, it is the opera. The operatic prima donna is not merely a lonely performer, like the piano virtuoso (Gemini 13°); he or she is the star in a collective effort. The opera is not only music, but a story, a *mythos*, which embodies some of the most basic images and emotions characterizing the culture that gave it birth. Euro-American culture is indeed extolled—or condemned—by its operas and their lurid and tragic passions. It is interesting to compare the opera with the equivalent type of social performances and their topics in India, Java or Tibet.

At this first stage of the twenty-third five-fold sequence of cyclic phases we find the drive toward individualization by means of concrete forms of cultural activity glorified in social and financial success. In its deepest sense the symbol refers to THE PRICE OF SUCCESS—for the individual, as well for as the collectivity acclaiming him or her. What is success really worth? A question few people ask.

PHASE 112 (CANCER 22°): A YOUNG WOMAN AWAITING A SAILBOAT.

KEYNOTE: *The longing for transcendent happiness in the soul opened to great dreams.*

Here the symbol pictures the imaginative youthful person who basically cannot be satisfied with what his or her ordinary social environment offers, and who instead is longing for the unknown visitation of which he or she has dreamed. From the unconscious beyond, the concretization of a spiritual image—spiritual because impelled by the "wind" (*pneuma,* spirit)—is hoped for and expected. The Beloved may come—not in a glittering opera house, but in the silence of the inner sea of consciousness.

At this second stage of this five-fold sequence the contrast with the first is strongly marked. Will the great dream become concrete? Will the emotion ready to well up in response to the Advent have its chance? Will the EXPECTANCY of the Eternal Feminine be rewarded with reality?

PHASE 113 (CANCER 23°): THE MEETING OF A LITERARY SOCIETY.

KEYNOTE: *An objective and critical approach to the common factors in our culture and to its psychological problems.*

The poets, novelists and critics of a society represent the endeavor by especially sensitive and intellectually gifted individuals to give form and meaning to the most characteristic situations and interpersonal relationships of their society and culture. They mirror society and at the same time influence and guide its development. It is their function to discuss the significance of what is, and to image what might be. They are both barometers and thermostats, reflectors and projectors of as yet mostly unconscious images.

With this third stage we reach the level of INTELLECTUALIZATION. Here the individual operates both as an objective mind an an emotional participant in the events and hopes of his day. He makes concrete what to most people may be only a subconscious aspiration or urge.

PHASE 114 (CANCER 24°): A WOMAN AND TWO MEN CASTAWAYS ON A SMALL ISLAND OF THE SOUTH SEAS.

KEYNOTE: *The focalization of complex inner potentialities in harmonic and concrete relationships.*

We are dealing here with a special phase of the process of integration. The woman and the two men represent the three-fold aspect of the human personality, particularly at this stage when one of these aspects—the emotional life (the woman)—is facing the possibility, if not the inevitability, of relating itself to both the spiritual and the mental. This confrontation occurs on a small island of the South Seas, and "south" always refers symbolically to the strong and passionate impulses of human nature. Somehow the three-fold consciousness has to develop a harmonious and well-integrated *modus vivendi* (a specific way of life). If successful, this will release powerful energies and will lead to the next symbolic scene.

We have reached the fourth stage of the twenty-third five-fold sequence. As is most often the case, we are introduced here to a specific technique—or at least to a problem of technique—in living. The three human beings should become integrated; but the form this integration will take seems left open. It has to be a concrete type of integration in terms of the emotional and biological drives of human nature (an island of the South Seas) and the field of integration is "small." The key to the problem of relationship should be the realization of INTER-DEPENDENCE.

PHASE 115 (CANCER 25°): A WILL-FULL MAN IS OVERSHAD-
OWED BY A DESCENT OF SUPERIOR POWER.

KEYNOTE: *The response of spiritual forces to the integration of personality through positive will-full endeavors.*

We are dealing here with a man who uses his will and positive
imagination in facing his life problems. To him comes a pen-
tecostal descent of power. He receives the "mantle of power,"
the grace (*baraka* in Sufi philosophy) or the Providential assistance which can make him a true leader in his culture.

In this fifth symbol we witness a more transcendent expression of
"success." It is not merely external success (as is given by society to its
prima donnas), but a spiritual response, a sign of inner strength and
uncommon ENDOWMENT.

THIRD LEVEL: INDIVIDUAL–MENTAL

PHASE 116 (CANCER 26°): GUESTS ARE READING IN THE
LIBRARY OF A LUXURIOUS HOME.

KEYNOTE: *The transference of social privilege to the level
of intellectual enjoyment.*

We now see the concretization of cultural excellence and
wealth at the level at which individuals can exercise their developed mental capacities in comfort. The process is individualized
because the library belongs to a private residence, the luxury of
which implies an individual's concentration upon the acquisition of wealth. This scene shows the result of such a concentration, including the acquisition of friends who can relax in and
enjoy intellectual pursuits.

This is the first phase of the twenty-fourth five-fold sequence which
here begins, and will end, on a note of social opulence and prestige.
We are not dealing now with leaders in the intellectual community,
but with wealthy guests who apparently seek to improve their minds
or to keep up with intellectual trends of the time, thus maintaining

CLASS STANDARDS OF INFORMATION. What is at stake here is the need
to conform to the requirements of one's social status.

PHASE 117 (CANCER 27°): A VIOLENT STORM IN A CANYON FILLED WITH EXPENSIVE HOMES.

KEYNOTE: *A confrontation with a social upheaval demanding the reconsideration of static values.*

The deeper implications of the scene depicted in the symbol are
that the sociocultural elite can always see its position and
security challenged by forces beyond its control, even if it may
be successful in protecting itself from destruction. The individual may not be able to depend on the standards and values he
has acquired through education and through a relatively shel-
tered and rich life. He has to rise to the occasion, and perhaps
to undergo an inner metamorphosis as a result of the crisis he
has been able to accept as a personal challenge.

The contrast between the two first phases of this twenty-fourth sequence is evident: peace in luxury and intellectual development in
terms of collective cultural values (reading books), then the challenge
to meet a crisis situation produced by uncontrollable karmic forces
that could lead to a successful CATHARSIS.

PHASE 118 (CANCER 28°): AN INDIAN GIRL INTRODUCES HER WHITE LOVER TO HER ASSEMBLED TRIBE.

KEYNOTE: *Inner rebirth through a total acceptance of the primordial values manifest in the human body and its natural functions.*

Even as this symbol was formulated in the clairvoyant's mind,
a few individuals belonging to the American intelligentsia were
trying to find in their absorption into the culture of the Indian
pueblos of the Southwest a solution to their intellectual artifi-
ciality and personal emotional emptiness. Fifty years later this

process has gained great momentum, especially among the disenchanted youth of our affluent middle class. The soul—or in Jungian terms, the "anima"—is leading the sophisticated and colorless (white!) intellect to a level of consciousness at which man can again operate in tune with the vast process of the biosphere and recover the simplicity and the inner peace which city life and business deny.

At this third stage of the twenty-fourth five-fold sequence the situations presented in the two preceding symbols can be seen combined and projected into a possibility of dramatic transformation. What is shown here is an emotional and warm commitment to the RETURN TO NATURE which today appeals so strongly to the new generation, but which Jean Jacques Rousseau, many great Romanticists and Gauguin long ago advocated and exemplified.

PHASE 119 (CANCER 29°): A GREEK MUSE WEIGHING NEW-BORN TWINS IN GOLDEN SCALES.

KEYNOTE: *The intuitive weighing of alternatives.*

This symbol seems to show that the "return to nature" pictured in the preceding symbol is only one of two possibilities. Somehow the repolarization of consciousness and life activities implied by that symbol may be more a dream or ideal than a practical reality. In any case, at this stage in the process of individualization two ways are open. The individual person may hesitate before making his decision. His "intuition" (the Muse) is able to show him what the choice is. Perhaps there can be a way of combining the two alternatives. But, as the next symbol implies, the one which in the end has the greatest appeal may not be the "nature" way. The "white boy" may rather bring the "Indian girl" to the city, as in Pocahontas' life story.

The fourth stage of this sequence of symbols reveals to us the pro and con operation of the mind when faced with a vital decision. Because it is the "Muse" that is doing the weighing, it is apparent that forces deeper or higher than the intellect are actually at work—the intuitive mind, or what Jung calls the "anima," i.e. the psychic function which relates ego-consciousness to the collective Unconscious. What we see happening, at the very threshold of a new cycle, is an INNER PRESENTATION OF ALTERNATIVES.

PHASE 120 (CANCER 30°): A DAUGHTER OF THE AMERICAN REVOLUTION.

KEYNOTE: *The prestige and conservatism of a long-maintained heritage.*

Here we have a symbol of the proud preservation of socio-cultural values in a tradition. After several generations the ancestor who was perhaps a violent revolutionist or rabble-rouser—or even a fugitive from justice—acquires a halo of respectability. The tradition that once was born of revolution now extolls "law and order," attempting to suppress any new forms of the same revolutionary spirit.

This is the last symbol of the section of the cycle referring mainly to the consolidation and concretization of life urges within a stable form of organization. In many instances the scenes presented picture social activities or events, yet at this stage it is the individual person and the problems attendant upon his development that are primarily considered.

This eighth scene with a keynote of "Consolidation," began with the study of a traditional symbol for personality integration, the Mandala; it ends with an example of what occurs when the individual chooses a path which totally embodies and glorifies tradition, a path which ends in a GLORIFICATION OF THE PAST.

SCENE NINE: *COMBUSTION*
(Leo 1° to Leo 15°)

FIRST LEVEL: ACTIONAL

PHASE 121 (LEO 1°): BLOOD RUSHES TO A MAN'S HEAD AS HIS
VITAL ENERGIES ARE MOBILIZED UNDER THE SPUR OF
AMBITION.

KEYNOTE: *An irruption of bio-psychic energies into the
ego-controlled field of consciousness.*

The occult tradition speaks of three kinds of "Fire": Electric
Fire, Solar Fire and Fire by friction. The three Fire signs of the
zodiac correspond to these. Aries refers to the "descent" of the
spiritual energy of the Creative Word. In its material aspect we
know this energy as electricity, and without electrical energy no
life processes could exist. Leo represents Solar Fire, the energy
which is released from an integrated person, either through
spontaneous radiations of apparently nuclear forms of energy,
or, at the truly human and conscious level (and also superhuman
in still more transcendent realms), through *conscious emanations* (e-mana-tions, from *manas* meaning "mind" in Sanskrit).
Sagittarius is related to the Fire by friction, because all social
processes are based on interpersonal relations, which imply polarization and often conflict.

The key symbol for Leo depicts a rising of energy from the
heart to the head, a "mentalization" process. However, this
process is a potentially dangerous one. Thus the original wording of the symbolic scene seen by the clairvoyant referred to "a
case of apoplexy"—just as a man standing with his head uncov-
ered for a long time in tropical regions could get sunstroke. The
sun can destroy as well as vivify. Without its symbolical mate,
water, it produces deserts on earth. The realization of *atman*,
the spiritual self, the existence of a formed and steady ego—
provided the ego can become a lens of pure crystal focusing the
all-pervasive cosmic light of the Brahman without introducing

the shadows of pride, possessiveness and showmanship. But this "provided" raises a very large question. The transmutation of "life" into "mind" is a difficult process.

This is the first stage of the twenty-fifth five-fold sequence of symbols which opens the ninth Scene. The keynote of "Combustion" for the entire series of fifteen phases hardly needs interpretation. In a general sense the key word for this first degree of the sign Leo could be ˙CONFLAGRATION. The energies of the biological drives as they irrupt, more or less forcefully, into the field of consciousness.

PHASE 122 (LEO 2°): AN EPIDEMIC OF MUMPS.

KEYNOTE: *The spreading power of individual crises through a collectivity.*

This symbol should be interpreted at two levels without evading the issues posed by its original wording. What does an epidemic imply, and why mumps? The broad meaning of an epidemic is that one individual, if infected by a certain type of disease, can spread the disease to a vast number of persons in his environment, and in some cases all over the globe. In the preceding symbol we were confronted with the individual crisis, and its dangerous possibilities *for the individual* were implied. Now we deal with a process that affects the entire society; this obviously points out that the whole of mankind is potentially affected by, and thus, consciously or not, cannot help being involved in the critical situations faced by any individual or special group of people. Why then an epidemic of mumps? A childhood disease is implied, but it may have very serious consequences for adult men who catch it, since it affects not only all lymphatic glands, especially in the neck region, but also the testicles. If the sign Aries symbolizes birth as a natural organism on this Earth, Leo represents (at least potentially) rebirth—at the level of the conscious and mind-based individuality. Thus in Leo man, in this sense, is as yet only a "little child"—one might say a would-be initiate, an infant in spirit. The relation of the mumps to the sexual glands is characteristic, for the entrance into the realm of the conscious and individualized mind can affect the sex force, either through overstimulation and irritation, or in terms of a deliberate ascetic deprivation.

This second stage symbol also provides a contrast with the first. What was an individual issue is now seen as a collective danger. Thus we are dealing with THE INFECTIOUS SPREAD OF INDIVIDUAL EXPERIENCES.

> PHASE 123 (LEO 3°): A MIDDLE-AGED WOMAN, HER LONG HAIR FLOWING OVER HER SHOULDERS AND IN A BRA-LESS YOUTHFUL GARMENT.
>
> KEYNOTE: *The will to meet the challenge of age in terms of our modern society's glorification of youth.*

While the original reading of the symbol over fifty years ago spoke of the mature woman having dared to bob her hair, today a similar kind of rebellion against aging and the customs of late middle age would manifest itself in different ways. The meaning of the symbol can be extended to any desire an individual woman would have to claim her right to experiences of youth which may have been denied to her, especially when according to the fashion of the day such experiences are considered highly valuable.

This third stage symbol implies a reorientation of one's ideal of action in relation to the collective mentality of the social environment; more particularly, a refusal by the individualized consciousness to be bound by biological or social standards. The Keyword: INDEPENDENCE.

> PHASE 124 (LEO 4°): A FORMALLY DRESSED ELDERLY MAN STANDS NEAR TROPHIES HE BROUGHT BACK FROM A HUNTING EXPEDITION.
>
> KEYNOTE: *The masculine will to conquer his animal nature and to impress his peers with his skill in performing the ancient traditional power rituals.*

This symbol may be interpreted at the strictly social level—the hunter's trophies, his pride in showing them to members of his high-class club, etc. But if one refers to the higher spiritual-mental implications of the sign Leo, one can see in this picture a reference to man's capacity to overcome the animalistic tendencies of his bio-psychic nature according to certain traditional procedures. The implication of being "formally dressed" is that an important, if not the most important, goal the individual had in developing this capacity has been to "prove himself"—to others, as well as perhaps to himself.

This is the fourth stage of the twenty-fifth five-fold sequence. The symbol can be referred to eagerness to show oneself to the best of one's advantage, which is characteristic of the Leo temperament: TO DRAMATIZE ONE'S ACHIEVEMENTS.

PHASE 125 (LEO 5°): ROCK FORMATIONS TOWER OVER A DEEP CANYON.

KEYNOTE: *The structuring power of elemental forces during the long cycle of planetary evolution.*

Dwarfing the time allowed to individual human beings, the vast periods of geological evolution not only awe our imagination, but allow the slow yet magnificent work of elemental forces as they mold landscapes and canyons, rocks and mountains. This symbol points to our need to acquire a much vaster perspective on what we are able to do—and on our yearning for prolonged youth and our pride in masculine achievements. The works of nature should make us feel humble and help us to "planetarize" our consciousness.

This fifth stage symbol concludes the first-level sequence. It stands in broad pictorial contrast to the first, or rather it seeks to impress us with our vanity as creators of forms and mental achievers. To the dramatic and proud Leo type, it presents a picture of IMPERSONALITY.

SECOND LEVEL: EMOTIONAL–CULTURAL

PHASE 126 (LEO 6°): A CONSERVATIVE, OLD-FASHIONED LADY IS CONFRONTED BY A "HIPPIE" GIRL.

KEYNOTE: *The need to transcend our subservience to fashion, in morals as well as in clothes.*

This refers to the ever-changing pageant of social values, as ideals of human relationship succeed one another, one generation facing in the next an antithetic picture of what it has been brought up to consider worthwhile and decent. The confrontation may lead to great bitterness, yet it should show us the impermanence of most of what society impresses upon our collective mentality.

This is the first stage of the twenty-sixth five-fold sequence of phases of the cyclic process. We are dealing now with cultural values and the emotional impact they have upon our character formation. Whereas the first degree of Leo dealt with an individual crisis of reorientation, the sixth degree refers to a collective, cultural and social crisis which challenges us to realize THE RELATIVITY OF SOCIAL VALUES.

PHASE 127 (LEO 7°): THE CONSTELLATIONS OF STARS SHINE BRILLIANTLY IN THE NIGHT SKY.

KEYNOTE: *The power of basic spiritual values which refer to man's common humanity and to all enduring archetypes.*

The experience of the night sky with its multitude of stars, especially brilliant in all the countries from which astrology came, is just as basic and archetypal an experience as that of sunrise, full moon and seasonal changes. Every people on this Earth has developed the concept of *constellations*, probably because of a need to find order in existence and to personalize everything that could be given a permanent form. Such personalizations can be called "psychic projections," but the projection concept should be worked out both ways. If man projects his basic human nature upon the star-filled night sky, is it not just as logical to say that the universe projects its own forever-evolving patterns of order upon human nature? In either case we deal with archetypal factors which endure through a long series of generations.

This second stage symbol once more stands in perfect contrast to the preceding one. The nearly unchanging patterns of star groups are opposed to the sequence of ever-changing fashions and social ideals. The Keyword here is PERMANENCE.

PHASE 128 (LEO 8°): A COMMUNIST ACTIVIST SPREADING HIS REVOLUTIONARY IDEALS.

KEYNOTE: *The emotional and ideological attempt to return to a state of non-differentiation and chaos as a prelude to a new type of order.*

This symbol, beyond all present-day socio-political controversy, represents the activity of destructive or catabolic forces (one aspect of the Indian god Shiva) in answer to the type of confrontation suggested by the symbol for Leo 6°. The old order is confronted by the youthful drive for a new way of life and a new sense of values. As the old order refuses to yield its prerogatives, this refusal polarizes violent revolutionary action. The revolutionary may have beautiful dreams of a "classless" society free from greed and harsh struggles for survival, but the first practical result of his activity almost inevitably appears as "chaos." Yet chaos is a state of being that calls for a new descent of the power to reorganize and differentiate. Alas, such a descent most often is still based on old concepts, and one witnesses a struggle for personal and dictatorial power.

This is the third stage of the twenty-sixth sequence of five phases, and ideally it could show how the vision of a cosmic order (stage two) might heal the potential conflict between an obsolete Establishment and its youthful challengers (stage one). But reality today presents a more cruel picture of CATABOLIC ACTION.

PHASE 129 (LEO 9°): GLASS BLOWERS SHAPE BEAUTIFUL VASES WITH THEIR CONTROLLED BREATHING.

KEYNOTE: *The need to involve one's most spiritual and vital energies in the creative act if it is to produce significant and beautiful new forms.*

The breath represents the power of the spirit, animator of all living manifestations. Because the glass blower uses his breath to shape the glass vessels, he is a fitting symbol of how deeply any creative individual has to involve his total being in his creation. He is also using the fire of the spirit—transpersonal inspiration—or, in another sense, the fire of deeply felt emotions. Any creative activity which does not involve both the "breath" and the "fire" cannot transform into beautiful artworks—or indeed into any new form of order—the raw materials, remains of the past (the "sand").

This fourth stage of the twenty-sixth sequence symbolically shows us the technique required in true and successful transforming activity. It always implies CREATIVE INTENSITY.

PHASE 130 (LEO 10°): EARLY MORNING DEW SPARKLES AS SUNLIGHT FLOODS THE FIELD.

KEYNOTE: *The exalted feeling that rises within the soul of the individual who has successfully passed through the long night which has tested his strength and his faith.*

The cold air of night having precipitated upon the field of man's consciousness the moisture of his deepest feelings, this widely spread dew is blessed with the light of significance by the rising sun of the new day. Even tears can be transformed into jewels in the light of victory over night and sorrow.

At this fifth stage of the present sequence we see the potential culmination of the process which began on a note of social and cultural crisis. The would-be reformer has to meet many emotional problems as he begins his work of creation. Creation means transformation; the reformer is actually a transformer if he is truly a creative and inspired individual open to the spirit that "makes everything new." The building of a new society, and of one's renewed personality as well, is just as much a process of artistic creation as the making of a delicate glass vase or a symphony. The Keyword is TRANSFIGURATION.

THIRD LEVEL: INDIVIDUAL–MENTAL

PHASE 131 (LEO 11°): CHILDREN PLAY ON A SWING HANGING FROM THE BRANCHES OF A HUGE OAK TREE.

KEYNOTE: *The power of tradition as it shelters the beginnings of individual self-expression.*

The great Tradition of mankind has been symbolized by a vast tree, every spiritual Teacher being one of its many branches issuing from the one trunk of a primordial Revelation. As a man begins his spiritual journey he is like a child in a state of excitement, playing with rhythmic up-and-down moods. He plays with words and concepts which "hang" from the "branches" of the Tradition—and often the whole quest is mainly a game for him. Yet he is securely held by the tree, protected by its foliage from too great and burning a light.

This begins the twenty-seventh five-fold sequence of symbols; it deals essentially with the release of emotional intensity at various levels of the individualized consciousness as it reacts to the newly developed potentialities of the mind. We are dealing at this first stage with the SPONTANEOUS ACTIVITY OF THE INNOCENT MIND.

PHASE 132 (LEO 12°): AN EVENING PARTY OF ADULTS ON A LAWN ILLUMINED BY FANCY LANTERNS.

KEYNOTE: *Group-relaxation in fashionable surroundings as an escape from work routine.*

While the preceding symbol dealt with the simple and spontaneous pleasure of children, this one refers to the more or less standardized and fashion-dictated relaxation of adults who have left behind their day's work and are exchanging pleasantries and gossip. The "lawn" and the "lanterns" are cultivated; the type of mind displayed in the animated conversations, stimulated by liquor, is thoroughly socialized and not always innocent. The great Tradition has become reduced to a mere social fashion.

This second stage symbol contrasts with that of the first phase. We have now reached a stage of SOPHISTICATION and involvement in externals and superficial intellectuality or wit.

PHASE 133 (LEO 13°): AN OLD SEA CAPTAIN ROCKING HIMSELF ON THE PORCH OF HIS COTTAGE.

KEYNOTE: *The quieted mind's recollections of crises and joys long past.*

The sea captain has steered the ship of his ego-consciousness through seas and storms, maintaining the integrity of his individual selfhood while in close contact with the collective Unconscious. Now retired, he may try to distill wisdom from his many experiences and from his victories over elemental forces. The "swing" of the child-consciousness has now become a "rocking chair" from which one can contemplate past as well as present scenes, gently moving as waves roll over the shore. Peace at last.

At this third stage we find the consciousness of old age, after having witnessed the spontaneous play of children close to protective nature (Leo 11°) and the fashionable social parties of escaping adults (Leo 12°): three phases of mental development. Keyword: QUIET RECOLLECTION.

PHASE 134 (LEO 14°): A HUMAN SOUL SEEKING OPPORTUNITIES FOR OUTWARD MANIFESTATION.

KEYNOTE: *The yearning for self-actualization.*

Behind the many rhythms and drives of individual existence, beyond the child, the adult and the old man, stands the soul seeking always to manifest itself *through* the personality. This is the transpersonal urge of the spirit, expressing itself in many ways during the whole life span. But most avenues are blocked, and the soul waits until it can wait no longer. Then comes the dramatic release, which may mean a joyous carnival or madness.

The fourth stage of this twenty-seventh sequence brings a transcendental clue to the technique of living: *Let* the soul speak out! Allow the power of the true tone of your being to manifest itself smoothly, easily, unobstructed—or expect a variety of consequences. LET the soul manifest!

> PHASE 135 (LEO 15°): A PAGEANT, WITH ITS SPECTACULAR FLOATS, MOVES ALONG A STREET CROWDED WITH CHEERING PEOPLE.
>
> KEYNOTE: *The more or less sensational release of energies in a form dramatizing the unconscious aspirations of man's primitive and instinctual nature.*

This last picture of the series dealing with the ninth scene, "Combustion," recalls in a collective sense the dramatic event represented by the first (Leo 1°). The street pageant, perhaps a tumultuous carnival, brings men and women to a peak of emotional excitement, and perhaps incandescence. But the pageant had to be planned carefully by individual minds that sought to express themselves in the process of giving a concrete form to the desires and expectations of the collective crowd. The theatricality of the Leo type is fully expressed here.

This is the fifth stage of the twenty-seventh five-fold sequence of phase. At this stage the mind of the individual is able to give a public DEMONSTRATION of his ability to sway the multitudes by a dramatic presentation of popularized ideals. This leads to a new scene on the cyclic journey around one's own universe, symbolized by the signs of the zodiac.

SCENE TEN: *RELEASE*
(*Leo 16° to Leo 30°*)

FIRST LEVEL: ACTIONAL

PHASE 136 (LEO 16°): THE STORM ENDED, ALL NATURE REJOICES IN BRILLIANT SUNSHINE.

KEYNOTE: *The surge of life and love after a major crisis.*

The symbol speaks clearly for itself. How brilliant the light after the long "night of the soul"! The battered but unconquered consciousness finds itself exalted in the marriage of sunbeams and rising sap. This indeed is "Release"—light and life singing in the cleansed and refreshed mind, flooded for a while by the waters of feeling.

This is the first stage in the twenty-eighth five-fold sequence. It is a sequence that reveals consciousness at its most inspiring moments of enjoyment. But these "peak experiences" can operate at several levels. The first and most basic level is that of life itself, and of the overcoming of its many crises—THE JOY AND POWER OF NEW BEGINNINGS.

PHASE 137 (LEO 17°): A VOLUNTEER CHURCH CHOIR SINGING RELIGIOUS HYMNS.

KEYNOTE: *The feeling of togetherness which unites men and women in their dedication to a collective ideal.*

Religion in its institutionalized aspect is the attempt to give a transcendental character to the feeling of community. The fellowship of common work needed for substance and security in a dangerous world is exalted in periodic rituals in which the co-workers participate. At such moments the consciousness and feelings of human beings flow into a common mold in which they become refreshed by the experience of shared values and beliefs.

This second stage symbol presents a contrast with that of the first only in that the collectively human aspect of experience is in contrast to the purely natural and fundamental character of instinctual life. The existence of a volunteer church choir implies a rather steady phase of culture and society. What is sung reflects the special way in which a particular community of human beings—extensive as it may be—interprets the deepest realities of human existence and man's longings for an ideal. The symbol expresses the idealized aspect of TOGETHER-NESS.

PHASE 138 (LEO 18°): A CHEMIST CONDUCTS AN EXPERIMENT FOR HIS STUDENTS.

KEYNOTE: *In inquiring into the hidden process of nature, the human mind experiences the thrill of discovery.*

Here we reach the level of intellectual analysis and the human ability to control natural processes. This ability is based on the inherited knowledge acquired by a community of men, generation after generation. The symbol stresses this fact, as it presents a teaching situation. The individual demonstrates his power, which is founded on a long series of efforts. He is one link in an ancestral chain which his activity prolongs into the future.

At this third stage of the twenty-eighth phase of the cyclic process we see man, as an agent of the collectivity of human beings, approaching nature in terms of the possibility of transforming it in order to satisfy his needs or his wants. At the highest level of this activity one can speak of ALCHEMY.

PHASE 139 (LEO 19°): A HOUSEBOAT PARTY.

KEYNOTE: *The enjoyment of temporary freedom from rigidly structured social behavior.*

This symbol in a sense duplicates the one for Leo 12°, except that it implies a less conventional and more youth-oriented type of gathering. The houseboat brings an intimacy and a "bohemian" character to the relationships between the participants, while "the evening lawn party" reflects a more socially respectable and superficial kind of interaction between middle-class sophisticates. The houseboat may be anchored, yet it floats on the river which—symbolically at least—extends far beyond the narrow social setup. What is suggested is that in such a gathering, men and women seek to at least get the feeling of the free flow of energies, as an escape from the routine activities of their business or student lives.

This fourth stage symbol indicates the possibility of finding "release" for natural energies in group entertainment and enhanced interpersonal contacts. It speaks of FREEDOM FROM SOCIAL RIGIDITY.

PHASE 140 (LEO 20°): ZUNI INDIANS PERFORM A RITUAL TO THE SUN.

KEYNOTE: *A return to the glorification of natural energies.*

While the first symbol of this five-fold sequence pictured the magnificence of the returning sun after a storm, in this last symbol we see, by implication, man returning to nature and glorifying the sun after the long crisis of "civilized" living in artificial cities. For many years now, the American Pueblo Indian has been for the weary city dweller and the dried-up intellectual a symbol of this "return to nature." After having ruthlessly destroyed him, we come to him as an exemplar of peaceful and harmonious group living.

This fifth symbol of the twenty-eighth sequence brings us the image of a reversal of our socialized activity and opens for us the way to the deepest release of our long-denied root energies. Natural man links himself consciously to the source of all life on earth. And this means IDENTIFICATION THROUGH WORSHIP—and the sanctification of the creative power.

SECOND LEVEL: EMOTIONAL–CULTURAL

PHASE 141 (LEO 21°): INTOXICATED CHICKENS DIZZILY
FLAP THEIR WINGS TRYING TO FLY.

KEYNOTE: *The often-negative and at times ludicrous first
experience with spiritual teachings.*

In Near Eastern symbolism wine, intoxication, and vineyards
always refer to ecstatic experiences and to the contact with
mystical or occult schools. "Chickens" here suggest that we are
dealing with human beings who are the standardized products
of their culture, and more or less undifferentiated specimens of
a social norm. Brought accidentally or prematurely to mystical
or occult experiences, they usually react to them in a highly
confused and "dizzy" manner. What reacts in them is the ego,
and the ego can never "fly" (i.e. experience spiritually transcendental realities in an effectual manner).

This first symbol of the twenty-ninth five-fold sequence presents to us
a picture of the unsatisfactory way many people today—especially
young people—approach what purports to be spiritual reality. The
"food" may be intoxicating, consciousness-expanding, but the inner
openings lack depth and constructiveness, whether or not they produce what appears to be wonderful feelings. One may speak here of
the danger of PREMATURE EXPANSION OF CONSCIOUSNESS.

PHASE 142 (LEO 22°) : A CARRIER PIGEON FULFILLING ITS
MISSION.

KEYNOTE: *Spirituality, in terms of training for service to
mankind.*

In contrast with the intoxicated chicken, we now have the successfully trained carrier pigeon delivering the message it was its
function to carry. Here the domesticated bird is seen endowed
with a special significance and purpose. This refers to spiritual
energies which are being used constructively and which bring
to the consciousness messages from other realms. Individual

realizations acquire their true meaning only as they fulfill a collective function.

This second stage symbol clearly presents a contrasting alternative to what the preceding picture revealed. The "release" of higher energies becomes effective and valuable to the extent to which it serves a higher, but concrete and definite, purpose. This is the ideal of the WORLD SERVER.

PHASE 143 (LEO 23°): IN A CIRCUS THE BAREBACK RIDER DISPLAYS HER DANGEROUS SKILL.

KEYNOTE: *The audacity and perseverance required to control and play with the powerful energies of the vital realm in human existence.*

The horse has always been the symbol of the vital energies. In a wild state the horse represents the magnificent, raw, impetuous energy of the libido in all its forms. When tamed, this energy is put to man's service. There are men who have dominated their natural energies so well that they can perform spectacular feats. Here these achievements are seen within the context of a social function and expressing a flair for dramatics.

At this third stage, the ego is in control; he is a great showman, but he serves a purpose. The performance stirs the imagination of the young consciousness. It raises the mind above the commonplace. The Keyword is VIRTUOSITY.

PHASE 144 (LEO 24°): TOTALLY CONCENTRATED UPON INNER SPIRITUAL ATTAINMENT, A MAN IS SITTING IN A STATE OF COMPLETE NEGLECT OF BODILY APPEARANCE AND CLEANLINESS.

KEYNOTE: *An interior focalization of energy and consciousness at the expense of all forms of outward activity and care.*

This traditional image of the Hindu holy man in the typical Western mind may well hide the fact that without proper training and intense concentration, what we usually consider spiritual attainment, self-realization and the "God experience" is not possible. The "intoxicated chickens" of the Leo 21° symbol must learn self-discipline if they want to "fly." There can be no halfway measures if the goal of true Yoga is to be reached.

This fourth stage symbol, as usual, suggests a certain kind of "technique," or at least an adequate means to reach an envisioned goal. The means is TOTAL CONCENTRATION.

PHASE 145 (LEO 25°): A LARGE CAMEL IS SEEN CROSSING A VAST AND FORBIDDING DESERT.

KEYNOTE: *Self-sufficiency in the face of a long and exhausting adventure.*

The camel here represents a living organism that is able to sustain itself independently of its environment at the start of a trying journey. (The original formulation of the symbol did *not* refer to "*a man* on camel back.") The organism carries within itself what is absolutely needed for survival. At the deeper human level of consciousness it is easy to see the value of self-reliance and self-sufficiency as one enters the occult Path leading to a more dynamic and more inclusive realm of existence.

The camel carries water within its body, and it is said that the dromedary is able to utilize the matter stored in its large protuberance as food. The suggestion here is that in order to be released from bondage to the "old world" we should be completely self-contained emotionally; having absorbed the mental food which this old culture has given us, we are ready to face "the desert," nothingness, *Sunya* . . . until we reach the "new world." We need TOTAL INDEPENDENCE from our surroundings and utter SELF–RELIANCE.

THIRD LEVEL: INDIVIDUAL–MENTAL

PHASE 146 (LEO 26°): AFTER THE HEAVY STORM, A RAIN-
BOW.

KEYNOTE: *Linking above and below, the Covenant with
one's divine nature, promise of immortality.*

In the Bible the rainbow is the sign of the Covenant established
by God with Noah (the cyclic "Seed man") guaranteeing that no
longer shall the destructive power of Spirit (the Shiva aspect of
the Divine) be used to destroy life on earth. As we come to the
third level of the scene of "Release," we find the man who has
been able to weather the cathartic storm face-to-face with his
divine Archetype; because he has been victorious, a link has
been established with his divine Soul-being. Both the human
and the divine partners should remain thus linked. H. P. Blavatsky's last words are said to have been: "Keep the Link un-
broken"—the Link she forged with the Trans-Himalayan
Brotherhood that had sent her into the darkness of nineteenth-century materialism for this purpose.

At the first stage of this thirtieth sequence, the symbol of the rainbow
shows us the need to maintain a state of open communication between
the Sky and the Earth within our total being—not for the sake of
finding an ever-elusive "pot of gold" at the end of the rainbow, for this
end is never to be reached, but in order to face the totality of our
individual selfhood as it is projected in the many-hued dome of our
sky-flung consciousness. After every successfully met crisis, the REVE-
LATION OF WORTH comes to us, and with it comes the promise of
success, if only we do our part.

PHASE 147 (LEO 27°): THE LUMINESCENCE OF DAWN IN THE
EASTERN SKY.

KEYNOTE: *The exalting challenge of new opportunities at
the threshold of a new cycle.*

While the rainbow marks the end of the crisis, early dawn indicates the real beginning of the new period of activity. In the

Biblical symbolism Noah plants his "vineyard"—he begins to teach the "secret doctrine" which he inherited from those *Ben Elohim* (Sons of God) who had not been sucked down into whirlpools of materiality. After the "peak experience" in which we touch our "divine" potentialities comes the struggle with everyday problems. But at first the state of deep inner exultation remains within us. We are aglow with its promise.

The crisis and the blessings it has brought to us are relatively unusual events; every day has its dawn, which we should meet with a pure heart and a clear mind. Alpha (dawn) and omega (the concluding peak experience) are opposites, yet the same. The Keyword here is ILLUMINATION.

PHASE 148 (LEO 28°): MANY LITTLE BIRDS ON A LIMB OF A BIG TREE.

KEYNOTE: *A wide, and perhaps confusing, openness to a multiplicity of inspiring potentialities.*

There is a stage in the spiritual life—which is not different from the everyday life—during which the consciousness, aspiring to greater realizations or more impressive forms of self-expression, feels itself flooded with new ideas and new possibilities. This can be very exciting, yet also quite confusing. It becomes necessary to focus oneself by limiting one's field of vision and activity.

This third stage of the thirtieth five-fold sequence brings us the results of the two preceding ones. We should try not to be OVERWHELMED WITH POTENTIALITIES, yet should enjoy the wonderful lightness of feeling this may bring after perhaps many days, months or years of frustration or darkness.

PHASE 149 (LEO 29°): A MERMAID EMERGES FROM THE OCEAN WAVES READY FOR REBIRTH IN HUMAN FORM.

KEYNOTE: *The stage at which an intense feeling-intuition rising from the unconscious is about to take form as a conscious thought.*

The mermaid personifies a stage of awareness still partially enveloped by the ever-moving and ever-elusive ocean of the collective Unconscious, yet already half formulated by the conscious mind. Any creative thinker or artist knows well the peculiar mixture of elation and anxiety characterizing such a stage. Will the intuitive feeling fade away reabsorbed into the unconscious, or will the inexpressible realization acquire the concreteness and expressible form of a concept or a definite motif in an art form?

This fourth symbol in the thirtieth five-fold sequence suggests that the fire of desire for concrete and steady form burns at the root of all techniques of self-expression. An unconscious energy archetype is reaching toward consciousness *through* the creator, as cosmic Love seeks tangible manifestation *through* human lovers. The whole prehuman universe reaches eagerly to the human stage of clear and steady consciousness. It is this great evolutionary urge, this *élan vital*, which is implied in this symbol of the mermaid seeking human incarnation —the YEARNING FOR CONSCIOUS FORM AND SOLIDITY.

PHASE 150 (LEO 30°): AN UNSEALED LETTER.

KEYNOTE: *The realization by the individual that all thoughts and all messages are inevitably to be shared with all men.*

Coming as it does as the end of this tenth scene and linked with the last degree of the zodiacal sign, Leo, this symbol seems at first quite puzzling; when it has been thought of as an isolated symbol, its essential meaning has not been apparent. The fact that a letter is unsealed does not imply a trust that other people will not read its contents, but rather the idea that the contents are for all men to read. The letter contains a public message in the sense that when man has reached the stage of true mental repolarization and development—which we see in the very first symbol for Leo—he has actually become a participant in the One Mind of humanity. Nothing can really be hidden, except superficially and for a brief time. What any man thinks and deeply realizes becomes the property of all men. Nothing is more senseless than possessiveness in the realm of ideas. If God speaks to a man, Man hears the word. Nothing can remain permanently "sealed."

As this thirtieth sequence of five symbols ends, it is made clear to us, and particularly to the inherently proud Leo type, that all that takes form within the mind of a man belongs to all men. Communication and SHARING must always prevail over the will to glorify oneself by claiming sole possession of ideas and information.

SCENE ELEVEN: *CHARACTERIZATION*
(Virgo 1° to Virgo 15°)

FIRST LEVEL: ACTIONAL

PHASE 151 (VIRGO 1°): IN A PORTRAIT, THE SIGNIFICANT FEATURES OF A MAN'S HEAD ARE ARTISTICALLY EMPHASIZED.

KEYNOTE: *The capacity to picture to oneself clearly the salient features and the overall meaning of any life situation.*

During the two preceding Scenes the "feel" of energy at work has been the dominant feature of a consciousness still strongly ego-centered yet at times eagerly and devotionally reaching up to a realization of divine or cosmic order. Now we have come in the seasonal cycle of the year to the sign Virgo. It is in a sense the symbol of harvesting, but it is also that of the Path of discipleship, and of all strongly determined processes of training, or retraining. Flooded with and having enjoyed and released *energy,* the personalized consciousness now has to learn the lesson of *significant form.* It must be able to see life situations as wholes of experience, and to discover their meaning by distinguishing their most characteristic features.

This is the first stage of the thirty-first five-fold sequence of symbols and its Keyword is DISCRIMINATION. Implied in discrimination is both analysis and intuition. The mind separates and identifies—and unfortunately often exaggerates—what makes a person or a situation different from another; but the intuitive responses of the whole person to what confronts him or her is also essential, for what matters is not only my or your "difference," but the place and function this difference occupies in the organic pattern of the evolution of "humanity as a whole," i.e. of Man.

PHASE 152 (VIRGO 2°): A LARGE WHITE CROSS DOMINATES THE LANDSCAPE.

KEYNOTE: *The wisdom and compassion which only the experience of suffering and isolation can bring.*

The individual must have gone beyond the state of ego-subjectivity in order truly and objectively to "see" and to discriminate. He must have learned detachment; and it is a lesson that no one can learn without the "crucifixion" of the ego-centered emotional life. In the occult tradition, the eye that "sees" must be washed by the blood of the heart. The experience of the Cross dominates the mystic Path that leads to Initiation, i.e. to the entrance into a greater realm of activity and participation with an exalted Company of perfected beings.

While the discovery of significant features in any situation implied the use of the mind, both analytical and intuitive, now a contrasting stage is reached at which the mind itself has to be left behind and perhaps even seemingly destroyed in order that compassion and understanding may rise from the depth of the innermost being: a LIBERATING ORDEAL.

PHASE 153 (VIRGO 3°): TWO GUARDIAN ANGELS.

KEYNOTE: *Invisible help and protection in times of crisis.*

Though the consciousness may not yet be able to realize this as a fact, man is as surrounded by spirit as fish by water. Angels, devas and the like are entitized forms of spirit. In a sense at least, they collectively constitute a realm of existence complementary to mankind. They are specialized fields of energy which are apparently conscious, but not "free" in a human sense —that is, free to be what they are not. We are told, by seers and even by merely clairvoyant persons, that they constitute hierarchies of energy-distributing forms which sustain all life processes—particularly in the vegetable and telluric realms—as well as protective agencies attached to human beings. Modern psychologists may think of them as symbols of as yet latent powers in man's unconscious. By being aware of their presence and sustaining power a man may avoid the desperate feeling of aloneness and alienation which usually pervades the "night of the soul" and the symbolic forty days in the wilderness.

This third stage symbol comes to those who may greatly need its reassurance. It is an answer to the symbol of the Crucifixion. The personal ego-centered feelings may be quartered and destroyed; in their place man may develop a sense of deep companionship with consciousnesses which, though utterly different from his, complement his assuaged mind. He may then realize STRENGTH WITHIN.

PHASE 154 (VIRGO 4°): BLACK AND WHITE CHILDREN PLAY TOGETHER HAPPILY.

KEYNOTE: *The overcoming of sociocultural prejudices.*

Freedom from all the forms, biases and idiosyncrasies of the particular culture and class in which one has been born and educated is a *sine qua non* of the consciousness truly "on the Path." The ideal of universal brotherhood underlies all great spiritual teachings, for they all are like branches of the One Tree, Man, in his divine state. This does not mean there are no racial differences, but rather that these differences have a *func-*

tional value in terms of the whole organism of Man—and of the planet Earth.

At this fourth stage the basic technique which applies to all truly spiritual progress is clearly stated. Every human being should be seen, approached and warmly met as a "child of God," or in less religious terms as an exemplar of Man. Such a status gives to every social and interpersonal group the character of a BROTHERHOOD.

> PHASE 155 (VIRGO 5°): A MAN BECOMING AWARE OF NA-
> TURE SPIRITS AND NORMALLY UNSEEN SPIRITUAL
> AGENCIES.
>
> KEYNOTE: *The opening of new levels of consciousness.*

In the first of this sequence of five symbols we saw the individual seeking to bring out of everyday contacts a consciousness of significant form and meaning. Now, as the sequence ends, a further stage of realization is shown in its initial and relatively primitive character. The consciousness is gradually reaching beyond physical characteristics and becoming aware of energy processes, i.e. of the dynamism of forces which externalize themselves as life forms.

This is the last stage of the thirty-first five-fold sequence of phases of the cyclic process of consciousness. The mind in its objectivizing and analytical character always tends to give "name and form" (*nama* and *rupa* in Sanskrit) to that which it contacts as energy process. It "images forth" energy or feeling, relating it to more or less familiar sense experience. We call this IMAGINATION.

> SECOND LEVEL: EMOTIONAL–CULTURAL
>
> PHASE 156 (VIRGO 6°): A MERRY-GO-ROUND.
>
> KEYNOTE: *The first experience of the dynamic intensity of*
> *life processes and of the possibility of using them to*
> *reach a characteristic ego-satisfaction.*

Several features connected with the old-fashioned type of mer-ry-go-round should be understood in their deepest symbolism.

Two stages of experience are distinguishable: that in which a very young child is seated with his mother or nurse in an open carriage—the only experience is that of circular, perhaps at first dizzying, movement—and the stage of riding a horse (or some other animal) which often goes up and down as well as around. As the horse always represents the vital energy (later understood as libido or "psychic energy"), the merry-go-round at this stage symbolizes or prefigures the awareness of the cyclicity and the ups and downs of the emotional life. In the fully developed merry-go-round the child on his horse is given some kind of handle to try and catch a ring hanging within his reach at a fixed point just outside the merry-go-round. If he succeeds in this rather difficult operation the child wins a prize or gets a free ride. The symbolism is sexual in its implications, but more generally it implies that any cyclic release of life energy provides us with the opportunity of demonstrating some type of skill and mastery.

This is the first stage of the thirty-second sequence of five symbols. In its broadest sense we see here a characterization of what the developing consciousness (and at a certain level, the "disciple on the Path") experiences: AN OBJECTIVE APPROACH TO THE LIFE FORCE.

PHASE 157 (VIRGO 7°): A HAREM.

KEYNOTE: *A fateful (even if sought after) subservience to the vagaries or desires of the emotional nature.*

In a sense this symbol is related to the preceding one, while revealing a deeply contrasting phase of the emotional and cultural life. The experience symbolized here is a *passive* one, while that for Virgo 6° was intensely *dynamic*. Yet there may be for the woman in the harem some sort of cyclic pattern and a prize to reach—the sultan's favor. In both cases the motive power is exterior to the experiencer, who is caught in a pattern of forces over which he or she has no control; yet the child may purposefully use his small allowance to get a ride, and the woman may use her charm to attract the attention of her master. The individual in both cases finds himself one with a number of other individuals all seeking or being subjected to the same type of experience or fate.

This second stage symbol contrasts with, but also supplements, that of the first stage. It supplements it in the sense that one may become addicted to the excitement of the merry-go-round of vital emotions and may become a slave to the hope of recapturing the exultation of the initial experiences; yet one may learn how *to put to use* even the EMPTINESS OF WAITING.

PHASE 158 (VIRGO 8°): A FIVE-YEAR-OLD CHILD TAKES A FIRST DANCING LESSON.

KEYNOTE: *Learning to use one's capacity for emotional self-expression according to cultural standards.*

The process of emotional experiencing under controlled situations is shown now to demand self-induced, active movement; yet the movements are still conditioned, if not totally determined, by cultural and thus collective patterns. The individual can express his own individual character *only* according to traditional modes. He is still entirely responsible to his teacher or guru. Yet new perspectives are now open to him.

At this third stage of the five-fold thirty-second sequence of symbols we witness at work the transitional phase which *may* lead to mastery. The child-consciousness is still dominated by some form of authority; but if the child is "five years old," the implication is that he is entering the level of conscious manhood, represented by the number 5, the five-pointed star which outlines at least the POTENTIALITY OF INITIATION.

PHASE 159 (VIRGO 9°): AN EXPRESSIONIST PAINTER AT WORK.

KEYNOTE: *The urge to express one's individualized sense of value regardless of tradition.*

At this stage the individual is seen reacting against cultural standards and stereotyped ways of interpreting his perceptions. This is a statement of uncompromising self-reliance, which may even imply a kind of defiance and a challenge to society. The mind is seeking to discover the character of the basic and true foundation of individual selfhood, the AUM tone (or logos) of individual being. In the process, however, what is expressed is usually the reflection of a deep catharsis with emotionally charged and often tragic overtones.

This fourth stage symbol brings to us the hint of a technique of transformation of the personality. What predominates is a sense of inner conflict and an overselfconscious attempt at "being oneself." But there is a great difference between being an origin of development pregnant with futurity, and deliberately sought for ORIGINALITY.

PHASE 160 (VIRGO 10°): TWO HEADS LOOKING OUT AND BEYOND THE SHADOWS.

KEYNOTE: *The growth of true understanding, born out of the transcendence of duality even while immersed in the world of duality.*

The mind operates inevitably in this world of conflicts, oppositions and duality. Yet when the opposites realize that they are complementary aspects of the one Reality which sustains and encompasses all dualistic modes of existence, they are able then to look away from internal conflicts and beyond the shadows these conflicts generate. They may come to realize the One Consciousness-Force, not in Itself (for this is, if not an impossible, at least an inexpressible experience), but as the Creative Unity, the New God, Ishvara, source of a new cycle of manifestation.

This is the last stage of the thirty-second sequence; it leads us to the new sequence, which deals with the characteristic features of the steadily progressing consciousness in the most critical part along its arduous Path toward transformation. In a deep philosophical sense we witness here the mind attempting to jump beyond the very shadow it inevitably casts upon all experiences; i.e. the SELF–TRANSCENDING ACTIVITY OF THE MIND.

THIRD LEVEL: INDIVIDUAL–MENTAL

PHASE 161 (VIRGO 11°): IN HER BABY A MOTHER SEES HER DEEP LONGING FOR A SON ANSWERED.

KEYNOTE: *The Spirit's answer to the vital needs of what-ever became individualized out of its infinite ocean of potentialities.*

All cycles of manifestation end in an essential duality of "suc-cess" and "failure," as every release of new potentiality at the start of a cycle is inevitably polarized in two opposite directions, becoming sharply differentiated at the mystical "separation of the sheep and the goat." But out of duality a new unity eventu-ally is produced: the child, the new God of a new universe. Subconsciously or consciously, during pregnancy, the mother dreams of the son-to-be and the imprint of the dream in time is revealed in the boy's structural being. The true disciple must become the Mother of the living God and should eventually fulfill the great need of humanity and of all his people. MAN is constantly renewed through the great dreams and sacramental pregnancies of all disciples of the One Master.

This is the first stage of the thirty-third five-fold sequence of phases of the cycle. At this stage the power to bring one's dreams and ideals to a clear and sharp focus of mental activity or imagination needs to be developed. It is the power of creative visualization *(Kriyashakti)* for which a significant word was coined during World War II: IMAGINEER-ING—a combination of "imagination" and "engineering." Alas, the word was there, but our statesmen failed to incarnate it in deeds.

PHASE 162 (VIRGO 12°): AFTER THE WEDDING, THE GROOM SNATCHES THE VEIL AWAY FROM HIS BRIDE.

KEYNOTE: *The penetrating and unveiling power of the trained mind.*

In contrast to the preceding symbol we have now a scene stressing a physical action with psychological and/or spiritual overtones. In ancient cosmologies the male god often appears in three roles as son, husband and father of the woman element of nature. Nature is fulfilled by the human mind and will that overcome her; she resists only better to be subdued by the power that transcends her, and by transcending her gives her a spiritual meaning. The element of "training" in the symbolic scene comes from the fact that there has been a marriage ritual; thus the sociocultural factor is in the background. The teacher-guru is here the priest who has performed the ritual.

At this second stage the rules are reversed, the masculine element assuming the dynamic positive part in the great play of polarity. The masculine *act* balances the feminine *dream visualization*. The Keyword is UNVEILING. There can also be an unveiling of mysteries, long protected by secrecy.

PHASE 163 (VIRGO 13°): A POWERFUL STATESMAN OVERCOMES A STATE OF POLITICAL HYSTERIA.

KEYNOTE: *The focusing of the collective need for order and structural interdependence into a personage who incarnates the answer to this need.*

The husband role of fecundator of nature here takes on a collective social significance. We are at the stage where a powerful realization of the very purpose of the cycle of existence faces the chaotic remains of a dis-structured past. The character of the leader is always delineated by the need, subconscious though it may be, of the unformed agglomeration of entities he is called upon by destiny to lead. In time the leader will be worshiped as the "divine Father" of the society he structured.

At this third stage of the thirty-third sequence we see a new type of characterization of the many-faceted polarization of positive and negative. We have before us a personage endowed with CHARISMA, this elusive and mysterious power that comes from a man's or woman's openness to the power of planetary evolution.

PHASE 164 (VIRGO 14°): AN ARISTOCRATIC FAMILY TREE.

KEYNOTE: *A deep reliance upon the ancestral roots of individual character.*

Stressed here is the fact that the power available to any man in time of crisis and decision has very deep roots in the past, whether the past of physical ancestry or the past outlined by a series of previous embodiments conditioned by some dominant purpose and by the many-phased development of a particular type of complex character. True spontaneity and creativity are always based on a structured sequence of antecedents if they are at all genuinely spiritual, i.e. if they are able to meet a collective need. Only the actions that are necessary—even if only in the long run—for meeting such a need can actually be called "spiritual."

This fourth stage symbol, strange as it may seem to many people—especially young people of our day—suggests a technique which, at critical times, must be used. It characterizes the means for true "success." One returns to the roots in order to produce the flowering of personality, if this flower is to bring forth a living seed. ROOT POWER is essential to seed-achievement.

PHASE 165 (VIRGO 15°): A FINE LACE HANDKERCHIEF, HEIR-LOOM FROM VALOROUS ANCESTORS.

KEYNOTE: *The quintessence of deeds well done.*

Root strength produces beautiful flowers. The neophyte who acts with determination, courage and discrimination while following "in the footsteps" of his predecessors receives a symbolic prize from the Brotherhood ready to welcome him when he has fully proven himself on the battlefield where he meets his past, which tries to block his way. The mystic Beloved hands him what she has woven for him out of spiritual threads.

This is the last stage of the thirty-third sequence which also ends the eleventh scene, "Characterization." This scene began with the revelation in a portrait of salient features in a man's face. It ends with symbols which bring out the ultimate validity of the many efforts of generations of men toward the building of a beautiful and significant CULTURE. The Man of Culture is, in the deepest and best sense of the term, the Aristocrat. He is the flowering of a line of ancestors who have accepted responsibility for a group or community. Likewise, the true "disciple" is the blossom that crowns a long series of incarnations.

SCENE TWELVE: *EDUCATION*
(Virgo 16° to Virgo 30°)

FIRST LEVEL: ACTIONAL

PHASE 166 (VIRGO 16°): IN THE ZOO, CHILDREN ARE BROUGHT FACE TO FACE WITH AN ORANG-UTANG.

KEYNOTE: *A direct confrontation with the "wild" power of primordial nature within oneself.*

During this twelfth subcycle closing the first half of the cycle we deal with phases of unfoldment which can be very broadly classified under the term "e-ducation," i.e. a leading out into the world of transcendent activity. Every hidden motive and depth energy has to be "led out" and objectively faced. According to the occult tradition, at least some of the ape species are actually throwbacks resulting from the perversion of the Man archetype when it belatedly came in touch with the elemental energies of an adolescent Earth. Likewise many of the so-called "primitive" tribes in places like Australia and New Guinea should be considered degenerate remnants of races which once had reached a much higher level of culture. In other words, the symbol refers to the confrontation of future-oriented modern children with the results of what one might refer to as an "original sin"—that is, with the degeneration of enormous vitalistic power once available to the human being. That power is now directed toward the mind, and has been immensely magnified by modern technology. Yet there are residual remains of this vitalistic power in modern man's nature, and we may well repeat at a higher level the "sin of the mindless." The candidate for Initiation must face this possibility; the whole of mankind, in a sense, is a candidate for a planetary Initiation.

This is the first stage of the thirty-fourth sequence of symbols. Its symbol speaks of KARMIC CONFRONTATION.

PHASE 167 (VIRGO 17°): A VOLCANIC ERUPTION.

KEYNOTE: *The explosive energy of long-repressed contents of the subconscious.*

We are dealing here with the dramatic release of energies which have been kept in check by the outer shell of the ego-controlled consciousness. It may be a spectacular catharsis, but it often takes paths of destruction. Yet unless some form of purification by fire is experienced, the inner pressure of the karmic past or of more recent frustrations would shake up perhaps even more destructively the very foundations of the personality.

At this second stage, the *objective* confrontation with an image of the karmic past is replaced by a *subjective* irruption of repressed memories and primitive cravings. Everything must be released from the psyche seeking to attain the transfigured state. The soul must become empty, the mind translucent. The Keyword is EXPLOSION.

PHASE 168 (VIRGO 18°): A OUIJA BOARD.

KEYNOTE: *The ability to contact deeper recesses of the unconscious psyche and sensitiveness to psychic intimations and omens.*

The ouija board is to be considered here a modern device similar to many ancient instruments used for divination and prophecy. Certain states of threshold consciousness are stimulated by such a use, and what the experience produces may vary greatly in quality and in origin. The release of unconscious material has lost the explosive force pictorialized in the preceding symbol, yet at this stage there is still no conscious and willful control over what reaches the ego-consciousness.

This is the third stage of the thirty-fourth sequence of symbolic phases in the life process. It is at best a stage of transition which stresses a passive openness to the unknown. The glamor of it may subtly pervert the mind of the aspirant; but in some cases, this can be the first manifestation of INNER GUIDANCE. The difficulty is to correctly evaluate what or who does the guiding.

PHASE 169 (VIRGO 19°): A SWIMMING RACE.

KEYNOTE: *The stimulation that comes from a group effort toward a spiritual goal.*

When man has become an expert swimmer he has symbolically learned how to operate in a new element. This element, water, represents the ever-flowing stream of psychic energy, and, in a sense at least, the "astral" world. In a still deeper sense man is now able, mystically speaking, to cross the river and reach "the other shore"—or to swim back toward the source. Whether or not the symbol should suggest the competitive spirit at work is questionable. At the biological level a host of spermatozoa are swimming toward the ovum, and each presses on toward the goal, the act of impregnation. A seeker after spiritual rebirth actually does not strive alone. It is Man who, acting through the most advanced individuals of the race, is taking a step toward "rebirth," or toward a new mutation. The personal ego-centered ambition to succeed and to be "first" is indeed a sign of expectable spiritual failure.

At this fourth stage we are confronted with a problem of interpretation. Is not ambition a subtle form of deviation under the pressure of ancient karma, and the competitive spirit so valued by our civilization a sign of failure to understand the deeper reality of existence? What is needed is EMULATION, not competition.

> PHASE 170 (VIRGO 20°): A CARAVAN OF CARS HEADED TO THE WEST COAST.
>
> KEYNOTE: *The need of cooperative effort in reaching any "New World" of experience.*

It is difficult to know, from the original formulation of the clairvoyant's vision, the type of caravan of cars that was visualized; what seems to be clearly implied is a process in which a group of persons are journeying together—thus linking their consciousnesses and energies (the "car" symbol)—in order to safely reach the goal of destiny. Here there is no longer any sense of competition, but an ordered and structured endeavor.

At this last stage of the five-fold sequence the past is entirely left behind; men cooperate in the great "adventure in consciousness" in a TOTALIZATION OF PURPOSE AND EFFORT.

> SECOND LEVEL: EMOTIONAL–CULTURAL
>
> PHASE 171 (VIRGO 21°): A GIRL'S BASKETBALL TEAM.
>
> KEYNOTE: *Physical training as a means to inculcate the feeling of participation in a collective culture.*

Basketball presents an interesting symbol. The ball must be thrown into a narrow opening high above the head of the player. The ego-consciousness (the ball) must be driven upward to a focal point or circle that is ready to receive it. In a sense, this parallels what the boy on the merry-go-round (Virgo 6°) can do if he succeeds in penetrating the ring with his stick, but there are notable differences. Here the players operate as a team; in the original formulation of the symbol there was no reference to two teams and thus to the competitive character of the game. What should be stressed here is the formation of a group acting as an organic whole and training itself to operate in a social context.

This is the first stage of a second-level sequence of five symbols, as was the symbol of the merry-go-round. A definite type of educational activity is implied with cultural, and as well emotional, overtones. It implies the training for GROUP INTEGRATION of "girls," i.e. of a type of consciousness more specifically receptive to collective forces.

PHASE 172 (VIRGO 22°): A ROYAL COAT OF ARMS ENRICHED WITH PRECIOUS STONES.

KEYNOTE: *The certification of aristocratic status, at whatever level "nobility" expresses itself in cultural eminence.*

Once more a reference to ancestral achievements occurs among these symbols for the sign Virgo. It is seen here in its most exalted character, for "royalty" is spoken of. Traditionally the king is the spiritual symbol of unity of an integrated nation; as a coat of arms is visualized, we are dealing with a status that is not merely personally acquired but has its roots in a notable past. Every great Adept has come out of a line of human beings who have made their marks upon human evolution. Spiritual attainment is the result of a series of long, repeated efforts; it is the end of a "royal road," *(raja yoga)* in the broadest sense of the term, *raja,* meaning king.

This second stage symbol contrasts with that of the first in that it refers to heredity rather than to the training of youthful raw material. Gautama the Buddha was known occultly as "He who comes after his predecessors." The coat of arms represents the collective status, the Spiritual Office. Whoever wears it assumes the responsibility of an

Office. As the French say, *"Noblesse oblige."* NOBILITY confers upon a man exacting responsibility. The question implied in the symbol is, Are you willing, able and ready to assume a "royal" office, at whatever level it may be?

PHASE 173 (VIRGO 23°): A LION TAMER DISPLAYS HIS SKILL AND CHARACTER.

KEYNOTE: *The need to tame one's vital energies in order to fulfill one's destiny.*

We see here the development of the concept of training. The true aristocrat is the individual who is in complete control of his vital and emotional energies; at the spiritual level this includes the overcoming of pride—pride in one's strength and mastery, and the pride attached to an exalted status or social Office.

This is the third stage of the thirty-fifth sequence of five symbols. The meaning of this phase of development is traditional and evident. The whole process of social-ethical and occult-spiritual conditioning of the individual aims at the control of man's "animal nature." The energies of this nature can be put to many uses. Implied in any successful process of taming and training is RESOLUTENESS and PATIENCE.

PHASE 174 (VIRGO 24°): MARY AND HER LITTLE LAMB.

KEYNOTE: *The need to keep a vibrant and pure simplicity at the core of one's being as one meets the many tests of existence.*

Coming after the preceding symbols this one tells us that, though great, spectacular and resolute efforts are needed in order to achieve one's higher goals of destiny, still the essential quality as one journeys on "the Path" is a pure, spontaneous, fresh and nonviolent approach to all encounters. This of course is Jesus' entreaty to his disciples—that they should be like "little children." Without such a deep, heartfelt simplicity the seeker after spiritual experiences or Initiation is bound to find himself glamorized by his own successes, and to see his ego feeding on the drama of struggle and victory.

This is the fourth stage of the thirty-fifth five-fold sequence and it presents us with a subtle hint of technique. Beyond individual prowess and social eminence, the individual whose innocence is fixed upon spiritual realization should genuinely radiate INNOCENCE.

PHASE 175 (VIRGO 25°): A FLAG AT HALF-MAST IN FRONT OF A PUBLIC BUILDING.

KEYNOTE: *The social acknowledgment of a job well done and a destiny fulfilled.*

As an individual who has accepted any significantly met public responsibilities reaches the end of his service to his community or to mankind as a whole, he gains social immortality, at least to some extent. In death he becomes identified with the archetype that ensouled his public office. He becomes a "culture hero," enshrined in the official memory of his race. He has found his place in history. The symbol implies the ability to carry any task to its ultimate fulfillment, provided this task is carried out with reference to the need of a collectivity, small or large as it may be.

In this final phase of the thirty-fifth five-fold sequence of symbols we are presented with an image of the end results of the individual's service to mankind. His personal failings may be forgotten but his achievements remain. They are given PUBLIC RECOGNITION.

THIRD LEVEL: INDIVIDUAL–MENTAL

PHASE 176 (VIRGO 26°): A BOY WITH A CENSER SERVES THE PRIEST NEAR THE ALTAR.

KEYNOTE: *The first stage of actual participation in the great ritual of planetary evolution.*

Whether we think of the ancient mysteries, or of a Catholic Mass, or of some still more transcendent ceremony in which great Beings charged with planetary responsibilities are involved, we are dealing with a type of archetypal activity. The ritual is archetypal in that it represents, in however small a field of activity, a portion of the evolving structure of the cosmos, as this structure is understood in its "sacred" sense. Every such activity is performed "in the presence of God." Menial as it may be, it nevertheless acquires a sacred meaning.

This is the first stage of the thirty-sixth five-fold sequence, which brings us to the close of the first half of the cycle. The individual is "e-ducated," i.e. led out into the world of transcendent activity, the world of archetypal performance. He must learn to serve, humbly and with intense attention, in what as yet is beyond his spiritual understanding. He learns to perform every action superpersonally. He learns to PRACTICE IN THE PRESENCE OF GOD.

PHASE 177 (VIRGO 27°): A GROUP OF ARISTOCRATIC LADIES MEET CEREMONIALLY AT A COURT'S FUNCTION.

KEYNOTE: *The ability to carry on a revered tradition in order to perpetuate cultural standards of excellence.*

At the highest peak of achievement of any fully developed culture the King considers himself in some manner a representative of the Power that controls the order of the universe. From him descends a hierarchy of offices performed by an aristocracy. On the feminine side, to be an aristocrat is to be able to act efficiently in the many rituals of a culture—from official tea parties to presentations at the Court. Dignity, elegance and respect for formal rules are essential. We may consider the formalism obsolete and meaningless, yet when it ceases to be observed the culture breaks down. Even now in this age of crisis and world transformation, there may be times when honoring formal procedures can be of great value for the disordered and rebellious mind.

This second stage symbol presents the contrast between the "profane" and the "sacred" ritual. But the two need not be antithetic. Our overindividualistic and confused new generations find it valuable to study Japanese tea ceremonies, flower arrangement, judo, etc. The undisciplined need to learn REFINEMENT.

PHASE 178 (VIRGO 28°): A BALDHEADED MAN WHO HAS SEIZED POWER.

KEYNOTE: *The sheer power of personality in times that call for decision.*

Whether at the religious or at the socio-political and cultural level there comes a time when obsolescent patterns of order and cultural refinement have to be radically and relentlessly challenged. Catabolic personages emerge to seize power and dictate decisions that alter the structures of society; or within an individual life, an intense urge for cathartic changes mobilizes the will, and traumatic decisions are made. At such times, the issue has to be met and, ruthless as the power may appear, it must be accepted.

At this third stage of the thirty-sixth sequence we face the unpostponable necessity for decision and transformation. Existence is motion. No static formation, however beautiful and inspiring, can remain long unchallenged. Everything bows to THE POWER OF THE WILL—divine, executively human, or Satanic.

PHASE 179 (VIRGO 29°): A SEEKER AFTER OCCULT KNOWLEDGE IS READING AN ANCIENT SCROLL WHICH ILLUMINES HIS MIND.

KEYNOTE: *After a crisis one should seek to realign the renewed consciousness with the primordial Revelation of the Truth of Man.*

Any revolutionary movement, once it has succeeded in overcoming the inertia of the past and in toppling obsolete structures, *needs* to tap the most essential realities of what Man represents and signifies in the universal Order; or else it merely reembodies in a superficially altered manner the very things it has destroyed. This is the crucial moment. In occultism the "Pattern of Man" is an archetypal Power that may be contacted. It must be sought with undeviating determination. After each revolutionary crisis this Pattern and this Power *can* be contacted—always the same, yet at each new cycle perceivable in a different light.

This fourth stage symbol presents us with the technique required to "reach the other shore." But each individual, and each group or racial unit, must come in its own way to the ROOT KNOWLEDGE which provides the only safe foundation for rebirth.

PHASE 180 (VIRGO 30°): TOTALLY INTENT UPON COMPLET-
ING AN IMMEDIATE TASK, A MAN IS DEAF TO ANY AL-
LUREMENT.

KEYNOTE: *The total concentration required for reaching any spiritual goal.*

This is the final symbol of the first half of the cycle. In the year cycle the fall equinox is now at hand; autumn begins. Through spring and summer many ways and byways have been experienced. The last message of this hemicycle of "Individualization" is that on all decisive occasions what must be done has to be done so intently that no outer voices can penetrate the mind, still less the soul. The neophyte stands at the gates of the sacred Pyramid. There is only one step he can take—ahead, or he is lost.

This is the culminating step, the decision that results from a myriad of small choices. Still a shadow of hesitation can remain. Attention may be distracted from the Now by a voice from the past, glamorizing some old memory. The outer doors of perception and thought must be closed, so the soul can complete its CONQUEST OF ILLUSION.

Second Hemicycle: The Process of Collectivization

◉

ACT III: GROUP-INTEGRATION

SCENE THIRTEEN: *TRANSFIGURATION*
(Libra 1° to Libra 15°)

FIRST LEVEL: ACTIONAL

PHASE 181 (LIBRA 1°): IN A COLLECTION OF PERFECT SPECI-
MENS OF MANY BIOLOGICAL FORMS, A BUTTERFLY DIS-
PLAYS THE BEAUTY OF ITS WINGS, ITS BODY IMPALED
BY A FINE DART.

KEYNOTE: *The immortal archetypal reality that a perfect*
and dedicated life reveals.

Just as the symbol for Aries 1° evoked the keynote of the entire
first half of the cycle, i.e. differentiation out of the undifferentiated "Ocean of potentiality," this symbol for Libra 1° reveals
to the intuitive consciousness the essential character of the sec-

ond hemicycle. In the yearly cycle we have reached the fall equinox, the symbolic time of bringing in the harvest in preparation for winter. It is the time consecrated to the seed, just as the spring equinox is consecrated to the germ, the new rise of life which in-forms the growth of individual organisms.

At this autumnal point, the drive toward individualization and self-assertion has lost much of its momentum, while a new trend is successfully and dynamically challenging its hegemony —the trend toward the formation of collectivities of individuals. But this new trend can be misunderstood if seen only superficially as the mere gathering together of individual persons. The process has a much deeper meaning, and indeed an inner source of power, for what is at stake is not merely an aggregation of separate units (simple or already complex, as in the case of "families"). At the core of this "coming together," the "descent" or externalization of archetypal realities is gradually occurring. At the Libra stage, these archetypal realities are "Forms"; at the Scorpio stage they will be "Powers." The symbol for this degree of the fall equinox thus describes a "perfect form"—the result of the metamorphosis of "worm" into butterfly, a process the symbolism of which has so often been used to indicate to man the possibility of his being transformed into "more-than-man," the transhuman being, the true Initiate, the Adept, the Perfect. The perfect butterfly is impaled by a fine dart; the symbol of "dart of wisdom" was used in Marc Jones's mimeographed course, while the original notation of what the clairvoyant had seen indicated "a butterfly made perfect by a dart through it," suggesting a process of perfection through sacrifice.

As I see it, the dart can hardly be said to have *made* the butterfly perfect, but it *keeps* it perfect by killing the living organism. The impaled butterfly is preserved by the dart which "fixes" it in perfection for a whole cycle, i.e. it makes an archetype of it. By thus escaping the normal process of dying and decay, the butterfly form (the "perfection") is kept. It is kept in the mystical Shamballah, where it is said that the Pattern of Man is kept, just as the perfect bar measuring exactly one meter is (or was) kept in a crypt in Paris, where the metric system was originally devised.

The perfect butterfly thus represents the outcome of the process of occult discipleship symbolized by the sign Virgo. From then on, a new process begins, that of collectivization; at the very core of that new process *the perfect Form of Man* must remain as a standard of value if this process is to be valid and meaningful.

This is the first statement in the thirteenth scene of the great ritual drama. It is an actional phase because in it the perfection of individual activity is revealed and immortalized. This is the symbolical Transfiguration; at the Mount of Transfiguration, Jesus, the Son of Man, was "impaled" by the ray of Divine Light, making of him a Son of God. It was at this very moment that he learned of the Crucifixion awaiting him. Thus the merely human individual is MADE SACRED, becoming the pure embodiment of an archetype.

PHASE 182 (LIBRA 2°): THE TRANSMUTATION OF THE FRUITS OF PAST EXPERIENCES INTO THE SEED-REALIZATIONS OF THE FOREVER CREATIVE SPIRIT.

KEYNOTE: *A repolarization of inner energies leading to a creative centralization of consciousness.*

The original formulation of this symbol was both "occult" and, I believe, confusing: "The light of the sixth Race transmuted to the seventh." It could be interpreted in terms of the process of mankind's development through the seven great Races (or evolutionary periods) outlined in the second volume of H. P. Blavatsky's *Secret Doctrine,* but there are no other symbols in the series having such a frame of reference. What seems more likely to be implied in the revealed image is a reference to the numerological and occult meaning of Number 6 and Number 7, especially geometrically expressed in the diagram (on page 32) in which seven circles, contiguous and of the same size, fill a larger circle whose diameter is three times that of the smaller one. The six circles touching the circumference of the larger one represent the six basic approaches to Truth and Reality possible to man's developing intelligence—thus the well-known Six Schools of Hindu philosophy, and at the level of energy the six fundamental colors, or "Rays." But *central* to this six-fold system is the hidden or occult "Seventh," the *Atma Vidya* of Hinduism, the unformulatable Truth of the Self which both includes and transcends the six approaches, Schools or Rays.

Number 6 (also Solomon's Seal) represents the synthesis of descending spirit and ascending matter. It represents the fruition of all past efforts; *within* the six-fold fruition the seed may be found, the seventh. Outer activity is fulfilled (the Six Days of Creation in the first chapter of Genesis); and the Supreme Actor can be seen in His changelessness and therefore his transcending all-inclusiveness.

All that was manifested in the plant is gathered in the hidden seed, which in due time becomes the foundation of a new cycle of existence. The fruit decays. For a brief moment the released seed may be seen; this is the "seventh" period that becomes the creative power fathering a new cycle. This symbol for Libra 2° refers to the process of centralization in the Self (the creative Reality) after the experience of fulfillment in the perfect Form of manifestation.

This is the second stage of the thirty-seventh five-fold sequence of symbols and phases. It refers to a dynamic process in contrast to the picture representing the first stage—a picture of maintained and immortalized, thus static, perfection of form. Formal perfection is now transcended through a process of CREATIVE CENTRALIZATION.

PHASE 183 (LIBRA 3°): THE DAWN OF A NEW DAY REVEALS EVERYTHING CHANGED.

KEYNOTE: *The ever-present possibility of beginning again on a new foundation of values.*

This symbol hardly needs to be interpreted, except for pointing out that these first three symbols beginning the second hemicycle of the cyclic process should be seen as a basic trinity. It can be related to the process of true Initiation: (1) The experience of the undying Form of perfection; (2) The release of the energy incorporated in the Form in order to reach "That-which-is-beyond-form-and-name"; (3) The reembodiment of energy in a new creative Act.

The third stage of this thirty-seventh sequence leads us to a vision of the fulfilled purpose of the first half of the cycle. What emerged hesitantly from the ocean of infinite potentiality (Aries 1°) now faces a totally new world in a truly individualized form of existence. He or she is ready to act significantly in the sphere of culture and social togetherness, the sphere in which an individual, aware of his archetypal essence and planetary function, can play his true role (dharma). In a basic sense it is always a new role, for no cycle repeats itself as far as its contents are concerned. The person who plays this role is always potentially an INNOVATOR.

PHASE 184 (LIBRA 4°): AROUND A CAMPFIRE A GROUP OF YOUNG PEOPLE SIT IN SPIRITUAL COMMUNION.

KEYNOTE: *The necessity to unite with kindred spirits as one enters unbeaten paths illumined by the still-insecure light of a dawning intuition of new values.*

As one partially visionary leader said a few years ago: "Beaten paths are for beaten men." The urge to create a new society and respond to new values leads the pioneer to the wilds, which represent the state of planetary possibility—i.e. the as-yet-uncultured, the virgin forest. Around the fire of a common dedication (or at least a common hope!) minds and bodies can commune, forming a "chalice" or Grail for the reception of creative inspiration.

At this fourth stage of this five-fold sequence of phases of development we find, as usual, a hint of technique. If a new society is to be built, those who yearn for it, or perhaps who have envisioned its outlines, should commune. But communion is useless where no central "fire" burns, IN-SPIRITING the group.

PHASE 185 (LIBRA 5°): A MAN REVEALING TO HIS STUDENTS THE FOUNDATION OF AN INNER KNOWLEDGE UPON WHICH A "NEW WORLD" COULD BE BUILT.

KEYNOTE: *The necessity for the youthful spirits to learn from a Teacher who through his long experience has been able to reach solid and illuminating truths, i.e. "seed ideas."*

An old saying is just as valid today as ever: When the pupil is ready, the Master appears. But he may appear in many disguises. What matters is not the Master, but the Mastery he "re-veals." It is veiled in his person. It has to be contacted *through* his person, rather than *in* his person. Devotion to a guru may be the way, but sooner or later it should be transmuted into reverence: the truth within the disciple saluting in true humility the truth in the Teacher.

This is the last stage of the thirty-seventh five-fold sequence and it marks the culmination of the four preceding stages. What is evoked by the symbol is the essential, withal rather mysterious, process of TRANSMISSION. What is transmitted, if the situation is really adequate and understood (at least tentatively) by all participants, is not merely knowledge. It is actually "being-ness."

SECOND LEVEL: EMOTIONAL–CULTURAL

PHASE 186 (LIBRA 6°): A MAN WATCHES HIS IDEALS TAKING A CONCRETE FORM BEFORE HIS INNER VISION.

KEYNOTE: *The need to visualize clearly one's dreams or ideals in order to make them truly effectual.*

According to a French proverb, "What is well conceived can easily be formulated." The process of interior visualization can be quite essential, except in the case of a creative individual who has become a totally pure channel for the descent of spiritual Power, and a clear lens *through* which the Archetype in the Mind of Man (or God) can be projected without distortion wherever needed. In other cases the creative act is less direct: a man projects into the world what he has "seen" reflected on the screen of his individualized consciousness.

This is the first stage of the thirty-eighth five-fold sequence of symbolized phases in the process of individualized existence. It is a phase of INTERIOR FORMULATION in preparation for a creative projection of one's ideals or concepts.

PHASE 187 (LIBRA 7°): A WOMAN FEEDING CHICKENS AND PROTECTING THEM FROM THE HAWKS.

KEYNOTE: *The need to face the antagonism of "powers of darkness" as one attempts to feed the mind of as yet helpless and frightened apprentices.*

The most basic "Law" of *our* universe is that every release of new potentialities (or modes of energy) brings about a polarization of effects—that is, the new potentiality will be used *both* for construction and destruction. It will arouse individuals (or groups and nations) to take a series of steps which will lead some to greater success, others to deeper failure. Whoever makes possible this new release has to accept the karma of *both* the success and the failure. When Jesus showered his immense love upon lukewarm, self-centered individuals, it inevitably came to be turned into violent hatred when these soul-minds were unable to cope with its frightening intensity. Jesus had to accept spiritual responsibility for those who crucified him.

At this second stage we witness the contrast between the ideal situation envisioned clearly by the creative consciousness (first stage) and what it will be in actual operation; thus the forever-present struggle involved in making it possible for the future-oriented actualizers of an ideal to survive the attacks of tradition-worshiping minds that can only follow the lines of automatic response. The keynote is GUARDIANSHIP.

PHASE 188 (LIBRA 8°): A BLAZING FIREPLACE IN A DE-
SERTED HOME.

KEYNOTE: *The need to realize that even through the most
empty hours a spiritual power is ever ready to welcome
and warm up the wayward consciousness returning to
center.*

Until the fire of the Soul within the human psyche totally dies
out—a rare and tragic occurrence—there is always hope of
recovery and rebeginning. Many disciples find themselves compelled to abandon their spiritual quest, even after having had
sense of essential being. Yet "the home" that once received
them—the guru's love—remains ready to welcome the return
of the "prodigal sons."

This is the third stage in the thirty-eighth sequence of five symbols. In
a sense it links the vision, catalyzed by the contact with an inspirer,
with the possible reaction of fear or shock that arises from such a
contact. Within the abandoned great dream, some intangible and
warm "presence" remains: the ever-renascent HOPE for a rebeginning.

PHASE 189 (LIBRA 9°): THREE "OLD MASTERS" HANGING
ON THE WALL OF A SPECIAL ROOM IN AN ART GAL-
LERY.

KEYNOTE: *The need to return to source during a confused
search for new value in a chaotic society.*

There are always moments which focus in our minds the longing to re-ground ourselves in the great achievements of the past.
The number 3 suggests completeness; esoteric traditions speak
of the three-fold Soul, or of three fundamental "Rays"—of
Power, of Love-Wisdom, and of Intelligence-in-action. Meditation, in its deepest sense, is a return to Source—an attempt to
reidentify oneself with one's archetypal essence of being, which
is triune in manifestation, and now, after confused but challenging wanderings, to identify oneself *consciously* with this "essence." The finer forms of one's culture provide the means to
do this. The great moments of the collective past become an

inspiration for new, yet sound, beginnings. The seed of tomorrow salutes the seed of yesteryear.

At this fourth stage of the thirty-eighth sequence it is suggested that in the process of "Transfiguration" the presence of the greatest moments of the past is called upon, as Moses and Elijah were invoked in Jesus' Transfiguration. The seed of the new day depends upon the seed of yesteryear for an experience of the cyclic continuity of spirit. This is the basis for the institutionalized ideal of APOSTOLIC SUCCESSION, the *guruampara* (an uninterrupted chain of gurus) of Indian tradition.

PHASE 190 (LIBRA 10°): HAVING PASSED SAFELY THROUGH NARROW RAPIDS, A CANOE REACHES CALM WATERS.

KEYNOTE: *The self-control and poise necessary to reach a steady state of inner stability.*

This symbol hardly needs to be commented upon. It could be related to the fifth symbol of the preceding five-fold sequence referring to guru-chela relationship at the actional level. Here we are dealing essentially with the emotional life and its crises. At the next—mental and individual—level, the concluding symbol will suggest the perfect and smooth working of the intellect ruled by logic and simplicity of means.

This is the fifth stage of the thirty-eighth sequence; it concludes what was begun at the first stage. The inner "revelation" which brought about dramatic confrontations can now be meditated upon as it is reflected on the calm waters of the mind. As a Keyword one may use the term RELIEF.

THIRD LEVEL: INDIVIDUAL–MENTAL

PHASE 191 (LIBRA 11°): A PROFESSOR PEERING OVER HIS GLASSES AT HIS STUDENTS.

KEYNOTE: *Problems attending the transmission of knowledge in a special cultural setup.*

This is a rather peculiar symbol for this phase of the process, and it reveals a rather humorous approach to what man's mind can accomplish at this stage. However, there seems to be no valid reason to make the image into some kind of a caricature, or to sentimentalize it by referring to a "kind old professor." Rather one should analyze the picture in order to discover its basic elements. The professor has dealt so much with books that he has greatly strained his eyes; in days when bifocal lenses were not widely used, he had to peer over his glasses in order to see his students. The symbol thus simply reveals two aspects of the condition of "professor-ship"—that is, of being able to transfer to the young generation the vast sum of knowledge accumulated by the past. The need to absorb this enormous amount of book knowledge affects the mind as well as the eyes; in order to meet the demands of the turbulent youth, the teacher in a sense has to look above this knowledge and to see his students simply as human beings.

This is the first symbol in the thirty-ninth five-fold sequence. It deals at the intellectual level with the teaching of accumulated collective knowledge, and the problem posed by the acquisition of that knowledge. This is what INSTRUCTION means—a process not to be confused with "education."

PHASE 192 (LIBRA 12°): MINERS ARE SURFACING FROM A DEEP COAL MINE.

KEYNOTE: *The need to carry on at ever deeper levels the quest for knowledge which keeps burning the fires of the collective mind of a society.*

The search for knowledge demands the dedication of many minds digging ever deeper into the realities of our earthly existence. It is a hard, often dark pursuit amidst great difficulties and the possibility of being spiritually *asphyxiated* by the constant intellectual effort and tension. When a person is confronted by this symbol it could be interpreted as showing the need for such an intellectual dedication but also as pointing to the advisability of emerging from it and leading a more natural life.

This second stage symbol is related to the first in that in both we see conditions of existence dealing with work for the sake of the collectivity. The opposition between intellectual and manual work is evident; less so is the fact that both classes of workers experience definite physical consequences as a result of their occupation: the eyes of the professor, the lungs of the coal miner. The professor digs in the intellectual past of mankind to find what may warm up the mental processes of his students; the coal miner brings to the surface the ancient remains of what once was living substance. Keyword: EXTRACTION.

PHASE 193 (LIBRA 13°): CHILDREN BLOWING SOAP BUBBLES.

KEYNOTE: *The cultural fantasies through which young minds dream of perfect fulfillment.*

This seems to refer to the use of the imagination and the value of fantasy in a collective setup. Men dream together as a preparation for acting together. Rituals related to the great aspirations of mankind are both sacred ceremonies and playthings for young minds; so also are court ceremonies and operas for the social elite, or baseball games for the crowds. Some men work hard at acquiring knowledge and providing society with what it needs to enjoy warmth and lighted palaces; others play at imagining themselves perfect spheres of multicolored radiance —soap bubbles so soon proven evanescent!

At this third stage of the thirty-ninth sequence we deal with another aspect of the cultural life made possible, in a sense, by the two just symbolized. It is a symbol of IMAGINATIVE PLAY, which foreshadows the idea of "global man," the man of plenitude.

PHASE 194 (LIBRA 14°): IN THE HEAT OF THE NOON HOUR A MAN TAKES A SIESTA.

KEYNOTE: *The need for recuperation within the social pattern of everyday activity.*

At the emotional-cultural level man today is not able to sustain constant activity. There must be rest periods, siestas or coffee breaks, during which the individual withdraws within his own sphere of selfhood, not only for physical relaxation but for allowing the strange, but evidently necessary play of dream fantasies. Social structuring cannot be maintained healthfully without breaks, in whatever climate man may live. Besides, the body needs quiet and relaxation fron nervous tension after what is often the main meal of the day.

This fourth stage symbol can be seen as emphasizing the need for techniques of RELAXATION, and the need to allow the functions of body and psyche to "digest," free from external pressures, the complex experiences of social living and particularly of business.

PHASE 195 (LIBRA 15°): CIRCULAR PATHS.

KEYNOTE: *Coming to terms with the inevitability of establishing steady rhythms of social activity.*

In his early course, "Symbolical Astrology," Marc Jones sought to concretize this abstract image by speaking of "machinery parts, new and circular." It is far better, however, to face the image in its most general sense, as he himself did later on. It is because everyday activities, whether in the home or in business, inevitably tend to repeat themselves in circular fashion that it is necessary for the individual to have rest times during which he can be released from repetitive patterns. It is only when the individual has become fully attuned to, and in a sense identified with the vast planetary and cosmic rhythms of the universe, and thus free from emotional and group tensions, that he can act serenely and at peace along "circular paths."

At this last stage of the thirty-ninth sequence of five symbols we find an abstract image which can be interpreted in a positive or negative manner. We deal with repetitive activity; but that activity may either bind or free the consciousness of the actor. It can mean BOREDOM or TRANSPERSONAL PEACE in action.

SCENE FOURTEEN: *RECONSTRUCTION*
(Libra 16° to Libra 30°)

FIRST LEVEL: ACTIONAL

PHASE 196 (LIBRA 16°): AFTER A STORM A BOAT LANDING STANDS IN NEED OF RECONSTRUCTION.

KEYNOTE: *The need to keep in operation steady links between the vast Unconscious and the ego-consciousness.*

Confrontation with broad issues of relationship and currents of energies released by man's contact with archetypal-spiritual realities often results in temporary destruction. "Boats" normally link distant regions, or enable men to draw food from the sea (i.e. new realizations which so far existed only in the unconscious realm of the planetary Mind). They may also be used to enjoy temporary excursions and the feel of the water and the waves. Any cultured society, however, may be wary of the danger inherent in venturing far away from the consciously defined and socially structured ways of life. Such adventures may indeed turn destructive; the points of contact between the vast Unconscious and the ego-consciousness molded by cultural assumptions and rituals may be wrecked by psychotic storms. The boat landings must then be slowly reconstructed.

This is the first stage in the fortieth five-fold sequence of cyclic phases in human experience. It brings to us vividly the realization that whatever men build in order to be able to venture away from solidly individualized and conscious bases of operation is likely to be damaged by as yet unfamiliar cosmic forces. The tenuous link between two realms constantly needs REPAIR.

PHASE 197 (LIBRA 17°): A RETIRED SEA CAPTAIN WATCHES SHIPS ENTERING AND LEAVING THE HARBOR.

KEYNOTE: *The capacity to gain an objective and calm understanding of human experiences in which one was once deeply involved.*

Old age may or may not bring to man this objective and calm understanding as one remembers the crises overcome and the quiet enjoyment of great life vistas or "peak experiences," but wisdom and inner serenity can hardly develop save on the basis of the overcoming of struggles and conflicts. The "sea captain" sailed his ship through storms and still waters of consciousness, his mind perhaps battered by gales, his ego-crew perhaps in revolt. Now there is peace and quietude. Another generation is sailing seas better charted perhaps, yet inherently nonrational and at times savage in their fury. He watches. He knows. Others are learning. At any age the ego-will may "retire" and contemplate, and be at peace before a greater voyage over even more poorly charted seas.

At this second stage we see a picture of true overcoming of storms, in polar opposition to the preceding one which revealed the destructive effect of psychic upheavals tearing apart the occult link—the *antakarana*—between the incarnate consciousness and the transcendent Soul-field, the CALM MIND beyond struggles and victories.

PHASE 198 (LIBRA 18°): TWO MEN PLACED UNDER ARREST.

KEYNOTE: *A breakdown in the constructive relationship between the individual and society, and the expectable result.*

If it is to remain steady and consistent, every form of order must be able to protect itself by the application of sanctions. Both a society and a personal ego constitute forms of order. Any form of order excludes what the form cannot securely and safely hold. It excludes, or exiles, the alien, the unassimilable; if it cannot send them to outer space, it must isolate them in a special type of inner space, a prison. The individual whose actions introduce unacceptable principles into the established order runs the risk of being "punished" or re-formed according to this order. The problem for a society is how to include in its patterns of order agencies or channels for transformation—and particularly how to keep them truly operative; for individuals, it is how to make their transforming vision or impulse acceptable to society. The symbol does not reveal what caused the breakdown in the relationship between the individual and society; but if one also considers the symbols that follow, one's thoughts may be led back to the image of the storm that wrecked boat landings (Phase 196). The suggestion is that whatever violence is released originates in *unconscious pressures* (the sea and the wind). A new step in the evolution of society—the Industrial and Electronic Revolutions of the last hundred and fifty years—caused a collective, world-wide upheaval which led to widespread violence. The fact that *two* men are pictured under arrest suggests a polarization and a purpose transcending a merely personal fit of recklessness.

This is the third stage of the fortieth sequence. Negative as the image may seem, one may see implied in it the power in every individual to assume social risks in order to express his convictions or deepest desires. Nevertheless, one thing is needed: FACING THE CONSEQUENCES.

PHASE 199 (LIBRA 19°): A GANG OF ROBBERS IN HIDING.

KEYNOTE: *Protest against disharmonic social privilege.*

It is questionable whether the formulation of the symbol at this place is adequate, but it is kept on general principle. One might rather think of Robin Hood and his band, or early Bolsheviks in Russia robbing banks to finance the revolution. The protest against an unbalanced society with its rigid stratification into classes can be seen as a positive factor, even if it challenges the principle of order, for it reveals dynamic qualities in individuals and the will to transformation. In another sense, it is the dark shadow of the ideal of "nonpossessiveness." The question is: How valid and effectual is this kind of protest?

The fourth stage in a five-fold sequence of symbols and phases usually presents us with at least a hint of technique. What can this mean at this level? Perhaps the fact that any effective resistance to the momentum of crystallized institutions should be organized if it is to be effective. Individuals alone are impotent in producing actual changes in social consciousness. A "group" must be formed. The Keywords are GROUP PROTEST.

PHASE 200 (LIBRA 20°): A RABBI PERFORMING HIS DUTIES.

KEYNOTE: *The ability to draw on the power of an ancestral tradition in order to serve and inspire one's fellowmen.*

Here we see at work the constructive use of rather rigid yet effectual sociocultural and religious patterns. The energies of the collective Unconscious are channeled through well-defined, age-old forms and formulas. This implies limitations and the possibility of sclerosis or inertia when confronted with new situations, yet there is beauty and wisdom in such a ritualization of behavior and of thinking.

This is the fifth stage of the fortieth five-fold sequence. At this stage the relation of man, the individual, to his community—and beyond it, the universe—is seen in stabilized and effective operation. INHERITED WISDOM can be focused through a person who accepts its limitations.

SECOND LEVEL: EMOTIONAL–CULTURAL

PHASE 201 (LIBRA 21°): A SUNDAY CROWD ENJOYING THE BEACH.

KEYNOTE: *A revivifying contact with the Mother-force of nature and of social togetherness.*

The sea is the vast matrix from which living organisms originally emerged. It also symbolizes the collective Unconscious, the "matricial" envelope of the biosphere within which conscious-ness takes individualized forms. The consciousness of human beings is given specific form by the culture in which they live and the particular occupations they carry on in everyday work. But it is very good and healthful for their minds to become revitalized by collective experiences and deep feelings of un-differentiated unity as they merge in the vast refreshment of the planetary "Mother" where "she" is most dynamic, unlim-ited and unconfined by boundaries.

At this first stage of the forty-first five-fold sequence of symbols we see the foundation on which coming developments will be based. It is in a sense a biodynamic foundation, but it reaches beyond even the biosphere to what in all cosmic types of organization is the Mother-principle—for instance, galactic Space. We may speak here of OCEANIC FEELING, born of attunement to the most basic rhythms of existence, at whatever level it might be.

PHASE 202 (LIBRA 22°): A CHILD GIVING BIRDS A DRINK AT A FOUNTAIN.

KEYNOTE: *The concern of simple souls for the welfare and happiness of less-evolved beings who thirst for life renewal.*

The original statement of this symbol is far more significant than the later formulation, for what is expressed here is a reversal of the operation mentioned in the preceding symbol. Man, who has built the fountain—perhaps on arid land and through skillful work—gives the life-bestowing water to the thirsting birds. He does not go to the sea, but he brings the purified, drinkable water to the birds needing it. The connection between "child" and "birds" implies a spontaneous, naïve rapport at the spiritual level, a soul-touch at the level of pure feelings.

At this second stage of the five-fold process the contrast with the first takes on a suggestive aspect. What you received from the Infinite, you can give to the finite beings that thirst for it. Man does not need to destroy nature's wilderness through greed and carelessness; he can transform this wilderness into a garden, whose singing fountains will attract birds. We can use here Marc Jones's Keyword for this degree: SOLICITUDE.

PHASE 203 (LIBRA 23°): CHANTICLEER'S VOICE HERALDS SUNRISE.

KEYNOTE: *A creative and joyous response to life processes.*

The cock that crows as the first coloring of dawn appears at the eastern horizon is a beautiful symbol of the ability, demonstrated by all pioneers and cosmically attuned individuals, to give voice to what is as yet unmanifested, but is on the way to manifestation. At the ego level, chanticleer may feel that he makes the sun rise; but someday he will learn through painful experiences that to create is only to reveal what essentially *is.* It is the vivid recognition of the as-yet-unknown in the known.

This third stage symbol should make us think afresh about issues we too often take for granted. At every "sunrise" there are a few isolated witnesses that herald the coming of a new day. What is at stake here is the individual's capacity of RESPONSE TO LIFE'S RENEWALS—renewals which are cyclic, predictable, yet always new, always creative.

PHASE 204 (LIBRA 24°): A BUTTERFLY WITH A THIRD WING ON ITS LEFT SIDE.

KEYNOTE: *The ability to develop, for inner strengthening, new modes of response to basic life situations.*

The butterfly is the ancient and traditional symbol of the results of the process of spiritual rebirth. If the butterfly has three wings instead of two, a special development of an aspect of the spiritual life is shown. Three is a symbol of fulfillment. Some power has been added to the normal spiritual life of the individual person. The left side usually refers to the instinctual field of the consciousness, but it is also the heart's side. A new strength is shown, perhaps as yet unrealized.

A fourth stage symbol usually refers to some kind of technique or technical achievement. What is implied here is that the contact with the revivifying Life-force (cf. the first stage symbol) can result in the appearance of a new faculty, the use of which may not as yet be consciously evaluated. Indeed it is the establishment of such a contact which constitutes a technique for ORIGINAL MUTATION.

PHASE 205 (LIBRA 25°): THE SIGHT OF AN AUTUMN LEAF BRINGS TO A PILGRIM THE SUDDEN REVELATION OF THE MYSTERY OF LIFE AND DEATH.

KEYNOTE: *The ability to discover in every experience a transcendent or cosmic meaning.*

The mind open to the multifarious wonders of natural processes, because it sees everything with fresh eyes, not only witnesses simple facts, but pierces through appearances and perceives the great rhythms of universal life. Without such a faculty the aspirant to spiritual realities is always looking for "elsewhere." Yet the spirit, life, God is ever present, here and now. And every death is an omen of rebirth.

At this fifth stage of the forty-first five-fold sequence of phases of the cosmic process, the implications of the four preceding stages are brought to a new state of consciousness which is truly the spiritual state. It is a state of CLAIR-SEEING, or "seeing through." This world is illusion only to the individual who cannot see through its phenomena and fails to apprehend the reality these phenomena reveal even as they conceal it.

THIRD LEVEL: INDIVIDUAL–MENTAL

PHASE 206 (LIBRA 26°): AN EAGLE AND A LARGE WHITE DOVE CHANGE INTO EACH OTHER.

KEYNOTE: *The interaction of the spiritual Will and of the Love principle when critical needs arise.*

This sequence of symbols concluding the Libra phase of the cycle deals with problems met by the seeker for the fulfillment of a higher life of Relationship. Implied here is a kind of Yang-Yin interplay. When the circle encompassing both principles rotates fast, they appear to change into each other. Consciousness operates beyond duality, because the polarized energies of the Soul (or spirit), Will and Love, though ever distinct, work for a single purpose.

This is the first stage of the forty-second five-fold set of symbolic phases. It represents a new, higher approach to the use of polarized forces within the personality which has been ever so little transformed and operating within a new framework. The Keyword ADEPTNESS fits this phase—but there are many levels of "adept-ship"!

PHASE 207 (LIBRA 27°): AN AIRPLANE SAILS, HIGH IN THE CLEAR SKY.

KEYNOTE: *A consciousness able to transcend the conflicts and pressures of the personal life.*

This picture symbolizes the capacity, latent in every individual, to contemplate the stress of existence in our world of duality from a higher level. Through the use of his mind, backed by the efforts and struggles of past generations and the cooperation of other men, the individual can gain a new perspective on human problems and reach freedom and peace in a supernal realm of being.

This second stage symbol contrasts with the first, for while the first dealt with the cooperation between polarized energies, this one introduces us to the realm of unity beyond polarity. It is a stage of TRANSCENDENT REALIZATION.

PHASE 208 (LIBRA 28°): A MAN BECOMING AWARE OF SPIRITUAL FORCES SURROUNDING AND ASSISTING HIM.

KEYNOTE: *The realization, at any level of existence, that one is never alone, and that the "community"—visible or invisible—is sustaining one's efforts.*

Every individualized organism is part of a larger organized whole, whether or not it is aware of this or of the sustaining power of the whole. A man, however, can deliberately choose to follow the dark path of ego-isolation which sooner or later always leads to destruction and self-loss in "matter." At the animal level, the whole biosphere is the community; for the ordinary human being, it is the tribe or family, the village community, the nation. As the individual expands his consciousness, he may become aware of a spiritual community, even beyond the "noösphere" (the one Mind of humanity), i.e. the realm of the pure light of the "Supermind," which is what the concept of the "White Lodge" suggests.

This is the third stage of the forty-second five-fold sequence. To the man who has ever so little transcended the world of conflicts, and, for a moment at least, experienced the oneness of all existence, this stage should bring the realization of "belonging" to a greater whole. This produces a state of INNER ASSURANCE.

PHASE 209 (LIBRA 29°): MANKIND'S VAST AND ENDURING EFFORT TO REACH FOR KNOWLEDGE TRANSFERABLE FROM GENERATION TO GENERATION.

KEYNOTE: *A deep sense of participation in, and commitment to, social processes which seek to bring to all men Truth and a greater Life.*

The most characteristic trait in human nature is the ability to "bind time" (as Korzybsky once stated): that is, to transfer to other men as yet unborn the harvest of his conscious experiences and his deliberate endeavors. This ability far transcends

instinct and biological mutuations, for it is based on consciousness, choice, will and self-sacrifice for the sake of future human
beings. It rests upon a deep feeling of the value of "community"; its use increases this feeling and eventually destroys the
roots of loneliness.

This fourth stage symbol suggests the technique that makes a life truly
"human." To join other men and women in the vast process of a *living*
civilization is to fulfill the basic implications of the human stage of
cosmic evolution—a stage characterized by CONSCIOUS PARTICIPA-
TION.

PHASE 210 (LIBRA 30°): THREE MOUNDS OF KNOWLEDGE
ON A PHILOSOPHER'S HEAD.

KEYNOTE: *The fulfillment of man's power of understanding at whatever level of existence the person operates.*

A true philosopher is a man who is able to "understand," not
merely "know," the processes of life as he comes to experience
them directly. He is the man of wisdom, different indeed from
the man of science; for while there must be knowledge before
understanding, knowledge alone can be both barren and destructive of wisdom. This peculiar symbol refers of course to
"phrenology," which is usually considered a pseudoscience, but
may provide significant indications. Number 3 always indicates
a state of completion. The symbol implies a fulfillment of philosophical understanding, which obviously has nothing to do with
academic degrees or the writing of successful treatises on abstract concepts.

This fifth stage symbol is the last of the Libra series. Understanding
and wisdom develop in terms of the life of community and through
experiences provided by interpersonal and group relationships. Cultural factors are always involved, even though true wisdom transcends
cultural values and is rooted in the essential nature of Man. What is
at stake here is A HOLISTIC APPROACH TO KNOWLEDGE, based on
universals.

SCENE FIFTEEN: *COMMUNION*
(Scorpio 1° to Scorpio 15°)

FIRST LEVEL: ACTIONAL

PHASE 211 (SCORPIO 1°): A CROWDED SIGHTSEEING BUS ON A CITY STREET.

KEYNOTE: *The fundamental human eagerness to expand one's social horizon and to experience the results of collective achievements and new ways of life.*

In this symbol we are dealing with a group-experience of a vast collective achievement, a city. Individuals coming from a variety of places and backgrounds "commune" in new awareness of a greater whole of human existence, an organized whole with its own rhythms of multifarious activity. New feelings and an expansion of consciousness result. What begins in the Libra phase of the cycle is given substantiation during the Scorpio phase. The process of "initiation" into collective values is now reaching the feeling nature.

This symbol begins the forty-third five-fold sequence. It refers to the first realization of what a larger whole of existence—a more encompassing frame of reference—implies, in very concrete and perhaps startling terms. What is at stake is A WIDENING OF EXPERIENCE.

PHASE 212 (SCORPIO 2°): A DELICATE BOTTLE OF PERFUME LIES BROKEN, RELEASING ITS FRAGRANCE.

KEYNOTE: *The accidental nature of opportunities that impel one to break away from a past, the remembrance of which is still poignant and cherished.*

A new and greater realization usually demands the sacrifice of something which has brought loveliness and fragrance to a lesser form of living and feeling. Old feelings are poignantly remembered, even as one moves into a new and wider sphere of experience. Old relationships may be left behind, but the memory of their essential moments lingers on, perhaps strong and nostalgic.

This is the second stage of the forty-third sequence. It contrasts with the first in that it reveals the difficulty of dealing with the past as one enters into a new realm of feelings. To the excitement of novelty answers the memory of the graciousness of the past one has SURRENDERED.

> PHASE 213 (SCORPIO 3°): A HOUSE-RAISING PARTY IN A SMALL VILLAGE ENLISTS THE NEIGHBORS' COOPERATION.

> KEYNOTE: *The feeling of community demonstrated in a basic joint effort.*

In rural neighborhoods, especially as the American West was being developed, the building of at least the framework of a house was often a collective, friendly enterprise. Newcomers building their home-to-be found friendly helpers in their neighbors. The sense of togetherness and participation in a common enterprise was developed by such collective work. The home remains "our" home, yet the whole community is involved in its erection and the welcome marking its completion.

At this third stage of the five-fold sequence, feeling becomes activity. The past and its memories are repolarized in terms of the expanded social consciousness. From that activity a new sense of reality will derive. The Keyword is COOPERATION.

> PHASE 214 (SCORPIO 4°): A YOUTH CARRIES A LIGHTED CANDLE IN A DEVOTIONAL RITUAL.

> KEYNOTE: *The educative power of ceremonies which impress the great images of a culture upon its gathered participants.*

A community of human beings is ensouled by a few basic symbols which structure and illustrate the group's particular culture and way of life. Rituals and social ceremonies of all types (from a baseball game to a ticker-tape parade for returning heroes, or a religious service in an old cathedral) incorporate these symbols in traditional forms of activity. As they participate in these collective presentations of commonly accepted values and ideals, the minds and feelings of young people are formed by these symbols. They take the values for granted until the day when they choose to assert their individuality—or their participation in a generation's revolt—by scorning the traditional rituals, including as well business rituals. Then they may poignantly search for new ones to participate in!

This fourth stage symbol pictures for us the method by which a community of feelings is built during the formative years of childhood and adolescence. The zodiacal sign Scorpio is especially related to rituals including the sex rituals which unite the communicants at the roots of their beings. In these sex rituals too, THE POWER OF SYMBOLS is evident, above and beyond the mere biological act.

PHASE 215 (SCORPIO 5°): A MASSIVE ROCKY SHORE RESISTS THE POUNDING OF THE SEA.

KEYNOTE: *The inertia of all institutionalized procedures.*

Slow is the rise of the land from the vast ocean, but once it is formed it develops a formidable resistance to change in spite of storms. Likewise, once a culture has expressed its basic symbols and its particular way of thinking, feeling and acting in concrete institutions, these change very slowly indeed. The individual who came to the great city (Scorpio 1° symbol) soon finds his life set by the rhythms of city living, which obliterate vaster life processes and the moving tides of evolution.

This is the last of the five symbols of the forty-third sequence. We see in it how binding and resistant a communal way of life can become. In this there is strength and stability, and these are necessary factors in the social life of man—until new horizons beckon. The Keyword is STABILITY.

SECOND LEVEL: EMOTIONAL–CULTURAL

PHASE 216 (SCORPIO 6°): THE GOLD RUSH TEARS MEN AWAY FROM THEIR NATIVE SOIL.

KEYNOTE: *The passionate search for new values which, at any level, promise a more abundant life.*

The greatness of man is that he can always be greater; likewise, at a national level, man's "greed" can more easily be aroused by whatever promises more wealth, more power, and ever-greater achievements at all levels, spiritual as well as material. Beyond this arousal of greed is the deep-seated desire to play a more important or spectacular role in one's society or community. Greed is the perverse intensification of the social sense, just as lust is the perverse intensification of the longing for love. Always at this Scorpio level the yearning is for an ever more intense and all-absorbing union with a person or a community—a yearning which motivates a search for more effectual means to achieve as total a feeling experience as is possible.

This is the first stage of the forty-fourth sequence of symbolic phases in the cycle of existence. It dramatizes the capacity in man to tear himself away from the known and the familiar, gambling everything on a vision or dream. A Keyword could be AVIDITY.

PHASE 217 (SCORPIO 7°): DEEP-SEA DIVERS.

KEYNOTE: *The will to explore the hidden depths of all experiences and to search for primordial causes.*

This symbol essentially refers to depth psychology—a coming to terms with the collective Unconscious and its contents. This type of depth-plumbing adventure is basically different from the one symbolized by the gold rush, for it can take place within the individual and with no relation to social value. It refers symbolically to a quest for "under-standing"—i.e. for what lies under the surface waves of daily living. This quest may lead to

great dangers. It demands a strong will and good breathing—
i.e. a degree of spiritual strength. It usually challenges powers
hidden in the depths of the unconscious.

The contrast between "deep-sea divers" and "men of the gold rush"
is significant. It presents in an interesting manner the opposition between a first stage and second stage symbol in the five-fold sequence
of cyclic phases. The inward quest opposes the outward search for the
great social symbol, gold. It should lead to a DEPTH REALIZATION of
the very roots of consciousness.

PHASE 218 (SCORPIO 8°): A CALM LAKE BATHED IN MOON-LIGHT.

KEYNOTE: *A quiet openness to higher inspiration.*

One could stress the romantic suggestions such an image
evokes, but even at the level of a love relationship what is
implied is a surrender of two personal egos to the inspiration of
transcendent feelings which are essentially impersonal. Love
expresses itself *through* the lovers, for real Love is a cosmic
undifferentiated principle or power which simply focuses itself
within the "souls" of human beings who reflect its light. The
same is true of the mystic's love for God. Man strives hard to
achieve great things through daring adventures, but a moment
comes when all that really matters is to present a calm mind
upon which a supernal light may be reflected.

This is the third stage of the forty-fourth five-fold sequence. It tells us
that beyond all efforts lies the need for peace and the readiness to
accept the illumination from above. The Keyword is QUIESCENCE.

PHASE 219 (SCORPIO 9°): A DENTIST AT WORK.

KEYNOTE: *Overcoming the negative results of social practices and ego-cravings.*

In order to properly evaluate and interpret this symbol, we should realize the meaning of the teeth. Permanent teeth appear normally at age 7, when, according to some occultists, the personalized individuality of the child—the ego—takes full control of the physical organism. The teeth are used to tear down foodstuffs so they can be digested and assimilated. Social living and cultural patterns impose upon us certain habits of eating, arouse desires for unwholesome or denatured food, force us perhaps to eat in tense circumstances and hurriedly. This results in tooth decay far more frequently than should be inevitable through aging. The symbol therefore shows us how society and civilization, which may indirectly cause tooth decay, then have to invent means to skillfully repair the damage.

At this fourth stage of the five-fold sequence we see once more a hint of technique. Life in society both perverts and repairs, destroys and rebuilds—truly a vicious cycle. Man is compelled by social needs to display INVENTIVENESS.

PHASE 220 (SCORPIO 10°): A FELLOWSHIP SUPPER RE-UNITES OLD COMRADES.

KEYNOTE: *The overtones of human relationships based on a community of work or experiences.*

This symbol pictures the essential nature of the bond that unites individuals who have participated in some common activity. The social feeling of communion, plus all that it engenders, arises *after* the act performed together. Activity is at the root of consciousness. Activity in common generates social consciousness and cultural patterns which become set in the form of institutions. A group-personality emerges, which displays characteristic features and gives birth to collective emotions and values.

This is the final stage of the forty-fourth five-fold sequence. Wherever the symbol appears, it suggests the importance of establishing or strengthening links with those with whom one has shared, or can share, living experiences. The value of COMRADESHIP is emphasized.

THIRD LEVEL: INDIVIDUAL–MENTAL

PHASE 221 (SCORPIO 11°): A DROWNING MAN IS BEING RES-CUED.

KEYNOTE: *The deep concern of the social group for the safety of individuals.*

This symbol should be interpreted as revealing the basic feeling of relationship between the individual and his fellow-men. What is pictured is the expression of this relationship rather than the experience of the person who, carelessly perhaps, ventured too far beyond his depth and then was given a "second chance" to live. A man risks his life to save another: this is love, based on a sense of responsibility produced by a vivid sense of interrelatedness. Sustained by this love, the individual may be more secure in venturing forth; but this assurance can also lead to unwarranted daring and trust.

This is the first stage of the forty-fifth sequence of five symbolic phases. It pictures the concern of the social whole for any one of its parts, even if this concern is merely the spontaneous act of rescue performed by a chance bystander. The HUMANITARIANISM thus displayed has deep cultural roots.

PHASE 222 (SCORPIO 12°): AN OFFICIAL EMBASSY BALL.

KEYNOTE: *Group-consciousness, as it flowers at the highest level in cultural interchanges between representatives of the elite of the ruling class.*

At present the largest unit of social organization is the nation. The symbol pictures the ruling class of such national wholes displaying at least the superficial forms of a concern for establishing permanent relationships in peaceful cooperation. What is evoked is the value of meeting other people at the highest possible level of cultural interplay (i.e. in "full dress"), rather than with an everyday type of consciousness and behavior.

In contrast to the natural spontaneity of the rescue operation shown in the preceding symbol, we have here the image of a ritualized DISPLAY of power, prestige and wealth. Relationship has been made hierarchical and is institutionalized. Phase 222 tells us that this too is an essential feature in the development of rhythmic give-and-take in order to achieve global peace.

PHASE 223 (SCORPIO 13°): AN INVENTOR PERFORMS A LABORATORY EXPERIMENT.

KEYNOTE: *The driving urge toward achievement, which is at the root of civilization.*

At whatever level, the development of more complete and efficient forms of social interplay—the essence of the process of civilization—demands ingenuity, inventiveness and the willingness to experiment within relatively secure test conditions. One must try to go to the roots of problems of interpersonal or international relations, as well as to discover the principles controlling the interaction between material particles and larger bodies. Modern technology is only one approach to an immensely complex problem. Intuition is as necessary to success as intellectual analysis.

This is the third stage of the forty-fifth sequence of five symbols. The symbol stresses the value of individual initiative, perseverance and caution in any attempt to understand how everything is related to everything else. What is most needed is the ABILITY TO RELATE SEEMINGLY UNRELATED FACTS.

PHASE 224 (SCORPIO 14°): TELEPHONE LINEMEN AT WORK INSTALLING NEW CONNECTIONS.

KEYNOTE: *The need to establish new channels of communication.*

The growth of community feeling among separated human beings requires the development of constantly more complex means of interchanging feelings and ideas. Wherever this symbol for Scorpio 14° is found, the indication is that such channels of communication are essential for the success of any interpersonal relationship. They are not only to be built, but to be used significantly and wisely.

This fourth stage symbol brings to our attention the essential value of communicating with our fellow-men and even our close associates— with whom such a communication may not always be easy. There can be no communion without communication *at some level*, including the level of biological attunement. Keyword: THE WILL TO ASSOCIATION or COMPREHENSION.

PHASE 225 (SCORPIO 15°): CHILDREN PLAYING AROUND FIVE MOUNDS OF SAND.

KEYNOTE: *Early steps in the development of a mind seeking to be attuned to the higher level of human evolution.*

This is a particularly cryptic symbol. It may be deciphered if one realizes that Man's essential destiny is to develop as a five-fold being, a "Pentagram" or five-pointed star. Number 5 symbolizes mind in its most creative and penetrating aspect, while number 4 refers to the life processes operating at present within the earth's biosphere. Our Western civilization has realized only the lower level of this vibration 5; i.e. mind contaminated by compulsive instincts and emotional involvement. Some individuals, however, are born with a special potential for development of the higher, creative mind, and in social circumstances favoring this development. In most cases, they are still "playing around" with their unusual capacity. They are in the kindergarten stage of this higher mind development.

In this final stage of the forty-fifth sequence of five symbols the transcendent possibilities of mental evolution, which require interpersonal communion in consciousness, are evoked. The free spirit of true scientific inquiry is only a foreshadowing of a such a type of mind, which demands dedication to mankind as a whole. What is seen here is FUTURE-ORIENTED GROWTH.

SCENE SIXTEEN: *FAITH*
(*Scorpio 16° to Scorpio 30°*)

FIRST LEVEL: ACTIONAL

PHASE 226 (SCORPIO 16°): A GIRL'S FACE BREAKING INTO A SMILE.

KEYNOTE: *The fervent reaching out on the part of the young of heart to new experiences.*

Faith in life and in other human beings enables us to go forth toward relationships with whatever attracts our senses or stirs our imagination. Smiling is perhaps a uniquely human characteristic because it implies a *conscious* acceptance of relationship, thus a choice. The animal, on the other hand, is compelled by unconscious instinct, at least in its natural state. It is not free to choose between love and hate.

This is the first symbol of the forty-sixth five-fold sequence. It introduces us to a series of responses to human experience and pictures a glowing WARMTH OF FEELING.

PHASE 227 (SCORPIO 17°): A WOMAN, FECUNDATED BY HER OWN SPIRIT, IS "GREAT WITH CHILD."

KEYNOTE: *A total reliance upon the dictates of the God-within.*

In contrast to the outgoing smile of the girl in the preceding symbol, here we see the result of a deep and complete concentration reaching to the innermost center of the personality where the Living God acts as a fecundating power. This reveals the potency of the inward way, the surrender of the ego to a transcendent Force which can create *through* the person vivid manifestations of the Will of God.

This second phase of the forty-sixth five-fold sequence brings to us the realization of normally hidden potentialities in the average human being of our day. Faith in the Divine is shown here being concretely justified. The human person becomes a "mother of the Living God." This is THE TRANSPERSONAL WAY of existence. It is the way that leads to creative mutations.

PHASE 228 (SCORPIO 18°): A PATH THROUGH WOODS BRILLIANT WITH MULTICOLORED SPLENDOR.

KEYNOTE: *The exalted feeling of a work well done and a truly consummated life.*

The person who has lived with faith the transpersonal life—the life *through* which spirit radiates creatively—can experience blessedness and peace, even though his or her cycle of experience nears its end. It has been a life full of seed. The seeds are hidden perhaps, yet they are filled with the power to overcome cyclic death. The soul is at peace. The clear autumnal sky silently intones the great message: "Well done, little man!"

In this third symbol of the five-fold sequence we see the smile of the youth brought to a more mature, more spiritual culmination. Human nature is a magnificent symphony of warm, rich colors, now that the

strictly biological green of vegetation experiences its TRANSFIGURA-
TION.

**PHASE 229 (SCORPIO 19°): A PARROT REPEATS THE CON-
VERSATION HE HAS OVERHEARD.**

KEYNOTE: *The capacity to transmit transcendental knowledge.*

To the individual who lives in a state of ardent and sustained
faith it may become possible to become a channel for the transmission of a knowledge or wisdom that transcends his normal
mental understanding. The mind that has learned to be silent
and attentive can become attuned to the rhythm of utterances
which he may not comprehend intellectually, yet which may
truly manifest superhuman realizations. Discrimination is
needed here to balance the overeagerness of faith.

At this fourth stage of the five-fold sequence of symbols we are given
a hint as to man's capacity to attune himself to sources of higher
wisdom if he can be sufficiently attentive and careful in channeling a
"higher Voice." To stress here the negative element of automatism
and unintelligent repetition is to use only one's intellect. All birds in
symbolism suggest spiritual faculties or forces. What is evoked is the
possibility of learning from higher Intelligences. Keyword: CHANNEL-
SHIP.

**PHASE 230 (SCORPIO 20°): A WOMAN DRAWS AWAY TWO
DARK CURTAINS CLOSING THE ENTRANCE TO A SACRED
PATHWAY.**

KEYNOTE: *The revelation to the human consciousness of
what lies beyond dualistic knowledge.*

The "Woman within"—the faith that is rooted in the deepest
intuitions of the soul—is seen here as the hierophant unveiling
the realities which the either-or, pro-and-con mind of man
alone cannot perceive. The path to the mystic's "unitive life" is

opened up once the darkness of fear, egocentricity and dualistic morality is removed.

This is the last symbol of the forty-sixth five-fold sequence. It reveals what a positive reliance upon faith and intuition can bring about. Courage is needed to go through the veiling darkness—the courage to venture beyond the familiar and the traditionally known, to PLUNGE AHEAD INTO THE UNKNOWN.

SECOND LEVEL: EMOTIONAL–CULTURAL

PHASE 231 (SCORPIO 21°): OBEYING HIS CONSCIENCE, A SOLDIER RESISTS ORDERS.

KEYNOTE: *A readiness to face the results of a refusal to follow the authoritarian patterns of an aggressive society.*

As a person finds himself involved in activities which are traditional in his particular culture—and in many instances in all societies at this stage of human evolution—he often faces a conflict between his own individual sense of value (his conscience) and the demands of society. The conflict may be most typical in terms of the armed services—thus this symbol. In it we find the individual asserting his own values, though he cannot escape the consequences of his decision. In such a case he has to be quietly ready to face these consequences, whatever the cost.

This is the first stage in the forty-seventh five-fold sequence of phases in the great cyclic ritual of activity. The issue it presents is clear. Society in this situation seems to be all-powerful; yet the individual need not be spiritually bound, even if imprisoned. He still can display INNER FREEDOM and prove himself an "individual."

PHASE 232 (SCORPIO 22°): HUNTERS SHOOTING WILD DUCKS.

KEYNOTE: *The socially accepted release of an individual's or a group's aggressive instincts.*

What this symbol clearly stresses is the socialization of man's primitive instincts according to a cultural ritual. Social hunting is a regulated seasonal outlet for male aggressiveness—a safety valve for emotional pressures in human beings in whom animal compulsions and biospheric values are still strong.

In this second stage symbol we find a strong contrast with the first. In the latter, the individual proved himself truly "man" by refusing to accept the practices of war imposed upon him by his society; in this symbol for Scorpio 22° it is society that willingly accepts—and in accepting, ritualizes and to some extent refines—the aggressiveness inherent in most individuals. The Keywords are SOCIALIZATION OF INSTINCTS.

PHASE 233 (SCORPIO 23°): A RABBIT METAMORPHOSES INTO A NATURE SPIRIT.

KEYNOTE: *The raising of animal drives to a higher level.*

The rabbit is traditionally a symbol of an overabundance of progeny, thus of a great stress on procreative and sexual processes. "Nature spirits," on the other hand, represent the higher aspect of life energies, as they are said to guide those normally invisible forces controlling the growth of all living organisms, particularly in the vegetable kingdom. Thus the symbol refers to the transmutation of the generative power into a more ethereal and subtle form of potency.

This is the third symbol in the forty-seventh sequence. It brings a new dimension to the preceding two. Whether it is the sexual desire for a progeny, or aggressiveness, the instinctual urge can be raised to a new level. The course can become subtle through a process of TRANSUBSTANTIATION.

PHASE 234 (SCORPIO 24°): AFTER HAVING HEARD AN IN-
SPIRED INDIVIDUAL DELIVER HIS "SERMON ON THE
MOUNT," CROWDS ARE RETURNING HOME.

KEYNOTE: *The need to incorporate inspiring experiences
and teachings into everyday living.*

Today we hear a great deal about "peak experiences" (Maslow).
The great problem facing everyone who has had such experiences is how to assimilate what has been felt, seen or heard, and
how to let it transform his everyday consciousness and behavior.
If this is not done the experience may turn confusing or toxic
and perhaps destructive of the integrity of the person.

This fourth symbol as usual suggests to us what has to be done or how
to do it. The "return home" from the high mountain, or from any
"upper chamber" of the consciousness, may lead to a sense of oppres-
sion by the normal realities of existence, or else the soul that has been
illuminated may retain enough of that light to transfigure every daily
situation. This is the great CHALLENGE TO TRANSFORMATION.

PHASE 235 (SCORPIO 25°) AN X-RAY PHOTOGRAPH.

KEYNOTE: *The capacity to acquire a knowledge of the structural factors in all existence.*

The true philosopher is able to grasp and significantly evaluate
what underlies all manifestations of life. His mind's eye pene-
trates through the superficialities of existence and perceives the
framework that gives an at least relatively permanent "form"
to all organized systems. Thus if the structure is weak, deformed
by persistent strain, or unbalanced, the basic causes of outer
disturbances and dis-ease can be discovered.

This symbol concludes the forty-seventh five-fold sequence. It gives an
added dimension to the preceding four. For instance, it provides the
conscience of the individual who refuses to obey his society with a
depth-understanding of what is wrong in the situation he faces.
Beyond the powerful feeling quality of "peak experiences," the mind
can understand the great Principles of which they were the manifesta-

tions. This is STRUCTURAL KNOWLEDGE in contrast to existential knowledge.

THIRD LEVEL: INDIVIDUAL–MENTAL

PHASE 236 (SCORPIO 26°): AMERICAN INDIANS MAKING CAMP AFTER MOVING INTO A NEW TERRITORY.

KEYNOTE: *The ability to adjust swiftly to a new situation by tuning in to its requirements.*

He who lives in harmony with nature, moving on as new needs arise, finds himself intuitively at home everywhere. He does not make demands upon life, for he has identified himself with the great ryhthms of the biosphere and he functions at peace with what they produce. This is the message of the American Indian culture which European invaders so wantonly and meaninglessly destroyed nearly everywhere. Western man has lost faith in life because he wants to dominate and enslave manifestations.

This represents the first stage of the forty-eighth five-fold sequence in the cycle of experience. It brings to us a message we greatly need today—the message of peaceful adaptation to nature, and through adaptation, of EFFICIENT FUNCTIONING in all life situations.

PHASE 237 (SCORPIO 27°): A MILITARY BAND MARCHES NOISILY ON THROUGH THE CITY STREETS.

KEYNOTE: *The aggressive glorification of cultural values.*

Every cultural-social collectivity sooner or later tries to impress the value of its achievements forcibly and noisily upon all those who belong to it, as well as upon foreign onlookers. At the individual-mental level the member of such a collectivity swells with pride and excitement when a display of the excellence of that in which his consciousness and personality are deeply rooted is publicly affirmed. Thus the feeling of social unity binds the individuals of a culture through collective pride.

This second stage symbol contrasts sharply with the first one. Our aggressive, tense, domineering Western civilization is indeed in opposition to the natural spontaneity and instinctive adjustment to nature of tribal societies. The Keyword here is POMP.

PHASE 238 (SCORPIO 28°): THE KING OF THE FAIRIES APPROACHING HIS DOMAIN.

KEYNOTE: *The capacity in man to recognize and to pay homage to an integrating Principle at the core of all existence.*

This rather peculiar picture tells us perhaps a good deal about the limitations of the mind of the clairvoyant who saw it, though it can be related to the symbolism of the various creatures of a spirit world mentioned in some alchemical and Rosicrucian books. What seems to be implied is that beyond both outer nature and the realm of the proud ego, a spiritual world exists to which the intuitive consciousness of man can pay allegiance. In that world, all manifested entities are seen as multiple aspects of a central Power and Consciousness. It is such a central principle of unity that human societies have sought to revere symbolically in human, all-too-human kings. In an individual sense, this principle is the Self.

This is the third stage in the forty-eighth five-fold pattern of symbols. It adds a new dimension to the two preceding ones. At this stage the presence of a spiritual unifying factor begins to be sensed by the individual perhaps weary of the outer shows of his culture. An INNER ALLEGIANCE begins to polarize the consciousness.

PHASE 239 (SCORPIO 29°): AN INDIAN SQUAW PLEADING TO THE CHIEF FOR THE LIVES OF HER CHILDREN.

KEYNOTE: *Love as a principle of redemption.*

Here the soul is presented as a mother whose sons (i.e. her active energies) have become disruptive forces in the collective life of the tribe. She seeks to counteract the karma of their misdeeds through her love and implorations. The soul is responsive to the experience of unity (the spiritual king or chief) but the energies of human nature often follow their self-seeking, divisive tendencies.

This is the fourth symbol of the forty-eighth sequence. It presents us with the value of prayer. The principle of wholeness in man—the soul —acts to offset or attenuate the dictates of karma. In a religious sense, Mary, the Mother, is seen as the Mediatrix, in constant acts of IN-TERCESSION for the sake of waylaid individuals.

PHASE 240 (SCORPIO 30°): CHILDREN IN HALLOWEEN COS-TUMES INDULGE IN VARIOUS PRANKS.

KEYNOTE: *The periodic outlets society furnishes within tra-ditional limits to still-immature energies.*

In the symbol for the first degree of Scorpio we see individuals beginning to be involved in the collective life of a large city. This leads them to a great diversity of experience which stimu-lates their sense of belonging to a vaster whole; or it may stimu-late their rebellious instincts. Some of the latter in most cases cannot be completely overcome, but society has built in several ways of allowing them to operate under ritualistic procedures that are sufficiently safe to the collectivity. Wherever this sym-bol is found, the need for such outlets is shown to exist. But the rules of the game have to be obeyed.

This is the last symbol referring to Scene Sixteen of the great ritual of cyclic being. It tells us that in any feeling experience of collective living and interhuman relationships one has to deal with unregenerated and centrifugal elements. These should be carefully managed. They can also be controlled by the power of mind—the Sagittarian way. The symbol points to an imaginative RELIEF FROM TENSION.

SCENE SEVENTEEN: *ABSTRACTION*
(Sagittarius 1° to Sagittarius 15°)

FIRST LEVEL: ACTIONAL

PHASE 241 (SAGITTARIUS 1°): RETIRED ARMY VETERANS GATHER TO REAWAKEN OLD MEMORIES.

KEYNOTE: *The will to reaffirm the value of the struggle upon which civilization and group-achievements are founded.*

Two important factors are revealed in this symbol: the men who have come together are Army men, and they are linked by actions and a type of consciousness that have roots in a common past. What we call "civilization" is built by constant struggles against nature, for it seeks to wrench *power* from nature. This element of power is seen in its most obvious aspect in the military consciousness. Moreover, all civilization is built upon the accumulated products of the experiences of past generations of dedicated men who agree to follow rather rigid procedures of work. Veterans' groups in all countries seek to rekindle in their members the old fire of well-fought battles; but the type of abstract or religious thinking normally related to the zodiacal sign, Sagittarius, also implies a special kind of "fire." It is a fire that burns the "now" of natural living in order to build a greater "tomorrow." It is future-oriented. It aspires to produce a greater, wider civilization, even though it finds its roots in the harvest of mankind's past. Comradeship and group activities are implied, but the togetherness is one of fighting spirits.

This is the first stage of the forty-ninth five-fold sequence of cyclic phases. The symbol should be understood in its widest and most basic meaning, not merely as the reunion of old comrades, but as referring to the very power implied in the process of civilization, as opposed to culture—thus to the PERPETUATION of the spirit of struggle for power.

PHASE 242 (SAGITTARIUS 2°): WHITE-CAPPED WAVES DISPLAY THE POWER OF WIND OVER SEA.

KEYNOTE: *The mobilization of unconscious energies under the pressure of superpersonal motives.*

Wind and sea are in constant interplay, and the results of that interplay are inspiring and beautiful. In symbolism, the wind (*pneuma* is the early Greek word for "spirit") is associated with spiritual dynamism; the stirring of deep energies this dynamism produces obeys cosmic or superpersonal rhythms, the power of which is irresistible.

At this second stage of the forty-ninth five-fold sequence we have a picture which contrasts the powerful but beautiful storms of nature with the often gory and hysterical crises of a civilization which progresses through war. The picture presented speaks of SUBTILIZATION THROUGH RHYTHMIC INTENSITY.

PHASE 243 (SAGITTARIUS 3°): TWO MEN PLAYING CHESS.

KEYNOTE: *The transcendent ritualization of conflict.*

Essential to sociocultural living is the transmutation of man's natural aggressiveness under most conditions of existence. Many rituals, sports and games have no other basic aim. In chess the complex types of energies which in their togetherness constitute a human person are symbolized by six kinds of pieces (king, queen, bishops, knights, rooks and pawns). The struggle between light and darkness (the Yang and Yin forces) is ritualized, ending in most cases with the checkmating of the king (the ego, the conscious self). In a dualistic world such a contest between polarized forces is omnipresent. The chess game trains men to be more objective, more careful, more aware of whole situations—and less impulsive and intent upon side issues.

This third stage symbol deals with conflict, but at the level of group culture and psychological symbolization. It brings to the objective consciousness the basic realities in interpersonal INTERPLAY.

> PHASE 244 (SAGITTARIUS 4°): A LITTLE CHILD LEARNING TO WALK WITH THE ENCOURAGEMENT OF HIS PARENTS.
>
> KEYNOTE: *The natural assistance of superior powers during crises of growth.*

At an early stage in its development, every living organism must make an attempt to overcome the power of gravitation, or rather to learn to use it in order to fulfill the purpose of its life. This implies passing through a critical state of growth—growth in freedom, potency and individuality, inasmuch as "walking" always symbolizes self-induced progress. In such a crisis the individual is not left alone. Some more evolved Power and Intelligence watches, encourages and gives examples to be followed.

As usual, this fourth stage symbol in the forty-ninth sequence gives a hint of technique. It presents a picture of the conditions under which a RESOLUTION OF CONFLICT can be ensured, whether at the organic, the personal or the superpersonal level of unfoldment.

> PHASE 245 (SAGITTARIUS 5°): AN OLD OWL SITS ALONE ON THE BRANCH OF A LARGE TREE.
>
> KEYNOTE: *A poised and wise approach to existence based on a clear perception of unconscious factors and their operation.*

The owl has always been a symbol of wisdom, and its hooting call has evoked a rise to mysterious and hidden elements in life. The owl functions lucidly in the night aspect of existence. His eyes see what men normally fail to perceive. He represents that consciousness which is active where the processes of life normally escape the attention of the personal ego and its intellect.

This is the last of the five symbols in the forty-ninth sequence. It suggests the possibility of developing a wisdom beyond tragedy, a peace and poise beyond conflict. One might speak here of TRANSLU-CIDITY.

SECOND LEVEL: EMOTIONAL–CULTURAL

PHASE 246 (SAGITTARIUS 6°): A GAME OF CRICKET.

KEYNOTE: *The development of skill in group-situations testing collective goals.*

Any society is built on the interplay between groups of people, each group united by an at least temporary aim. The individual person within the group is assigned a particular role in the play, and definite rules have to be obeyed. The game teaches not only personal skill, but fairness and cooperation. Where this symbol is found, the value of making individual-will or ego-will subservient to collective cultural patterns is emphasized. Several symbols belonging to Scene Seventeen (Sagittarius) relate to games or group rituals, because these are "ab-stracted" from everyday social behavior and used as educative means to develop group-consciousness and an individual sense of responsibility to the group.

This is the first symbol of the fiftieth five-fold sequence. It refers to the importance of developing GROUP SOLIDARITY.

PHASE 247 (SAGITTARIUS 7°): CUPID KNOCKS AT THE DOOR OF A HUMAN HEART.

KEYNOTE: *A stirring-up of individual longings for romantic love.*

In contrast to the preceding, this symbol refers to what one might call a personal initiation through an ideal love. Far from being related to social value, ideal love tends to exalt individual characteristics in that it glorifies what seems able to fill poignant and often unconscious needs. Such a love is a projection of the anima or animus Images which in a sense complement the outer character of the one who loves. It is a subjective event which tends to bring to the lover a crisis or emotional chaos. Such a love often turns asocial if not antisocial and is blocked or frowned upon by society.

This second stage symbol is in direct opposition to that of the "cricket game." Intensely romantic love knows no rules and ignores collective purpose or dictates of reason. Yet it may bring to the individual an intensity of feeling which no group togetherness can arouse, at least at the ordinary social level. What is implied is a challenge to EMO-TIONAL REBIRTH.

PHASE 248 (SAGITTARIUS 8°): WITHIN THE DEPTHS OF THE EARTH NEW ELEMENTS ARE BEING FORMED.

KEYNOTE: *The alchemical fire which both purifies and transforms the very substance of man's inner life.*

Forces are at work in the deepest layers of the psyche which in their own way respond to the outer stimulation produced by a strong involvement in group ambitions and emotions, and even more by the powerful tensions and releases of love. An alchemical process goes on, usually unnoticed by the conscious ego, until it becomes obvious that a kind of mutation has taken place and a new level of awareness and of responses to life has been reached.

At this third stage of the five-fold sequence we deal with both the basic rhythm of growth of the human being and the reaction to more in-dividualized experiences which aroused the emotions. The very sub-stance of the person's nature undergoes modifications, on the basis of which a new step may be taken. The symbol draws our attention to the inner changes. We have to become aware of them. What is implied is a kind of PSYCHIC GESTATION.

PHASE 249 (SAGITTARIUS 9°): A MOTHER LEADS HER SMALL CHILD STEP BY STEP UP A STEEP STAIRWAY.

KEYNOTE: *The need in any social situation to assist the less evolved in their management of the problems which society requires its members to solve.*

A staircase does not present a *natural* difficulty to a very young child. Man builds stairs and therefore is responsible for assisting the child to climb them step by step. Social and cultural living is not "natural." The child must first be taught by example, then helped along as he imitates as well as he can the grownup's behavior. Climbing stairs is only an illustration of a general process. Every generation must involve itself in teaching the next even the simplest skills needed for social existence.

At the fourth stage of the preceding five-fold sequence we saw parents encouraging a little child to walk. Walking is a natural human function; climbing stairs is a skill made necessary by the building of several-storied houses—a product of civilization. What is implied here is SOCIAL CONCERN for the less evolved of society's members.

PHASE 250 (SAGITTARIUS 10°): A THEATRICAL REPRESENTATION OF A GOLDEN-HAIRED GODDESS OF OPPORTUNITY.

KEYNOTE: *Society's efforts at dramatizing the greatness of what it offers to the ambitious person.*

Civilization as a process demands the goading of individuals to spend their vital energies in the pursuit of achievements which, while fulfilling the individual's ambition and greed, nevertheless generate various forms of what we call "progress." This sequence of symbols mainly refers to the drive for advancement along "human, all too human" paths of growth.

This is the last symbol of the fiftieth five-fold sequence. We see in it how sociocultural forces operate by dramatization and propaganda. The result is all too often a process of FORCED GROWTH.

THIRD LEVEL: INDIVIDUAL-MENTAL

PHASE 251 (SAGITTARIUS 11°): IN THE LEFT SECTION OF AN ARCHAIC TEMPLE, A LAMP BURNS IN A CONTAINER SHAPED LIKE A HUMAN BODY.

KEYNOTE: *The value of the "return to the body" advocated by modern thinkers in order to balance the stress on intellectuality and objective consciousness.*

This sequence of five symbols confronts us with rather mysterious images, which nevertheless can be given very profound and important meanings for today. The original formulation of this symbol spoke of "physical enlightenment," but what seems to be implied, in contemporary terms, is the need to rely upon "the wisdom of the body" of which so much is made in sensitivity training and Gestalt psychotherapy. This refers to the process of deconditioning a consciousness that has become a prisoner of intellectual concepts with their total reliance on quantitative values, objectivity and conformity to the official patterns of our culture.

This represents the first stage of a challenging process—the fifty-first sequence of five symbols. It stresses the importance, for many individuals, of RELYING UPON ORGANISMIC RESPONSES in meeting life's challenges.

PHASE 252 (SAGITTARIUS 12°): A FLAG TURNS INTO AN EAGLE; THE EAGLE INTO A CHANTICLEER SALUTING THE DAWN.

KEYNOTE: *The spiritualization and promotion of great symbols of a New Age by minds sensitive to its precursory manifestations.*

In the background of this strange allegory we can recognize the deep-seated belief that the American nation and its basic democratic institutions were constituted to be the cradle for a new step in human evolution. The "flag" is the abstract symbol of the nation; it becomes an "eagle"—another U.S. symbol—when the concept is made alive by bold and transcendent action. The eagle symbolizes spiritual will and the power to rise to the highest possible altitude of consciousness and purpose. Flying at such an altitude, the eagle is the first living creature to perceive the rising sun. Having perceived it, it heralds it—and by so doing is identified with the crowing chanticleer, who had convinced himself that his resonant cry was responsible for the rise of the sun and the coming of a new day.

This second stage symbol contrasts with the first in that it is completely future-oriented. It speaks of "peak experiences" instead of the wisdom found in the organismic depth of the body-consciousness. It urges us to bring our noblest ideals to actual life through the power of the spiritual will. A Keyword might be ANNUNCIATION.

PHASE 253 (SAGITTARIUS 13°): A WIDOW'S PAST IS BROUGHT TO LIGHT.

KEYNOTE: *The karma of past actions as it affects opportunities presented by a new cycle.*

What the "widow's past" is remains obscure but the point is that even as a past cycle is closed—a phase of married life ends—the karma of whatever deeds or misdeeds this cycle witnessed will almost inevitably intrude into the new life period. Also, once a cycle of activity is concluded, much that was unclear or unconsciously motivated in the events it witnessed can now more easily come to the clear consciousness of the mind. It is possible to joyously herald the dawn from high above the actual stresses of existence (the preceding symbol), but the new day may be found loaded and darkened by the unfinished business of many a yesterday.

This is the third stage of the fifty-first five-fold sequence. Mankind is "the widow," because our soon-to-be-concluded Piscean Age has buried most of the ideals it once revered and proclaimed. Yet the New Age will have to deal with many oppressive ghosts. This is a symbol of RETRIBUTION.

PHASE 254 (SAGITTARIUS 14°): THE GREAT PYRAMID AND THE SPHINX.

KEYNOTE: *The enduring power of occult knowledge and of its quasi-divine Custodians, "Seed-men" of a previous cycle of existence.*

The belief in an Original Tradition based on the perfect knowledge of the archetypal principles and forms which underlie all manifestations of life on this Earth (and by extension in the cosmos) is deeply rooted in man's consciousness. The Great Pyramid and the Sphinx are witnesses to such a Tradition, especially for the Western world. The symbol implies that such an archetypal knowledge remains the foundation upon which men's minds can still build solid and valid formulations, as new evolutionary developments are pending.

This fourth stage symbol suggests that this occult knowledge and the traditional process of acquiring it is still available, and that by accepting their principles modern man can best meet the challenge of our present world crisis. The symbol, interpreted from a personal point of view, points to the greatness of a Soul's past achievements and the value of trying to reevoke this past. What is revealed is THE POWER OF SPIRITUAL ANCESTRY.

PHASE 255 (SAGITTARIUS 15°): THE GROUND HOG LOOKING FOR ITS SHADOW ON GROUND-HOG DAY, FEBRUARY 2.

KEYNOTE: *The value of anticipating new turns of events and ascertaining future prospects.*

In our modern industrial society where policy changes and decisions often take several years to reach full actualization, it has become essential to plan with an eye on probable future developments. Such planning requires a study of past trends and the extrapolation of the results. What above all is implied in the symbol is a sensitivity to social or planetary rhythms, and the need to ensure at least relative safety by planning ahead.

This is the last symbol in this fifty-first sequence. Something of the meanings of the first four is involved in the process it suggests. In its highest form the knowledge required is "eonic consciousness"—in modern terms the new science of PROSPECTIVE.

SCENE EIGHTEEN: *TRANSFERENCE*
(Sagittarius 16° to Sagittarius 30°)

FIRST LEVEL: ACTIONAL

PHASE 256 (SAGITTARIUS 16°): SEA GULLS FLY AROUND A SHIP IN EXPECTATION OF FOOD.

KEYNOTE: *The easily acquired dependence of psychic desires upon the stimulation of social circumstances.*

Animals drawn into the circle of what human society produces find it easier to depend on man's handouts than to pursue their usually difficult search for sustenance. The sea gulls here symbolize the more wild and normally untamable energies of the human soul, but they too can develop a kind of domesticated dependence upon the by-products of man's adventures within the realm of the unconscious (the sea). Natural instincts feed on the reactions, and often perversions, of the socially conditioned mind-ego.

This is the first stage in the process represented by the fifty-second sequence of five symbols. It shows us how nature can readily become subservient to man's restless ambition to dominate the entire biosphere through an all-human planetary socioeconomic organization. This is a symbol of DEPENDENCE.

PHASE 257 (SAGITTARIUS 17°): AN EASTER SUNRISE SERVICE DRAWS A LARGE CROWD.

KEYNOTE: *The culturally stimulated longing for group participation in a process of rebirth.*

Since the very early days of man's evolution, religions and cults of various types have used the most significant periods in the year's cycle to dramatize the deepest longings of human nature, thus giving them direction, meaning, and through group action, a greater dynamic intensity. Easter is the Chritian way of celebrating the coming of spring and the rebirth of life on this earth after the hardships of winter.

At this second stage of the five-fold sequence we see, in contrast to the first, man discovering in nature's cycles great movements that stimulate his spiritual quest for the psychic and mental equivalent of solar light and warmth. The obvious Keyword here is REBIRTH.

PHASE 258 (SAGITTARIUS 18°): CHILDREN PLAYING ON THE BEACH, THEIR HEADS PROTECTED BY SUNBONNETS.

KEYNOTE: *The protection society affords to as yet immature individuals as they begin to deal with the powerful energies of their unconscious nature.*

What we call "culture" is an attempt to limit and define the areas of consciousness and interpersonal or group behavior within which growth and exploration into superphysical realms can be considered safe and sound. Sun and sea are powerful forces; they can kill as well as illumine and inspire, as can various kinds of forces within man's unconscious. The cultural and religious institutions of society aim to act as protective agencies, especially for the youth. Overprotection and hypocritical behavior by supposed grownups defeat this purpose, and today we are witnessing an at least partially healthy rebellion against the protective paternalism of social institutions. This, however, does lead to many a symbolic "sunstroke."

This is the third symbol in the fifty-second five-fold sequence. It brings to us a realization of the value of PROTECTIVENESS, yet also evokes the negative possibility that too much protection may be unhealthy and defeat its purpose.

PHASE 259 (SAGITTARIUS 19°): PELICANS MENACED BY THE BEHAVIOR AND REFUSE OF MEN SEEK SAFER AREAS FOR BRINGING UP THEIR YOUNG.

KEYNOTE: *The need for people concerned with the future to discover a new way of living and more wholesome surroundings.*

The evident reason for using "pelicans" at this stage of the cyclic process is that tradition tells us that these birds are so concerned with their young that they give their own blood and flesh to feed their progeny. Whether this is fact or symbol, the meaning of this picture refers to a situation that lately has acquired great urgency. Our technological society is polluting not only our global environment, but the mind and feeling-responses of new generations as well. The search for a new way of life is seen by many people to be imperative.

In this fourth symbol of the fifty-second sequence we are told that the race's SURVIVAL has become a matter of extreme importance. Whole animal species may be destroyed by our civilization; mankind itself is in danger. Going to distant planets is hardly the answer. A generation may have to sacrifice itself for the sake of its descendants.

PHASE 260 (SAGITTARIUS 20°): IN AN OLD-FASHIONED NORTHERN VILLAGE MEN CUT THE ICE OF A FROZEN POND FOR USE DURING THE SUMMER.

KEYNOTE: *The foresighted use of natural resources to supply future human needs.*

At the close of this series of symbols we again see a reference to the relationship between man and nature. Man's ingenuity and foresight make it possible for him to plan for the future in terms of his knowledge of the seasonal rhythm of cold and heat and, by implication, of even larger cycles of change. Quiet and relaxation may have to be sacrificed, and some hardships endured, in order that another type of problem, which may involve survival through proper feeding, may be met at some later time.

This is the fifth and last phase in the fifty-second section of the cycle. It stresses the value of actively planning for future need, and of foresight based on the knowledge of cyclic processes. Keywords: ASSURING SUPPLY.

SECOND LEVEL: EMOTIONAL–CULTURAL

PHASE 261 (SAGITTARIUS 21°): A CHILD AND A DOG WEARING BORROWED EYEGLASSES.

KEYNOTE: *The use of imagination and make-believe in anticipating higher stages of development.*

This rather peculiar symbol seems to imply here that by imitating features belonging to a level of consciousness as yet unreachable, the process of growth may be accelerated. Eyeglasses symbolize intellectual development; the chiefs of primitive tribes in some instances have sought to impress their people by wearing spectacles without glass, or Western hats—simply because these objects seemed characteristic of a race of superior people. This is similar to the process of growth by identification with a "Master" or guru. In a sense it is mere pretending or make-believe, yet by wearing the "mask" of a god the medicine man at the time *becomes* for all practical purposes the incarnation of the god. Growth is always a hierarchical process, even if the growing entity is not aware of it.

This is the first of five symbols constituting the fifty-third sequence. It suggests the value of LEARNING THROUGH IMITATION.

PHASE 262 (SAGITTARIUS 22°): A CHINESE LAUNDRY.

KEYNOTE: *Making use of one's special racial-cultural background in order to survive and prosper in an alien environment.*

There are many life situations in which because of his ancestral or personal background, or his special interests, an individual finds himself separated from the people in the midst of whom he has to live. Yet he often can use this background as a valuable foundation for smooth operation and for acceptance by the alien environment, without losing his own natural character.

This second stage symbol stands in contrast to the one for the first stage. There is no longer a question of imitating the ways of a superior group, but instead of maintaining one's own integrity in situations which neither give value for, nor favor what one basically is. What is asked here is SELF-CONTAINMENT . . . and good humor!

PHASE 263 (SAGITTARIUS 23°): A GROUP OF IMMIGRANTS AS THEY FULFILL THE REQUIREMENTS OF ENTRANCE INTO THE NEW COUNTRY.

KEYNOTE: *Consciously accepting the ways of a new stage of experience, in readiness for the opportunities it will present.*

As we pass any threshold leading to a new realm of existence we have to meet certain requirements and the necessity to adjust to new ways of life—in action, thought and feeling. At times this may seem an ordeal, but it is inevitable. Everything that will follow depends largely on how we cross this threshold, and on the spirit in which we meet unfamiliar and perhaps shocking experiences.

At this third stage of the fifty-third five-fold sequence we face a combination of the two preceding symbols. We find ourselves in a period of TRANSITION. We have to imitate, yet retain our inner integrity.

PHASE 264 (SAGITTARIUS 24°): A BLUEBIRD PERCHED ON THE GATE OF A COTTAGE.

KEYNOTE: *The reward which meets every effort at integration into a social environment for those who remain true to their own selves.*

The bluebird is a well-known symbol of happiness, but also it refers to what one might call a spiritually oriented mind—to which the color blue relates, especially when a "bird" is mentioned. A cottage is normally part of a community, and the implication is that its inhabitants are well-adapted, either to the life of the community, or to their more or less isolated togetherness.

This is a fourth stage symbol, and it suggests that the essential technique for successful living is the development of a consciousness in which peace and happiness dwell. There is also a hint that GOOD FORTUNE is going to bless your life.

PHASE 265 (SAGITTARIUS 25°): A CHUBBY BOY ON A HOBBY-HORSE.

KEYNOTE: *The anticipatory enjoyment of powers one can only as yet dream of utilizing.*

The horse has always been a symbol of power and, in many instances, of sexual energy. Until very recently the horse gave man a greater possibility of conquering more space and what that space contained. Mounted on his hobby-horse and experiencing the to-and-fro rhythm of its motion, the well-fed boy unconsciously, and perhaps nowadays half-consciously, may anticipate the rhythm of the sexual act. In a sense it is also a kind of make-believe and growth through the imagination, but here —in contrast to what was shown in the symbol for Phase 261— the imagination is active at the organic body level. There is something of an initiation in the play.

This is the last symbol of the fifty-third sequence of five. It ends in a mood of play, but it is a play filled with cultural and emotional expectation, unconscious though this expectation may be. We see here the FORESHADOWING of the mature experience of manhood.

THIRD LEVEL: INDIVIDUAL–MENTAL

PHASE 266 (SAGITTARIUS 26°): A FLAG BEARER IN A BATTLE.

KEYNOTE: *The nobly accepted subservience of the individual to collective values and goals.*

A flag symbolizes an organized collectivity of human beings, a nation or even a social class. In the old-fashioned type of battle, whoever carries the flag has to feel himself the representative of the integrity and unity of his group. His personal life and his welfare should therefore be totally submerged in and identified with the welfare of the "greater Whole" of which he carries the standard. In certain circumstances, every person can act as a conscious and responsible agent for mankind. In substance, the symbol asks: Are you ready to assume this role?

This first stage of the fifty-fourth five-fold sequence presents a picture of what social consciousness can mean in its highest implications. The flag bearer is unarmed, defenseless; yet he can be the rallying point for the total effort of a large collectivity. This is a symbol of CONSECRATION TO AN IDEAL.

PHASE 267 (SAGITTARIUS 27°): A SCULPTOR AT HIS WORK.

KEYNOTE: *The ability to project one's vision upon and to give form to materials.*

At this stage we see the individual creatively expressing his own particular individuality. He takes the materials available in his social-geographical environment and shapes them so they reveal to other people something of his inner life and purpose.

This second phase in the fifty-fourth sequence is, as usual, in contrast to the first. The "flag bearer" symbolizes the selfless representative of a *collective* tradition or of national unity; the "sculptor," on the contrary, represents man as a creative *individual* intent on making his mark upon society. This is a symbol of man's capacity to transform raw materials according to his personal vision—thus a symbol of SELF-PROJECTION INTO A WORK.

PHASE 268 (SAGITTARIUS 28°): AN OLD BRIDGE OVER A BEAUTIFUL STREAM IS STILL IN CONSTANT USE.

KEYNOTE: *The enduring elements in a society which reveal its ability to significantly link the genius of its individuals to the everyday needs of the collectivity.*

This symbol brings together, as it were, the essential values implied in the two preceding ones. The mastery over material factors of a few imaginative and trained individuals enables their community to remain well-integrated and able to function easily in the best possible environment. The work of these sculptor-engineers allows their people to develop a relatively permanent culture. A tradition is built which enables men to link their outer nature with the highest vision their leaders can conceive and objectively demonstrate.

This third symbol of the fifty-fourth sequence also suggests the way in which the works of man can blend harmoniously with natural environment in producing beautiful and enduring shapes of profound meaning. Reacting against the ugliness of our commercial and chaotic cities and highways, today we tend to long for "wilderness." But the combination of natural beauty and human skill and imagination is the true ideal to strive for. As Keywords we might use the title of an excellent book by the architect Claude Bragdon: THE BEAUTIFUL NECESSITY.

> **PHASE 269 (SAGITTARIUS 29°): A FAT BOY MOWING THE LAWN OF HIS HOUSE ON AN ELEGANT SUBURBAN STREET.**
>
> **KEYNOTE:** *The need to attend to everyday tasks which both ensure social worth or respectability, and benefit one's constitution.*

This rather trivial picture becomes quite significant if related to the preceding three symbols. It brings down to a very concrete and commonplace level what the "flag bearer" and the "sculptor" symbols have presented. A well-attended front lawn is a symbol of the homeowner's concern for his social position, and of his desire to give beautiful form to the growth of natural forces, thus revealing his appreciation of order and esthetic values. The "fat boy" suggests that constructive working habits are needed to compensate for self-indulgence in the amenities of social living.

This fourth stage symbol speaks of one of the commonplace technical imperatives which face an individual belonging to a social elite. It reveals another phase in the cycle relationship between the individual and the community, and the need to maintain SOCIAL RESPECTABILITY.

> **PHASE 270 (SAGITTARIUS 30°): THE POPE, BLESSING THE FAITHFUL.**
>
> **KEYNOTE:** *The need to pay homage to traditional values upon which the Invisible Community of the spirit is built.*

The concrete integration of myriads of human individuals within a great religious institution with a long tradition reflects, as well as having produced century after century, an invisible spiritual Community. The "flag bearer" has now become the "Pope," who assumes the role of God's representative on earth. It is a role, but culture is based on embodying great Images and deeply moving symbols in physical reality. The symbol asks of the individual: "Are you willing to live a transpersonal life as a symbol?" This is the final and supreme statement of that section of the cycle of the year represented by Sagittarius.

This concludes Scene Eighteen. A collectivity of human beings is seen having "transferred" their sense of spiritual value to a man who has become an incarnation of their common ideal. Keywords: PERSONAL-IZED WORSHIP. It can be a blessing or in some cases, a curse.

ACT IV: CAPITALIZATION

SCENE NINETEEN: *CRYSTALLIZATION*
(Capricorn 1° to Capricorn 15°)

FIRST LEVEL: ACTIONAL

PHASE 271 (CAPRICORN 1°): AN INDIAN CHIEF CLAIMS POWER FROM THE ASSEMBLED TRIBE.

KEYNOTE: *The power and responsibility implied in any claim for leadership.*

The religious ideal implied in the preceding symbol has now materialized or crystallized into sheer power—the power to lead the community and to ensure its welfare or even its physical survival. The energies released through group cooperation (Libra), deepened and emotionally experienced as forces of great potency (Scorpio), and given meaning and conscious purpose (Sagittarius) are now stabilized and hierarchized. The power of the group is turned into a measurable and carefully managed "capital." The words "chief" and "capital" come from the same Latin word, *caput*, meaning "head." A time comes in many lives when the individual finds himself placed in a situation that allows him to assume power over his comrades, however limited this power may be. Is he ready to do this effectively and responsibly? This is the supreme test of man in society. It complements its polar opposite (summer solstice degree), which refers to the acceptance by the individual of a new kind of allegiance as a foundation for the integration of his mature personality. Such a foundation may, but need not, refer to establishing a home.

This represents the first stage in a five-fold process—the fifty-fifth sequence of five symbols. It refers to the capacity latent in every individual to claim and assume AUTHORITY in a vital group-situation.

PHASE 272 (CAPRICORN 2°): THREE ROSE WINDOWS IN A GOTHIC CHURCH, ONE DAMAGED BY WAR.

KEYNOTE: *The necessary realization by any individual making a violent use of collective power that it will lead to the inevitable destruction of some of the values ensuring group-integration.*

It seems obvious that the interpretation of this symbol should refer to the disruptive consequences of war. The "chief" who claimed power from his tribe in order to lead or save it must reckon with the consequences of a too-impulsive use of this power in terms of violence. The integration he seeks to maintain or enhance may be partially destroyed if in his ambition he yearns to be the victorious war leader glorified by his people. A "rose window" is not absolutely essential to a cathedral, yet it symbolizes that through which the "light of the Spirit" enters into the edifice. Man's soul is said to be three-fold. Which part of man's inner trinity of principles tends to be destroyed by the use of violence? Evidently the principle of love and compassion.

This second stage symbol is in contrast to the preceding one because it opposes the power to destroy to the power to build. The "capital" of group-energies is partially squandered in armaments and death. WASTE is the opposite of group-integration.

PHASE 273 (CAPRICORN 3°): A HUMAN SOUL, IN ITS EAGER-
NESS FOR NEW EXPERIENCES, SEEKS EMBODIMENT.

KEYNOTE: *A powerful yearning for whatever will increase
the scope and depth of one's contacts with other living
beings.*

One wonders what the clairvoyant "saw" and said to the re-
corder of this symbol. How did she visualize a "human soul" or,
as Marc Edmund Jones recorded it, its being "receptive to
growth and understanding"? What is implied in the position of
this symbol seems to be the strong drive in every human consciousness or will toward new experiences, *whether they are
constructive or destructive.* Man may grow and gain understanding and wisdom through both types. Yet the yearning
needs to be tempered by an instinctive evaluation of the end
results of the experience.

This is the third phase of the fifty-fifth five-fold process. It shows us
what is behind all uses of power, anabolic or catabolic: a strong DESIRE
TO PROVE ONESELF.

PHASE 274 (CAPRICORN 4°): A GROUP OF PEOPLE OUTFIT-
TING A LARGE CANOE AT THE START OF A JOURNEY BY
WATER.

KEYNOTE: *The ability to use natural resources and basic
skills in order to achieve a group-purpose.*

As this scene was recorded in the original version only in imprecise terms, it seems merely to indicate the start of a journey
undertaken by a cohesive group of people, who perhaps together have built this large canoe. Thus we see here a common
enterprise which may be an answer to the need for a change of
locality. A social group more strongly than ever reveals its
homogeneity and common will when it decides to move away
from its familiar habitat. The zodiacal sign Capricorn brings this
common will to a focus in concrete actions. It does so in terms

of socio-political expediency and under a definite type of executive direction, even though the decisions are arrived at by common consent.

As this is the fourth symbol in the fifty-fifth five-fold sequence, we find in it a hint of how to do something concrete. The "canoe" may also have a special technical meaning, as it uses water in order to move. A common *feeling-response* to a specific situation may be implied. The main emphasis is nevertheless on GROUP-ACTIVITY in circumstances implying a need for change.

PHASE 275 (CAPRICORN 5°): INDIANS ON THE WARPATH. WHILE SOME MEN ROW A WELL-FILLED CANOE, OTHERS IN IT PERFORM A WAR DANCE.

KEYNOTE: *The mobilization of physical and emotional energies in a spirit of conquest.*

War is often undertaken mainly to mobilize the common will and avoid individualistic disintegration. The "Indian chief" in the symbol for Capricorn 1° may find it convenient or necessary to arouse the war spirit—perhaps under a very slight provocation—in order to more firmly establish his authority. The scene presents an extremely dynamic situation. The group (or the nation) affirms its solidarity and unity of purpose by taking the offensive. The group-life demands constant activity and challenges in order to remain healthy.

This is the last symbol of the fifty-fifth sequence. It suggests that AGGRESSIVENESS may be a necessary ingredient in the activation of the potential of growth inherent in any social group.

SECOND LEVEL: EMOTIONAL–CULTURAL

PHASE 276 (CAPRICORN 6°): TEN LOGS LIE UNDER AN ARCHWAY LEADING TO DARKER WOODS.

KEYNOTE: *The need to complete any undertaking before seeking entrance to whatever is to be found beyond.*

Number 10 is a symbol of completion; it symbolizes even more the revelation of a new series of activities just ahead. Yet unless the concluded series is brought to some degree of fulfillment, nothing truly significant is likely to be accomplished by a restless reaching out toward the as-yet-unknown. Number 10 is a symbol of germination, but the seed (Number 9) must have matured well. No natural process can be accelerated safely beyond certain limits.

This represents the first stage in the fifty-sixth five-fold sequence. It establishes a foundation for what will follow. Here man reaches a THRESHOLD in which he may have to pause in order to safeguard his further advance.

PHASE 277 (CAPRICORN 7°): A VEILED PROPHET SPEAKS, SEIZED BY THE POWER OF A GOD.

KEYNOTE: *The ability to act as a mouthpiece for the revelation of a transcendent will and truth determining future action.*

Here we witness the deepest manifestation of that Power which operates within all relatively permanent social units, especially at the level of tribal organization. A tribe is a bio-psychic whole (or organism) integrated by a collective superphysical Power, the god of the tribe. In the Hebrew tradition this god is YHWH (Yahweh-Jehovah); in earlier tribes it may have been a deified more or less mythical "Great Ancestor." All these tribal gods are local manifestations of the very power of "Life" within the earth's biosphere. It is this deified Power which psychically "seized" especially sensitive or religiously trained men or women, who became Its mouthpiece—prophets, seers, oracles. That Power operates in our days as well, but in different ways because of the individualization and intellectualization of modern man's consciousness. It binds together and helps to maintain the integration of organized social collectivities. It guides their development by releasing and focusing through especially open persons the visionary expectation of developments about to occur.

At this second stage of the fifty-sixth subcycle the future interacts with the present to release it from the inertial power of the past. Thus this symbol stands in contrast to the preceding one. At the threshold of tomorrow man is allowed to have a vision or revelation of the essential elements of the as-yet-unknown next step in evolution. The key word is MEDIATORSHIP.

PHASE 278 (CAPRICORN 8°): IN A SUN-LIT HOME DOMESTICATED BIRDS SING JOYOUSLY.

KEYNOTE: *The wholesome happiness which subservience to the ideals and patterns of a well-established culture brings to those who accept them unreservedly.*

In various ways this section of the cyclic process brings to us images glorifying the power and benefits which a steady and well-integrated society brings to its members. Saturn rules Capricorn; Saturn was the ruler of the Golden Age before he became a symbol of binding limitations. He who accepts willingly or—even better—takes for granted the value of these limitations can lead a serene and happy existence, whatever his social status.

The third stage of this five-fold sequence suggests to us how we can enjoy our life condition by allowing the spiritual values it embodies to fill our consciousness. In every condition provided by a healthy culture —which hardly refers to our present chaotic world!—human beings can find ENJOYMENT in the roles they are born to play.

PHASE 279 (CAPRICORN 9°): AN ANGEL CARRYING A HARP.

KEYNOTE: *The revelation of the spiritual meaning and purpose at the core of any life situation.*

This picture simply says that "heaven is within us." All we have to do is to be open and listen to the total harmony of life, a harmony in which we play a part that is necessary to the completeness and meaning of the whole. In order to do this we have to surrender our separative ego-consciousness and flow with the universal current which, to the religiously minded person, is the Will of God.

This is the fourth symbol of the series. The technique it implies is that of ATTUNEMENT to the rhythm of universal life. Angels are to be considered personalizations of various aspects of this life, and totally subservient to its rhythms and purposes.

PHASE 280 (CAPRICORN 10°): AN ALBATROSS FEEDING FROM THE HAND OF A SAILOR.

KEYNOTE: *The overcoming of fear and its rewards.*

The man who radiates perfect harmlessness can call the wildest creatures to him and can establish with them a partnership based on mutual respect and understanding. Every living entity plays a role in the world's ritual of existence; beyond these specific roles, which too often separate one entity from another, the communion of love and compassion can bring together the most disparate lives.

At this last stage of the fifty-sixth sequence we are presented with a picture extending the ideal of peace and happiness through culture so it now includes all living organisms on this planet. The power of such a culture of harmlessness and compassion generates TRUST everywhere.

THIRD LEVEL: INDIVIDUAL–MENTAL

PHASE 281 (CAPRICORN 11°): A LARGE GROUP OF PHEASANT ON A PRIVATE ESTATE.

KEYNOTE: *The refinement and propagation of aristocratic values by means of which man participates in the evolution of life toward ever more perfect forms of existence.*

All life implies a hierarchy of values, from the crude to the subtle, from the rough and the ugly to the beautiful. By the use of biological techniques, man is able to develop new species, or at least to greatly improve those found in the wild. This ability is at the root of all cultural processes. Wilderness is turned into the gardens of an aristocracy having the leisure, taste and money to produce or encourage the creation of beautiful forms. This is what the social process produces in its highest aspect.

The first symbol of the fifty-seventh five-fold sequence shows us how man can cooperate with nature in creating beauty and elegance by capitalizing on skill and opportunity. The Keyword is ARISTOCRACY.

PHASE 282 (CAPRICORN 12°): AN ILLUSTRATED LECTURE ON NATURAL SCIENCE REVEALS LITTLE–KNOWN ASPECTS OF LIFE.

KEYNOTE: *The ability to explore unfamiliar realms and discover the laws underlying the complex processes of nature.*

The aristocratic garden of the preceding phase has become the laboratory and lecture hall of a modern college. The emphasis here is on the acquisition of extensive knowledge, the satisfaction of intellectual curiosity. Nevertheless, there is also an aristocracy of science: this is the modern type. Its use of acquired knowledge can pose as many problems as the use of hereditary aristocratic wealth. But it is man's essential function to become fully conscious of all life forms and processes on this earth. Mankind is the conscious mind of the planet.

At this second stage the intellectual search for empirical knowledge contrasts with the display attendant to the wealth and culture of an elite. Civilization is founded on an ever-extended capitalization on knowledge and use of technology. It features EXPLORATION preeminently at all levels.

PHASE 283 (CAPRICORN 13°): A FIRE WORSHIPER MEDITATES ON THE ULTIMATE REALITIES OF EXISTENCE.

KEYNOTE: *The subjective quest for ultimates beyond the interplay of life and death processes.*

Beyond cultural enjoyment and the passion for accumulation of often-unusable data of sense knowledge stands the willful and determined "adventure in consciousness" of the occultist, the yogi, the mystic. The mystery of fire has always captured man's imagination because it is the mystery of all transformations wrapped in the enigma of death. In times when collective, perhaps total, death could be in store for mankind, the process of subjective meditation is fascinating an ever-greater number of people.

This is the third symbol in the fifty-seventh sequence. It brings us to a stage beyond life itself. Are we ready to take this step which the masters of yoga claim to have taken: to experience death and return to the same body? Are we ready to demonstrate man's WILL TO TRANSCENDENCE?

PHASE 284 (CAPRICORN 14°): AN ANCIENT BAS-RELIEF CARVED IN GRANITE REMAINS A WITNESS TO A LONG-FORGOTTEN CULTURE.

KEYNOTE: *The will to unearth, in our culture as well as in any culture, what has permanent value, and to let go of nonessentials.*

At a time when in nearly every land men are questioning and challenging the validity of traditional beliefs and customary attitudes, it becomes necessary to separate permanent values and great principles or symbols from the many individual habits and the socio-political developments which more often than not have perverted or even negated the original ideals of the culture. We must strive to free these ideals from the wild growth of personal and class selfishness, from the greed and ambition so prevalent in human nature, and learn to appreciate the excellence of what is the immortal seed-foundation, as well as the spiritual harvest, of any culture—and by extension of every sustained and complete work produced by a man's indomitable effort to achieve creative perfection.

In this fourth stage symbol we are shown the procedure which enables us to gain a deep and thorough appreciation of sociocultural processes in their most enduring forms. What is needed is a penetrating and courageous insight founded upon a valid HISTORICAL PERSPECTIVE. This applies to the past of an individual's life as well as to the history of a nation or a group.

PHASE 285 (CAPRICORN 15°): IN A HOSPITAL, THE CHILDREN'S WARD IS FILLED WITH TOYS.

KEYNOTE: *The responsibility of society to ensure the welfare and total health of the new generation.*

The sociocultural process must look to the future as well as to the past. It has created conditions which may harm the children who will carry forward its work, and it must try to repair these negative conditions through love as well as through physical care. In personal life, the individual should take great care of his fresh intuitions and his dreams of future growth. They are often fragile developments which the pressures of everyday life can easily distort or destroy.

This is the last stage of Scene Nineteen, which began with a powerful claim for socio-political power. The exercise of such a power can indeed produce social conditions which endanger the healthy and spiritual unfoldment of a community, and especially of its children. There is therefore constant need for TENDER CARE as well as skill to neutralize the destructive tensions of social living.

SCENE TWENTY: *GROUP–PERFORMANCE*
(Capricorn 16° to Capricorn 30°)

FIRST LEVEL: ACTIONAL

PHASE 286 (CAPRICORN 16°): SCHOOL GROUNDS FILLED WITH BOYS AND GIRLS IN GYMNASIUM SUITS.

KEYNOTE: *The need for physical activity and play, especially in adolescence.*

Society has learned that a balanced combination of intellectual study and physical activity is necessary for the harmonious development of the human personality. Adults often forget this under the pressure of money-making and other duties, and this symbol reminds us of it.

This is the first stage of the fifty-eighth five-fold sequence which begins Scene Twenty of the cyclic ritual. It shows how we normally depend upon physical stimulation and EXERCISE for the maintenance of our health, and therefore of an equally healthy society.

PHASE 287 (CAPRICORN 17°): A REPRESSED WOMAN FINDS A PSYCHOLOGICAL RELEASE IN NUDISM.

KEYNOTE: *The escape from bondage to social inhibitions and a reliance upon the wisdom of the body.*

Under the pressure of religions that have created a sharp and unwholesome division between soul and body, society has produced strict codes of values regarding the play of natural instincts, and has glorified them under the name of "decency" and "modesty." The growing trend toward nudism—which of course has nothing to do with the "pornographic" display of one's body—is a welcome protest against the depressing and neurosis-generating puritanism of the past. Men and women are demanding a psychologically as well as physically healthful freedom of the body as a means of overcoming the hypocrisy and constrictions of social behavior.

In this second stage symbol we see how our society has been able to repress and distort the natural activity of the human body and its sensitivity to the elements. Thus a contrast is established between healthy youth at play and the neurotic subservience to a socio-religious tradition. The symbol is a call for RELEASE FROM INHIBITIONS.

PHASE 288 (CAPRICORN 18°): THE UNION JACK FLAG FLIES FROM A BRITISH WARSHIP.

KEYNOTE: *The protection afforded to individuals and groups by powerful institutions in charge of maintaining order.*

This symbol reflects conditions prevailing in the past when Great Britain's fleet was policing the seas under the international principle of the freedom of the seas. Times have changed, but the concept remains valid. Power is required to maintain social order and relatively peaceful interpersonal as well as international relationships. Alas, this power can easily be misused under the pretext of preserving "law and order." Justice and compassion must balance social power, and especially the power of privileged groups. Where this symbol appears, the need for protection may be in evidence—or it may be a warning against using power for selfish advantage.

This is the third symbol in the fifty-eighth five-fold sequence. It brings to us a realization of the ambivalence of POLITICAL POWER, its value and its dangers.

PHASE 289 (CAPRICORN 19°): A FIVE-YEAR-OLD CHILD CARRYING A BAG FILLED WITH GROCERIES.

KEYNOTE: *Rising to the occasion when asked to assume social responsibilities ahead of one's normal development.*

What seems to be implied at this stage of the cyclic process is the value of early conditioning in teaching one how to fulfill the responsibilities of everyday life in our modern society. This twentieth scene of the complete process has been entitled "Group performance," and today it is evident that children at an early age are expected to assume a family role which at times will strain their natural capacities. This is part of the accelerating pace of our technological society.

This fourth stage symbol evokes the possibility of meeting a certain type of social opportunity which normally may seem premature. A pattern of ACCELERATED GROWTH can thus be established, with both positive and negative aspects. Rushing ahead of one's natural development may be damaging; yet we are living in a particularly dynamic period of man's evolution.

PHASE 290 (CAPRICORN 20°): A HIDDEN CHOIR IS SINGING DURING A RELIGIOUS SERVICE.

KEYNOTE: *The fulfillment of the individual's creative function through his participation in a group performance consecrated to a transcendent realization of unity.*

In great cathedrals and other religious edifices the choir is normally hidden behind the altar or above the nave. It symbolizes thus more perfectly the supernal harmony of "heaven"—or the music of the spheres. The ideal of social participation is exalted to its highest manifestation, for the choir also represents the multifaceted and polyphonic unity of the communiry in its transcendent state of perfect harmony. Within this harmony the individual who has overcome his egocentric separativeness and developed his higher consciousness finds fulfillment in superpersonal togetherness.

This is the fifth and last symbol of this fifty-eighth sequence. It presents us with the purest form of group-harmony, the most basic yet most difficult fulfillment of the social state. At the level of the individual person this "hidden choir" would refer to the polyphonic integration of all faculties in their most spiritual manifestations: the ideal of PLENITUDE of being.

SECOND LEVEL: EMOTIONAL–CULTURAL

PHASE 291 (CAPRICORN 21°): A RELAY RACE.

KEYNOTE: *The value of competition in developing group-consciousness.*

Here we are no longer dealing with competition between individuals, but with competition between groups of individuals who take turns sucessively in order to maximize the group effort and the possibility of outstanding results. The whole of civilization is a vast kind of relay race in which groups of people and generations carry the torch of what we call "progress." Major achievements result from the sum total of human strivings.

This first symbol of the fifty-ninth sequence stresses one especially dynamic aspect of "group performance." Wherever this symbol appears, it emphasizes the value of group cooperation and of necessary give-and-take. One must seek to relate and adjust one's strength to the challenge presented by competitors in DYNAMIC INTERCHANGE.

PHASE 292 (CAPRICORN 22°): BY ACCEPTING DEFEAT GRACEFULLY, A GENERAL REVEALS NOBILITY OF CHARACTER.

KEYNOTE: *The realization that one may grow through defeat as well as, and perhaps more than, through success.*

While the preceding symbol referred to the drive toward success in culturally organized collective endeavors, this one presents us with the possibility of turning apparent external defeat into an inner spiritual achievement. We have recently seen how totally vanquished nations (Germany and Japan) have leaped forward and achieved great economic success. Much depends on the quality of the will and the inner integrity of the person.

At this second stage we find what seems to be a paradox, but the spiritual life is always paradoxical. The great sinner can become the most renowned saint, and a medieval Pope a criminal. What matters most always is INNER STRENGTH.

PHASE 293 (CAPRICORN 23°): A SOLDIER RECEIVING TWO AWARDS FOR BRAVERY IN COMBAT.

KEYNOTE: *The reward offered by society for the fulfillment of individual responsibility.*

The fact that "two" awards are emphasized makes us believe that this may refer subtly to the recognition by the community that, whether he succeeded or failed, an individual who discharged his duty nobly under unusual circumstances is entitled to the respect and appreciation of the collectivity he served so well. What is implied here is a constant give-and-take between society and the individual person. Each one should be able to trust the other.

This third symbol of the fifty-ninth five-fold sequence extracts, as it were, a common element from the two preceding scenes. The Keyword here is RECOMPENSE, i.e. a compensation for a well-done performance—a balancing of accounts.

PHASE 294 (CAPRICORN 24°): A WOMAN ENTERING A CONVENT.

KEYNOTE: *Total commitment to a transcendent goal.*

A convent is a place made available by a community which believes in the possibility of reaching a world-transcending state of consciousness. It is made available to individuals who may be variously motivated. To some it is an escape from the intolerable pressures of family and society; to others it represents the possibility of pursuing in peace a spiritual ideal to which the whole being aspires and is totally dedicated. The important point, in this phase of the cyclic process, is that the existence of a convent expresses another aspect of the relationship between the society (its religion and culture) and the individual. In the preceding symbol society rewarded the individual for a noble performance in its service; here society accepts the fact that beyond its daily normal patterns of behavior and commitments, another way of life exists which, in a higher sense, also has social value. In the old Hindu society dominated by a rigid caste system, the ideal embodied in the *sannyasi*—the wandering holy man or yogi meditating in a forest or a cave, who had entirely given up all that caste implied—was seen to be the very culmination of the social process.

In this fourth stage symbol we see the paradoxical nature of the social process operating more strongly than ever. This derives from the fact that man's nature contains in seed the possibility of overcoming and transcending itself in acts of complete denials and of surrender to a "higher" Law or quality of being. All spiritual techniques are indeed paradoxical. Rigid discipline conditions pure inner freedom. The final goal is the attainment of TRANSCENDENT SECURITY.

PHASE 295 (CAPRICORN 25°): A STORE FILLED WITH PRECIOUS ORIENTAL RUGS.

KEYNOTE: *The use of cultural and artistic processes as a means to enhance personal comfort and appreciation.*

Coming after the preceding symbol this one brings us back to the material, yet esthetic, aspect of the benefits a society can bring its members. A "rug" always implied to some extent something on which a person stands or sits. It is a foundation for cultural "under-standing," and as such it can have a magical or sacred meaning, as in the case of prayer rugs. The "woman in a convent" probably knows only the bare floor, because her goal is one of transcendence, of surrendering comfort as well as cultural patterns. But to the social elite, or even to the oriental devotee praying to his god, society offers the relative comfort of beautiful rugs so he may meet the universe, not merely in terms of the support the natural soil gives, but protected by and securely established on the mental-spiritual as well as manual achievements of those who keep the cultural symbols alive.

This is the last symbol in the fifty-ninth five-fold sequence. It shows the beautiful products of dedicated and inspired group performance at the level of tradition. It emphasizes the value of RELIANCE ON TRADITION.

THIRD LEVEL: INDIVIDUAL–MENTAL

PHASE 296 (CAPRICORN 26°): A NATURE SPIRIT DANCING IN THE IRIDESCENT MIST OF A WATERFALL.

KEYNOTE: *The ability to perceive the hidden and creative spirit of natural phenomena.*

The Sabian symbols make several references to nature spirits. Here we are dealing with the revelation of the spiritual or psychic forces related to the element water. Water binds all living cells in a wholesome interplay. It symbolizes the constant flow of vital energies, the fluidity of a consciousness which finds itself stimulated by change. The great cycle of water within the earth's biosphere (oceans, clouds, rain, river) symbolizes the basic phases of universal life processes, the ascent and descent of emotional energies and of love. We can personify these phases and speak of "the soul of nature," and at a cosmic level of "the World-Soul," *anima mundi*. Water is the substance of the telluric manifestations of this soul. It is a magical substance, and modern chemists are rediscovering in their study of its unusual behavior in certain situations what old Alchemists in their own way no doubt understood.

This is the first stage of the sixtieth subcycle, and it presents us with a deep intuition of superphysical energies which at the end of this five-fold sequence we will see fully mastered (Phase 300). The consciousness here becomes sensitized to the downward flow of OCCULT ENERGY in its bountiful natural aspect.

PHASE 297 (CAPRICORN 27°): PILGRIMS CLIMBING THE STEEP STEPS LEADING TO A MOUNTAIN SHRINE.

KEYNOTE: *The ascent of the individualized consciousness to the highest realizations reached by the spiritual leaders of its culture.*

We hear a great deal now about "peak experiences," but this symbol tells us that they depend to a very great extent upon following a path which many have trod before, under the inspiration of the great Teachers and Sages of our race. The shrine is built by the unceasing dedication of perhaps generations of men. The pilgrimage is hallowed by the devotion of many, even though each person finds on his own mountaintop what to him seems a unique and transcendent revelation.

In this second stage symbol we witness the rise of the human consciousness; the preceding symbol spoke of what one may picture as the "descent" of the energies of nature which, like water, flow down toward a lower level of intensity. It is man's supreme task to rise like fire, impelled by a vision he shares with his companions. The Keyword: UPREACHING.

PHASE 298 (CAPRICORN 28°): A LARGE AVIARY.

KEYNOTE: *The enjoyment of spiritual values by the soul able to familiarize itself with their implications.*

Birds symbolize spiritual forces, and the aviary presents us with a picture of these forces or desires contained within a mind open to the light of psychic or Soul realities, and bringing joy and harmony to the consciousness. The strenuous ascent represented by the preceding scene changes into a picture of familiarity with inspiring experiences. Yet this familiarity may also suggest a lack of spontaneity and of the thrill of discovery. To use modern terms, the peak experiences have become those of a high plateau, at which level one may lose one's sense of direction at times.

This is the third stage in the sixtieth sequence of phases which lead to group mastery of cosmic energies. The youthful effort to reach the summits of cultural and spiritual attainment has settled down into a complex state of inspiration—a state which at times may bring confusion because of the multiplicity of the voices to which one has become open. One may speak here of CLAIRAUDIENCE, meaning a capacity for being responsive to many inner voices.

PHASE 299 (CAPRICORN 29°): A WOMAN READING TEA LEAVES.

KEYNOTE: *The ability to see the Signature of hidden meaning in every occurrence drawing one's attention.*

Man has always sought to interpret the meaning of events or situations which baffle him in terms of specific omens or "Signatures." The reading of tea leaves is only a commonplace modern version of a certain type of procedure used by priests of all ancient religions. The practice is based on a realization of "the relation of everything to everything else"—a definition of astrology given by Marc Jones. Dream interpretation in depth psychology belongs to the same category, as it is based upon the establishment of a close connection between the unconscious and the conscious. But in dream analysis the *individual* unconscious, at least at first, is mainly referred to, while in omens (or modern fortunetelling at its best) one relies upon the power of occult forces or entities to convey the information that will clarify confusing situations.

This fourth stage symbol can be referred to a specific "technique" of understanding or evaluation. What is implied is the ability not only to perceive the facts of everyday existence, but to see *through* these facts and discover how they are related to the realm of basic meanings or archetypal processes. This is essentially what is meant by true CLAIRVOYANCE, the capacity to see in everything the Signature of deeper realities.

PHASE 300 (CAPRICORN 30°): A SECRET MEETING OF MEN RESPONSIBLE FOR EXECUTIVE DECISIONS IN WORLD AFFAIRS.

KEYNOTE: *The power to assume responsibility for crucial choices arrived at after mature discussions with those who share this power.*

We are all aware now of the work of secret committees in the White House and at all levels of the government. The student of esoteric philosophy believes in the existence of what has been called an "inner Government" which has the power to direct or guide the evolution of our planet and of mankind. Some people speak of "occult Hierarchy," or of the "White Lodge." Here again what is at stake is a "seeing through" the facts of telluric processes and human history—assuming that these facts are at least in part the outcome of the decisions of a supreme Council of quasi-divine Beings. Obviously the symbol can also refer to what occurs at the more ordinary level of business and politics. At any level, it refers to the highest form of social interaction.

This is the last symbol belonging to Scene Twenty and related to the zodiacal sign Capricorn. We see in it the culmination of social responsibility and a reference to EXECUTIVE POWER.

SCENE TWENTY-ONE: *CONTRIBUTION*
(*Aquarius 1° to Aquarius 15°*)

FIRST LEVEL: ACTIONAL

PHASE 301 (AQUARIUS 1°): AN OLD ADOBE MISSION IN CALIFORNIA.

KEYNOTE: *The power inherent in all great human works to endure far beyond the workers' life spans.*

The works and spirit of the Spanish priests who directed the building of the California missions have had a lasting influence on the development of this land; these remain as a monument to the men who were able to make their mark upon this alien environment. While the zodiacal sign Capricorn begins with a symbol of socio-political power, Aquarius at its start presents a more spiritualized and idealistic or creative picture of the social forces at work. Moreover, it stresses the enduring character of human achievements ensouled by a great vision. At least within the frame of reference of our Western civilization, the symbol speaks of the projection of a noble ideal into concrete forms of beauty and significance, thus of the radiation of a "civilizing" power into an institution offering to primitive men the opportunity to reach a higher, more organized and productive, level of activity.

This is the first stage in the sixty-first five-fold sequence. It speaks to us of THE CONCRETIZATION OF AN IDEAL. This also implies the "immortalization" of an individual within a great collective and cultural enterprise.

PHASE 302 (AQUARIUS 2°): AN UNEXPECTED THUNDERSTORM.

KEYNOTE: *The need to develop the inner security which will enable us to meet unexpected crises.*

An interesting connection can be made between the symbols for Taurus 1° and 2°—"A clear mountain stream" and "An electrical storm"—and those for Aquarius 1° and 2°, two hundred and seventy degrees apart (a "waning" square, in terms of a cycle of relationship such as the lunation cycle). In the first case we deal with energies or activities that can be related to the natural development of the individual. But here we are primarily concerned with social, collective processes and the function of the individual within them. The symbol itself—"An unexpected thunderstorm"—could be given a very positive meaning in an arid environment, but the emphasis on "unexpected" tends to accent the sudden and dangerous character of the event. Such a thunderstorm in a region of dry hills can cause a devastating flood. At any rate, it refers to an event for which *one is not prepared*—a menace to men's works.

Seen as a second stage symbol—thus in contrast to the preceding one —this scene stresses the fact that nature may reduce to impermanence the seemingly most permanent endeavors and constructive activities of men. Under a downpour of rain, adobe brick can return to mud. All human institutions and their achievements can be washed away, even in their day of great glory. "Dust you were, dust you must become." This is NATURE'S CHALLENGE.

PHASE 303 (AQUARIUS 3°): A DESERTER FROM THE NAVY.

KEYNOTE: *The individual's self-realization through a crucial repudiation of a collective status which has become unbearable.*

This symbol recalls the one for Scorpio 21°, but the fact that actual "desertion" is emphasized and reference is made to "the Navy" suggests that the crisis symbolized here is one implying an irrevocable change of *status*. Man refuses to accept the type of cultural patterns derived from his society's specific approach to local circumstances and to the universe as a whole, and in another sense, from its particular relationship to the all-human collective Unconscious. (The Navy refers to the ocean, symbol of primordial and unconscious evolutionary forces.) He not only refuses to obey orders, he deliberately turns his back on his collective social status; he becomes an outcast, and through this decision he may definitely individualize his consciousness.

This is the third stage of the sixty-first five-fold sequence. Something with collective social value is being potentially destroyed, but nature is not the destroyer (as in the preceding symbol). Man, the individual, steps out of his bondage to collective patterns and ideals. He may thus "find himself" by means of a sharp renunciation of his social birthright, i.e. by a crucial process of DESOCIALIZATION.

PHASE 304 (AQUARIUS 4°): A HINDU YOGI DEMONSTRATES HIS HEALING POWERS.

KEYNOTE: *The disciplined use of spiritual energies in re-storing the natural harmony disturbed by man's in-harmonic attempts to transcend nature through mind.*

Civilization implies a process of transcending compulsive and rigid biological drives while making use, in a refined and men-talized way, of what it cannot control. The goal of a *true* civiliza-tion—Western civilization being to a large extent a caricature of it—is the development of a humanity composed of self-motivated and responsible individuals freely associating accord-ing to harmonic patterns in order to produce a vast spiritual chord of consciousness fully actualizing the potentialities inher-ent in the archetype, MAN. The process of individualization and civilization is full of dangers, and for a very long time it is obsessed by karmic shadows, the results of individual and collec-tive deviations and perversions. Such results most often lead to disease. It is the spiritual duty of individuals who have been able to tap the vast reservoir of spiritual forces pervading our planet to use these energies for healing their less-fortunate comrades.

This fourth stage symbol refers to a technique which not only can be used for the healing of physical illnesses but for the "making whole" of whatever has lost its natural root integration and has not yet reached the holistic state of perfect harmony and identification with the "divine" whole. Self-discipline, purity of motive, compassion, faith in the divine order are required—and the FOCUSING OF SPIRITUAL ENERGY.

PHASE 305 (AQUARIUS 5°): A COUNCIL OF ANCESTORS IS SEEN IMPLEMENTING THE EFFORTS OF A YOUNG LEADER.

KEYNOTE: *The Root foundation of past performances which power and sustain whatever decision is made in a crisis by an individual.*

The whole past of mankind stands behind any individual effort, especially in times of critical decisions. The endeavor of the priests who built the California missions had behind it the whole past of Catholic proselytizing, i.e. the attempt to bring the "Good News" to all people of the Earth. Every individual is far more dependent upon the strengh of his ancestors' achievements—or oppressed by their failures and lack of vision—than he usually believes. This can mean a hidden foundation of individual strength, or the inertia of a tradition unable to transcend its limited origins.

This is the last symbol in the sixty-first five-fold sequence. It suggests that in many situations RELIANCE UPON PRECEDENTS will enable the aspirant to greatness to tap the power of his deepest roots.

SECOND LEVEL: EMOTIONAL–CULTURAL

PHASE 306 (AQUARIUS 6°): A MASKED FIGURE PERFORMS RITUALISTIC ACTS IN A MYSTERY PLAY.

KEYNOTE: *The individual's involvement in long-established patterns of activity aiming at the release of collective power.*

The great Mysteries of the past were created by inspired Seers and Adepts for the purpose of transferring to a mentally conscious and humanly significant level of group operation what in the lower kingdoms of life we call instincts. Biological and cosmic energies can thus be used to ensure that social processes do not lose touch with the deeper realities of planetary and universal Life. Rituals are binding, and often the performers wear masks, for they do not act as human persons but as focal points for the release of transpersonal forces.

This first symbol of the sixty-second five-fold sequence presents to us social processes in their deepest occult aspect. The individual is seen having assumed a TRANSPERSONAL RESPONSIBILITY.

PHASE 307 (AQUARIUS 7°): A CHILD IS SEEN BEING BORN OUT OF AN EGG.

KEYNOTE: *The emergence of new mutations according to the great rhythms of the cosmos.*

The ancient symbolism of the Cosmic Egg *(Hiranyagharba* in Sanskrit) out of which a new universe is born can be interpreted at several levels. Here we see the appearance of a new type of human being who is not born from "Ancestors" and who therefore is free from the inertia of mankind's past. He is a new product of evolution, a mutant. He constitutes a fresh projection of the creative Spirit that emanates from the cosmic or planetary Whole, and not from any local culture and racial tradition.

This second stage symbol is in contrast with the preceding one. It can be said to announce the EMERGENCE OF GLOBAL MAN for the New Age. The power of the whole is focused within him in perfect freedom from ancient standards of value based on local conditions.

PHASE 308 (AQUARIUS 8°): BEAUTIFULLY GOWNED WAX FIGURES ON DISPLAY.

KEYNOTE: *The inspiration one may derive from the appearance of Exemplars who present to us the archetypes of a new culture.*

We are dealing here with the fixed symbols upon which a culture is based, with *mental* archetypes. They are kept and made available as patterns to imitate, or at least from which to draw new motives for inspiration. We are at the stage of vision: new forms are revealed to the consciousness, as well as new ways of meeting other people in social relationships.

This is the third stage in the sixty-second sequence of five symbols. In a sense the generic human past and the future are implied here. The wax figures are impersonal forms. The gowns constitute a static presentation of ideal patterns; yet they are the PREFORMATION of what will be experienced in the culture being born. They herald new collective developments.

> PHASE 309 (AQUARIUS 9°): A FLAG IS SEEN TURNING INTO AN EAGLE.
>
> KEYNOTE: *The dynamic incorporation of new social values in individuals who exemplify the spiritual potential and greatest significance of these values.*

This symbol nearly duplicates the one for Sagittarius 12°, but in this five-fold sequence it has a somewhat different meaning—especially since the last term of the mysterious transformation (i.e. the crowing of the eagle in chanticleer's fashion) is omitted. All that is implied here is the vitalization of a powerful symbol, its embodiment in a living reality, i.e. in a person able to fly in consciousness to the highest spiritual realm. The archetype is given living substance and wings. The Image has become a Power.

This fourth stage symbol, as usual, gives us a technical suggestion. To "see" the new archetype, to perceive the new standard of value with one's mind is not enough. The seer must become the doer. The impersonal is dynamized and brought into focus. We have here the ACTING OUT of the vision.

> PHASE 310 (AQUARIUS 10°): A MAN WHO HAD FOR A TIME BECOME THE EMBODIMENT OF A POPULAR IDEAL IS MADE TO REALIZE THAT AS A PERSON HE IS NOT THIS IDEAL.
>
> KEYNOTE: *The need to deal with human beings as persons rather than as screens upon which one projects one's dream and ideal.*

Here we have a final statement on the relationship between mental-spiritual vision and living reality, between persons and the ideal they appear to incarnate, between the "great lover Image" and one's need for love—a love his presence stimulated and aroused. The "star" on the movie screen is not the actual person. The star's popularity fades away, the person remains. What has this episode of popularity actually done to the person? This is a question that can be applied to a great variety of circumstances.

This fifth symbol in the sixty-second sequence brings to our attention an issue that is basic and may confront us in various forms. Person versus archetype. This can mean a critical need for SELF-REVALUA-TION.

THIRD LEVEL: INDIVIDUAL–MENTAL

PHASE 311 (AQUARIUS 11°): DURING A SILENT HOUR, A MAN RECEIVES A NEW INSPIRATION WHICH MAY CHANGE HIS LIFE.

KEYNOTE: *The need to rely upon inner inspiration and guidance at the start of new developments.*

What is implied here is the essential value of keeping open to the descent of spiritual or Soul forces, especially when a new period of individual activity is about to begin. The individual should not depend mainly on outer circumstances and on tradi-tional—and in a sense external, because collectively formulated —incentives. There is a creative power within, a power that can be tapped, or rather that should be allowed to flow into the brain-consciousness or the hands which write or fashion materi-als into original forms.

This is the first stage in the sixty-third sequence of five phases of activity. It refers to the OVERSHADOWING of the individual conscious-ness by an inner, yet transcendent, Power.

PHASE 312 (AQUARIUS 12°): ON A VAST STAIRCASE STAND PEOPLE OF DIFFERENT TYPES, GRADUATED UPWARD.

KEYNOTE: *The necessity of recognizing differences of types and levels of development wherever human beings live and work together.*

This symbol obviously refers to the ascending process of evolution of life forms and consciousness. It seems to apply especially to the fact that differences of levels exist among human beings. The ideal of equalitarianism has to be balanced by a realization that hierarchy of levels is a fact of nature. Each person should be aware of the level at which he (or she) stands, even as he strives to move toward a higher one. He should look up for inspiration and examples, while helping the human beings of the next lower level to reach up. This is the great give-and-take of evolution, and it applies to *sociocultural* evolution as well as to the progression of biological species.

At this second stage of the sixty-third sequence we find a symbol of "ascent," contrasting with the preceding one which implied a "descent" of spiritual forces. It warns us against sentimentally overstressing our Western equalitarianism which essentially applies to the spiritual core of all individual persons, considered "sons of God" or spiritual monads. Every human being is *potentially* divine as an individual person, but THE NATURAL PROGRESSION OF STATES OF CONSCIOUSNESS is an unavoidable reality to accept at the social-mental level.

PHASE 313 (AQUARIUS 13°): A BAROMETER.

KEYNOTE: *The ability to discover basic natural facts that allow us to plan in advance for action.*

Here we are no longer dealing with ascent or descent, but with natural laws which involve causal relationships and the passage of one natural condition into another. The barometer registers air pressure, and a change of pressure today gives some indication of what the weather will be tomorrow. In a sense this is the modern scientific equivalent of archaic prognostication through omens. Likewise, animals grow a more or less thick fur in early autumn according to whether the winter will be more or less severe. Planning for the near future is a possibility because the potential (or seed) of the future is already operating at the core of the present.

This third symbol of the sixty-third sequence tells us that it is most important to seek—by whatever means and at whatever level of consciousness—a knowledge of causal progression. In the broadest sense this implies an awareness of cyclic processes, and this includes astrology. The Keyword is ANTICIPATION.

PHASE 314 (AQUARIUS 14°): A TRAIN ENTERING A TUNNEL.

KEYNOTE: *The ability to short-cut the process of natural evolution by the exercise of will, mental skill and physical self-discipline.*

In this symbol we see a condensation of what is implied in the three preceding ones. Man must be inspired by a vision of what is possible for him to achieve; he has to organize a schedule of necessary activities if the work is to be done in terms of successive moves, each requiring a specialized type of skill and strength (i.e. a hierarchy of functions); he has to find a propitious time for beginning the work. The end result is an acceleration of the evolutionary process, whether at the psychobiological level (that of yoga and other similar disciplines) or at the social level, i.e. the level at which, in its external aspect, civilization proceeds.

This fourth stage symbol presents a picture of what can be achieved by a combination of social and cultural, and even personal, techniques. It implies the possibility of shortening the length of time needed for progress by cutting through obstacles and delays. The Keyword is PENETRATION.

PHASE 315 (AQUARIUS 15°): TWO LOVEBIRDS SITTING ON A FENCE AND SINGING HAPPILY.

KEYNOTE: *The blessing bestowed upon personal achievements by the spiritually fulfilled consciousness of the Soul.*

This symbol can be interpreted at various levels of significance, but it evidently suggests a state of being in which two complementary aspects of spiritual reality—however we may conceive them—are united; this union results in happiness or bliss *(ananda)*. As the two birds are "sitting on a fence," and a fence separates two fields or gardens, the implication is that the separative consciousness of the ego can thus be blessed, perhaps as a spiritual reward for long-sustained and well-done work.

This is the last symbol of the sixty-third five-fold sequence which completes Scene Twenty-one. Inner happiness is seen to be the reward for all individuals who have made a valuable "contribution" to their community or to mankind as a whole. In its highest aspect this happiness is indeed BEATITUDE.

SCENE TWENTY-TWO: *MANAGEMENT*
(Aquarius 16° to Aquarius 30°)

FIRST LEVEL: ACTIONAL

PHASE 316 (AQUARIUS 16°): A BIG BUSINESSMAN AT HIS DESK.

KEYNOTE: *The ability to organize the many aspects of an enterprise involving a large group of human beings.*

A great deal of what is glowingly written about the Aquarian Age is probably sheer glamor. The New Age should be one in which man learns to use the power generated by human togetherness and group interplay—that is, *to use it harmoniously* for the welfare of the whole of which all individuals are parts, humanity and the planet Earth. This has never been achieved and only very rarely attempted. Mankind today must make a thorough and irresistible attempt, or be nearly destroyed—except for a creative "remnant" of seed-persons who would have to begin again from new foundations. In the field of big business, of huge war undertakings (like the Normandy landing in World War II) or of major national efforts (like the Moon landings) great results have been achieved, but the motive and the quality of the human interrelationships involved were neither of permanent significance nor invested with a truly harmonic quality. The character of the techniques used were totally unsatisfactory from a "human" point of view. Nevertheless there is much to learn from modern large-scale management and systems analysis, even in terms of personal endeavors of very limited scope.

This is the first stage in the sixty-fourth five-fold subcycle. It introduces the concept of management which is basic at this period of the cyclic life process which the zodiac symbolizes, yet which needs to be totally reevaluated if mankind is to actualize the spiritual potentialities implied in the evolutionary transformation just ahead. ORGANATION should be the Keyword, rather than mere "organization"; for humanity now can and should realize that it is indeed an "organism."

PHASE 317 (AQUARIUS 17°): A WATCHDOG STANDS GUARD, PROTECTING HIS MASTER AND HIS POSSESSIONS.

KEYNOTE: *The development of the capacity to protect oneself and to safeguard one's individual rights under complex social pressures.*

What seems to be implied in this symbol, considering its position in the entire cycle, is that under present-day social conditions the individual person needs protection against the ever-growing encroachments of society upon his theoretically recognized right to lead a private life free from public interference. Seen in this light the symbol stands in contrast to the preceding one depicting the power of big business and the totalitarian implications of large-scale organization. At a deeper occult level of interpretation it also reveals the need to protect oneself against "astral" intrusions and perhaps "black magic," the more so as one ventures into supernormal states of consciousness. It is said that the Adept trains certain subhuman entities ("Elementals") to protect him. The Christian religion speaks of Guardian Angels in a related sense.

At this second stage we see the individual able to master natural energies which he enlists in his service, so he may pursue his individualized work of destiny in security. This is another aspect of the relationship of individual-to-society. Individuals of course do also seek to rob or injure other persons, but the state of affairs resulting from a society glorifying competition, ambition and success at any cost is largely responsible for individual violence. The more creative the person, the greater his or her NEED FOR PROTECTION.

PHASE 318 (AQUARIUS 18°): A MAN'S SECRET MOTIVES ARE BEING PUBLICLY UNMASKED.

KEYNOTE: *The difficulty for the modern individual to keep secret his private past or his deeper motives.*

This symbol logically follows the two preceding ones. Today, struggle between the power of society and the rights of the individual leads in the end to the defeat of the latter. The media and innumerable governmental agencies are nearly always able to find access to remains or records of past actions; modern psychologists and psychiatrists are increasingly adept at penetrating the deepest secrets of a life through "analysis" and all kinds of more or less allowed techniques involving drugs and the subconscious reactions of muscles and nerves. The individual whose activities have to remain unrecognized is engaged in a constant struggle; he needs the help of higher Powers as well as of the protective agencies he may have placed at his service.

This is the third stage in the sixty-fourth five-fold sequence of archetypal images of the cyclic process. It refers to the UNMASKING of hidden motives and personal secrets. It may refer to the publicizing of past behavior.

PHASE 319 (AQUARIUS 19°): A FOREST FIRE IS BEING SUB-DUED BY THE USE OF WATER, CHEMICALS AND SHEER MUSCULAR ENERGY.

KEYNOTE: *The skill and courage necessary to bring under control the destructive potential of carelessness of karmic "visitations."*

Forest fires may be caused by human carelessness, by lightning or by the by-products of modern technology. Every individual —at least once in his lifetime, if not repeatedly—may perhaps have to face spectacular reactions to seemingly insignificant acts. These are to be considered means to test his strength, ingenuity or emotional stability. Every faculty at his disposal must be made use of—emotional, mental, physical. He needs faith in himself and in superior Powers.

At this fourth stage of the five-fold series we are shown man in action in a crucial and potentially devastating situation. There is need for a total mobilization of energy and a deep sense of INDOMITABILITY.

PHASE 320: (AQUARIUS 20°): A LARGE WHITE DOVE BEAR-ING A MESSAGE.

KEYNOTE: *The answer of spiritual agencies to thorough, sustained and victorious individual efforts.*

This concludes most significantly this series of five symbols. The individual who has gone courageously and with indomitable spirit through his crucial crisis receives, as it were, a deep spiritual blessing from the Soul-realm: "Mission accomplished. Peace be with you." And in this blessing a secret prophecy of what is yet to come may be seen by the perspicacious and spiritually sensitive mind of the recipient. Every real spiritual step a man takes in his development is the result of a victory over forces of inertia or destruction. The Divine is totally "present" in the heart of all true victories.

This is the fifth and last symbol of the sixty-fourth series. What the "message" is depends on the particular situation, but the white dove always signifies peace; at the very heart of this peace is the CERTIFICATION of individual worth and victory.

SECOND LEVEL: EMOTIONAL–CULTURAL

PHASE 321 (AQUARIUS 21°): A DISAPPOINTED AND DISILLUSIONED WOMAN COURAGEOUSLY FACES A SEEMINGLY EMPTY LIFE.

KEYNOTE: *The capacity to meet emotionally upsetting experiences in human relationships with strength of character and personal integrity.*

The man who manages vast and complex business enterprises most often reaches power and achieves success because of his ability to deal with crises and temporary reverses of fortune. At the emotional level we now see a "woman" confronted with sharp disappointment and forced to face the vanishing of cherished illusions, presumably in terms of a close personal relationship. She has to learn to manage such crises, which are really tests of inner strength and perhaps compassion. We all have within ourselves the power to learn through emotional crises. But like any other faculty it needs development.

This is the first symbol in the sixty-fifth five-fold sequence. It urges us to develop RESILIENCE under adversity.

PHASE 322 (AQUARIUS 22°): A RUG IS PLACED ON THE FLOOR OF A NURSERY TO ALLOW CHILDREN TO PLAY IN COMFORT AND WARMTH.

KEYNOTE: *The warmth of understanding which comes to those who, early in life, are open to new possibilities.*

Man is never left without assistance when eagerly seeking to grow emotionally and spiritually. Even if he does not consciously realize the intent and value of what sustains his self-development and cushions the shocks which life provides his growth in understanding, still the assistance is there. He may think: No one understands me. But the understanding is there if he does not egotistically take for granted that life and society owe him everything.

This second stage symbol contrasts the kindness inherent in so many of life's situations with the tragic feeling of disillusionment represented by the first stage symbol. Through a warm APPRECIATION of basic opportunities and even small comforts, we can safely and happily grow into personal maturity.

> **PHASE 323 (AQUARIUS 23°):** A BIG BEAR SITTING DOWN AND WAVING ALL ITS PAWS.
>
> **KEYNOTE:** *The self-discipline which results from an intelligent development of individual faculties under proper training.*

What constitutes the proper training of children or animals is a complex and much-disputed problem. The symbol seems to state simply that powerful life energies *can* be trained adequately—the implication or extension of the idea being that no training is really successful unless it leads to the realization of the value and power of self-discipline. We are constantly faced with situations which, whether we are aware of it or not, are in fact training situations; God or the Soul is the trainer. Much depends on the attitudes we assume in these situations.

This is the third symbol in the sixty-fifth sequence. We see in it the outcome of what is suggested in the two preceding ones. Character and a warm "under-standing" of what is involved in the process of growth and overcoming of emotional heaviness can be taught. We can learn to discipline our natural impulses and to use them for a more-than-personal purpose. This is DISCIPLESHIP in the true sense of the term.

PHASE 324 (AQUARIUS 24°): A MAN, HAVING OVERCOME HIS PASSIONS, TEACHES DEEP WISDOM IN TERMS OF HIS EXPERIENCE.

KEYNOTE: *The constructive use to which difficult past experiences can be put as examples for those who are still striving to overcome their passions.*

Every type of experience can be made to serve a spiritual purpose. Every man or woman, however humble his or her status, can be an example to younger people who are still struggling to overcome or control the compulsive drives of their emotional-biological natures. Whoever has managed a difficult performance contributes to the collective wisdom of his community and of mankind. Every achievement is to be passed on to those who may be inspired by it to greater and more adequate efforts.

At this fourth stage of the sixty-fourth subcycle we are given a never-to-be-forgotten hint: it is the responsibility of anyone who has taken one step ahead in his evolution to help others to take that step. This is true education. The Keyword is COMMUNICABILITY.

PHASE 325 (AQUARIUS 25°): A BUTTERFLY WITH THE RIGHT WING MORE PERFECTLY FORMED.

KEYNOTE: *The capacity to develop the rational and fully conscious aspect of the mind ahead of normal evolution.*

What seems implied is a kind of mutation, and more specifically the special development of whatever is symbolized by the "right side" of the organism. Here, however, the *spiritual body* (the butterfly) is what the Image represents. A strong process of conscious individualization is suggested, perhaps at the expense of the instinctual-emotional aspect of the personality (its "left side").

This last symbol fittingly concludes this sixty-fifth sequence, which began with "A disappointed woman . . ." The five-fold set deals with the management of human energies at the emotional level; here management means overcoming—this, on the basis of negative or ego-challenging experiences. This fifth symbol refers thus to the results of a TRANSMUTATION OF EMOTIONAL ENERGIES.

THIRD LEVEL: INDIVIDUAL–MENTAL

PHASE 326 (AQUARIUS 26°): A GARAGE MAN TESTING A CAR'S BATTERY WITH A HYDROMETER.

KEYNOTE: *Skill in applying knowledge of natural laws to the solution of everyday problems resulting from life in our technological society.*

Here we see a man using his analytical mind to check up on the operation of the machines his inventive genius produced. This simple commonplace operation is used here as an indication of how deeply technology involves us in small matters, yet matters which in some circumstances could make the difference between life and death—i.e. a mechanical failure in a car on a crowded freeway. The need for "management" therefore is seen to affect every detail of our individual lives; this applies as well to the complexities of interpersonal, social or political relationships, because our modern society is indeed like a huge machine speeding on dangerous ground. Safety depends on available power.

This is the first of five degree symbols in the sixty-sixth sequence. It tells us that we constantly need the use of our intellectual power of observation and analysis to check on the effectiveness of the energies at our disposal. It is a symbol of MENTAL EFFICIENCY.

PHASE 327 (AQUARIUS 27°): AN ANCIENT POTTERY BOWL FILLED WITH FRESH VIOLETS.

KEYNOTE: *The importance of traditional skills and artistic values deeply rooted in man's instinctive feelings as frames of reference for man's most authentic emotions.*

This symbol contrasts with the preceding one just as personal reticence and a simple love of natural beauty contrast with the rush, gawdiness and intellectual efficiency characterizing so much of our modern existence. Violets have often been considered symbols of modesty and humility—values which were understood to be the mark of true womanhood . . . long ago, it seems!

In this symbol we see pictured the dependence of the purest feelings of natural living upon the traditions within which they find their most adequate and effective setting. It is a symbol of DELICACY OF FEELING.

PHASE 328 (AQUARIUS 28°): A TREE FELLED AND SAWED TO ENSURE A SUPPLY OF WOOD FOR THE WINTER.

KEYNOTE: *Knowledge and skill used in its natural surroundings for the satisfaction of vital basic needs.*

This symbol combines, as it were, the implications represented in the two preceding ones. It relates to natural living the human capacity to prepare for the future and to use both physical strength and mental ingenuity. In meeting the hardships inherent in an existence close to nature, strength, efficiency and intelligence are needed, but they are incorporated in a life in which every act can be part of a harmonic and beautiful ritual permeated with deep significance.

This is the third in the sixty-sixth five-fold series of symbols. It refers to the efficient use of natural resources for insuring man's well-being. Such a use is based on INTELLIGENT FORESIGHT.

PHASE 329 (AQUARIUS 29°): A BUTTERFLY EMERGING FROM A CHRYSALIS.

KEYNOTE: *The capacity to utterly transform the character of one's consciousness by radically altering the structural patterns of everyday living and the types of relationships one enters upon.*

This is the second time within a very short span of the cycle that the butterfly symbol appears (cf. Aquarius 25°). Here what is emphasized is the process of metamorphosis itself. It is the fourth symbol of a five-fold sequence and it stresses the essential character of the activity required at this stage of the cycle; i.e. nothing short of a complete renewal of all the implications of being alive as a human individual will do. A radical change is needed. At this stage, this change is individual and mental, and it should be seen against the background of humanity as a whole. What is revealed is the potential ability of every human being to participate in a higher realm of evolution AFTER his or her emergence from a critical state of transition.

At this fourth stage of the sixty-fifth subcycle the Keyword is META-MORPHOSIS. In spiritual terms, this implies "Initiation," i.e. entering a higher realm of conscious existence and there joining a sacred Company.

PHASE 330 (AQUARIUS 30°): DEEPLY ROOTED IN THE PAST OF A VERY ANCIENT CULTURE, A SPIRITUAL BROTHERHOOD IN WHICH MANY INDIVIDUAL MINDS ARE MERGED INTO THE GLOWING LIGHT OF A UNANIMOUS CONSCIOUSNESS IS REVEALED TO ONE WHO HAS EMERGED SUCCESSFULLY FROM HIS METAMORPHOSIS.

KEYNOTE: *The ability for the person with an open mind and a deep feeling for self-transcendence to come in contact with higher forms of existence.*

The originally recorded Sabian symbol stated: "The field of Ardath in bloom," which referred to a scene in an occult novel by

Marie Corelli centering upon ancient Babylon. The reference may well have been a "blind" inasmuch as Marc Jones has stressed his inner contact with a Brotherhood with Babylonian (or "Sabian") roots. A spiritual Brotherhood consitutes a state of "multi-unity"—i.e. a *multiplicity* of individuals, if one thinks of the paths they trod to reach their final metamorphosis, but a *unity* of consciousness and "Soul"—thus unanimity ("anima" meaning Soul). In this spiritual Whole each unit is a recognizable "form" or entity if one looks at it with the eyes of personality; but when seen through a unified spiritual vision or from a distance, the Whole appears to be one single area of radiant light. Similarly, when studied by the modern physicist, light can be apprehended either as a stream of identifiable particles (photons) or as one continuous wave. Whether it is seen as one or the other depends on the point of view.

This is the last and culminating symbol of Scene Twenty-two of the cyclic ritual. This is indeed a fitting symbol, as the number 22 symbolizes all forms of mastery. At any level, it is a symbol of spiritual group fulfillment—of CONSCIOUS TOTALITY OF BEING.

SCENE TWENTY-THREE: *FEDERATION*
(Pisces 1° to Pisces 16°)

FIRST LEVEL: ACTIONAL

PHASE 331 (PISCES 1°): IN A CROWDED MARKETPLACE FARMERS AND MIDDLEMEN DISPLAY A GREAT VARIETY OF PRODUCTS.

KEYNOTE: *The process of commingling and interchange which at all levels demonstrates the health of a community.*

In any twelve-fold division of a complete cycle (for instance the 12 zodiacal signs and the 12 Houses of a birth chart) the twelfth section often has been given a negative significance. It can refer to oppressive conditions as it represents a "closing of accounts," a final evaluation of the harvest of the cycle. A very bad harvest may lead to bankruptcy; a premature revolt may bring the rebel to jail; the dissolute may end in a hospital. In this section of the cycle a man reaps what he has sown. But it may also be honors, social prestige, the interests of well-managed wealth. In this twenty-fourth scene what is stressed is the coming together, in a final experience of community, of all factors previously experienced; this means constructive interaction and an interchange of the products of social activity. In a practical sense, the symbol, whenever it is found, emphasizes that the time has come to take full advantage of the social opportunities to bargain and to trade.

This is the first stage of the process related to the sixty-seventh five-fold sequence of symbols. It refers to all that can be gained from social interplay and especially, in the broadest sense of the word, from COMMERCE.

PHASE 332 (PISCES 2°): A SQUIRREL HIDING FROM HUNTERS.

KEYNOTE: *The individual's need both to ensure his future subsistence and to protect himself from aggressive social elements.*

The squirrel not only has to hide and store food for the winter, but to be on the lookout for the dangers involved in gathering this food supply. Social processes always cast strong shadows. The individual is never certain of being safe among his fellowmen, once the process of individualization—with its negative aspects, competition, social aggressivity and greed—forces the breakdown of the organic tribal state of mankind during the archaic ages.

This second stage symbol contrasts with the first. It warns of the dangers of life in society during an era of exacerbated individualism, when violence is a possibility never to be dismissed. The need for SELF-PROTECTION and caution is ever present.

PHASE 333 (PISCES 3°): PETRIFIED TREE TRUNKS LIE BROKEN ON DESERT SAND.

KEYNOTE: *The power to preserve records of their achievements which is inherent in fully matured cultures.*

When a vast group of men succeed in building a culture with strong institutions which express themselves in significant symbols and works of art or literature, such an effort of many generations is rarely lost altogether. In one form or another, records of this culture endure or are mysteriously preserved, simply because they reveal the place and function of this particular culture in the long process of unfoldment of the potentialities inherent in archetypal MAN. It is such a concept that has been mythified and popularized in the religious idea of the resurrection of the dead on the Last Day. The symbol of petrified wood in the Arizona desert, however, tells us that the *actual* preservation of the records is never perfect or total. Only fragments remain, significant enough to reveal the essential archetypal form.

This third symbol of the sixty-seventh five-fold sequence brings the promise of social immortality—i.e. the preservation of the enduring (because archetypally meaningful) factors in whatever man attempts within his culture. A symbol of INDESTRUCTABILITY.

PHASE 334 (PISCES 4°): HEAVY CAR TRAFFIC ON A NARROW ISTHMUS LINKING TWO SEASHORE RESORTS.

KEYNOTE: *The mobility and intensity of interchanges which make possible and characterize complex social processes.*

Here we see the concept of commerce and social interaction in a new form. What is stressed is the need to establish unceasing dynamic relationships between all aspects and functions of the social life. The more complex the relationships, the more dynamic and restless the society. In this symbol the "isthmus" refers to a geographic situation found near San Diego, California, where these Sabian symbols were produced—also in Florida and elsewhere. A narrow strip of land separates the sea from a lagoon and on this strip, houses are built and roads are constantly filled with moving cars. The proximity of the sea stresses the collective nature of social experiences and of what may appear to be "individual" achievements.

This fourth stage symbol evokes many aspects of what at several levels can be called TRAFFIC. The technique for achieving social results is always based on an interchange of ideas and interplay of activities. Often, however, confusion ensues and traffic jams are ever-present possibilities.

PHASE 335 (PISCES 5°): A CHURCH BAZAAR.

KEYNOTE: *The value of giving a spiritual or transcendent sanction to even the most commonplace interchanges between social persons and individual minds.*

This is the last of five symbols emphasizing the interaction between people constituting a social group, small or large. It brings in the element of religious sanctions. The purpose of any organized religion is primarily to meet the need of giving a more permanent significance to interpersonal relationships within the framework of a particular way of life and culture. It helps to keep the society "whole" by making it "holy"—at least in principle and ideal. It justifies human behavior by blessing it with a divine Revelation of what is good and valuable. It idealizes biological and social needs by ritualizing them.

This ends the sixty-seventh five-fold sequence on a note of RITUALIZED BENEFICENCE. It stresses the possibility of the "Presence of God" in even the most material human activities.

SECOND LEVEL: EMOTIONAL–CULTURAL

PHASE 336 (PISCES 6°): A PARADE OF ARMY OFFICERS IN FULL DRESS.

KEYNOTE: *The dedication of human beings to the service of their community, and the assurance that it will be emotionally sustained by the people at large.*

Here we see at work the emotion-rousing appeal of social activities which demand the surrendering by the individual of his personal way of life, his opinions and his comfort. The socializing process is pictured in all its intensity but what is implied even more is the support that the socialized person can expect from the collectivity if he is ready to act and to sacrifice himself for the nation or the group.

This is the first symbol of the sixty-eighth series. It allegorizes the power generated by a totally accepted and enforced collective discipline, and the exaltation and mass response which he who has achieved this self-surrender to a social tradition can expect in return. The Keyword is GROUP–RESPONSIBILITY.

PHASE 337 (PISCES 7°): ILLUMINED BY A SHAFT OF LIGHT, A LARGE CROSS LIES ON ROCKS SURROUNDED BY SEA MIST.

KEYNOTE: *The spiritual blessing which strengthens individuals who, happen what may, stand uncompromisingly for their own truth.*

Men who do not depend upon collective values, traditions or support but seek at any cost to be true to their individual self and destiny almost inevitably face some kind of crucifixion. They are sustained only by the power within them, to which a light above answers. The symbol tells us: "Be true to thine own self, and in the midst of the outer confusion displayed by those surrounding you, you will realize what you really are as an individual—a son of God."

This second stage symbol presents us with a realization in polar opposition to that evoked by the preceding scene. It implies the supreme worth of a life guided by an inner voice and manifesting a high degree of SELF-ASSERTION.

PHASE 338 (PISCES 8°): A GIRL BLOWING A BUGLE.

KEYNOTE: *A call to participation in the service of the race, as an evolutionary crisis approaches.*

This symbolic picture presents another aspect of the emotional relationship between the individual and the collectivity of human beings. It can also be related to the old feminist movement or the present women's liberation. In traditional symbolism the woman refers more specifically to the biological and psychic aspect of human life; she is seen primarily as the mother, and/or the intuitive or "psychic" type of person. A new race of human beings may well be slowly unfolding some of its potential of consciousness and fulfillment. The individual who envisions this evolutionary development "sounds the call." He or she is both seer-herald and mutant. In that sense such a human being is both an individual true to his original nature and a dedicated person—dedicated to the future he or she holds in latency as does a seed in mutation.

At this third stage of the sixty-eighth five-fold sequence the two preceding phases blend in a new form of consecration of the individual to the Whole. Tomorrow acts through today; it SUMMONS men to rebirth.

PHASE 339 (PISCES 9°): A JOCKEY SPURS HIS HORSE, INTENT ON OUTDISTANCING HIS RIVALS.

KEYNOTE: *Intense mobilization of energy and skill in the drive for success in any social performance affected by the competitive spirit.*

Since the end of the archaic ages and the stressing of individualism, especially in our American society which worships the material images of "success," the desire to win any kind of "race" engenders an often-feverish release of energy controlled by technical skill and long practice. Wherever this symbol is found, it indicates the need to spur one's total being toward speedy attainment of whatever goal it may be.

This is the fourth symbol in the sixty-eighth series; its technical significance is quite evident. Every superfluous "weight," every unnecessary consideration is to be dismissed in the one-pointed attempt to reach one's social goal. SELF–QUICKENING may be the Keyword.

PHASE 340 (PISCES 10°): AN AVIATOR PURSUES HIS JOURNEY, FLYING THROUGH GROUND-OBSCURING CLOUDS.

KEYNOTE: *Man's ability to develop powers and skills which by transcending natural limitations allow him to operate in mental-spiritual realms.*

This symbol in a sense synthesizes the implications of the four preceding ones: the dedication to the community of men (present and future), self-assertion and the ambition to reach a social goal. Man is seen mastering difficulties implied in a type of operation transcending his organic limitations and the narrow boundaries of a localized "living space." He does so as an individual in command of powerful energies, but also as heir to the industry of countless innovators and managers.

This is the last symbol of the sixty-eighth five-fold sequence of evolving stages of consciousness and human activity. It evokes the achievement of MASTERY.

THIRD LEVEL: INDIVIDUAL–MENTAL

PHASE 341 (PISCES 11°): MEN TRAVELING A NARROW PATH, SEEKING ILLUMINATION.

KEYNOTE: *The capacity inherent in every individual to seek at whatever cost entrance to a transcendent realm of reality.*

This refers to the ancient and eternal symbol of the Path of Discipleship. The greatness of man is that he can always be greater; and the belief—deeply rooted in men's inner nature—that if he fulfills the necessary conditions he can find "Elder Brothers" who have already attained a higher level of consciousness and will transfer their attainment and light to him. The Path is always open to the pure in heart, the mentally aware, the conqueror of emotions and the spiritually self-mobilized.

This symbol opens the sixty-ninth five-fold sequence and a new level of consciousness. Man is always in the making and remaking. He can always go further, reach beyond. But he has to take the first step. Someone can show him the Path, but he alone can do the walking. Thus the Zen injunction: WALK ON.

PHASE 342 (PISCES 12°): IN THE SANCTUARY OF AN OCCULT BROTHERHOOD, NEWLY INITIATED MEMBERS ARE BEING EXAMINED AND THEIR CHARACTER TESTED.

KEYNOTE: *The ever-repeated challenge presented to the individual by the group in which he has claimed acceptance—the challenge to prove himself and his ability to assume responsibility effectively.*

At any level of activity, sooner or later life itself demands of the individual that he or she stand up clearly and unequivocally to the ideal he himself has declared publicly his own. At the occult level the testing seems to be controlled and irrevocable. The "initiate" has become a constituent part of an integrated field of mental-spiritual activity. He is therefore controlled by the structural order of the group. He is no longer seeking; having found his place, he must prove himself able to fulfill the function associated with it. He is no longer "free" as an individual, for he has become a part of an integral Whole operating under structural principles of immense antiquity.

This second symbolic stage of unfoldment stands in contrast to the first in that the individual is now bound by collective laws and traditions. At a mundane political or business level he is the junior executive incorporated in a hierarchical institution. He has at all times to prove his worth. QUALIFICATION is an apt Keyword.

PHASE 343 (PISCES 13°): AN ANCIENT SWORD, USED IN MANY BATTLES, IS DISPLAYED IN A MUSEUM.

KEYNOTE: *Through the effectual use of his will a consecrated man can become a symbol of courage for all those who follow in his footsteps.*

Will power is the ultimate spiritual weapon, and its undeviating use is the certification of individual worth. Wherever found, this symbol emphasizes the imperative need to make use of the will in meeting the basic challenges of the inner life as well as outer adversaries.

With this third symbol of the sixty-ninth sequence we see singled out and strongly emphasized the one power in man which is an assurance of victory in the contests generated by social (or occult) processes in which he has become an active part. The individual must use that WILL POWER, yet it is not really his own once he operates at a spiritual level. It is God's will operating *through* his mind which focuses its thrusts. It is, occultly speaking, the power of the Brotherhood—the energy of the Whole operating through the one-pointed individual who has made this Whole aware of the need for its use in a particular situation.

PHASE 344 (PISCES 14°): A LADY WRAPPED IN A LARGE STOLE OF FOX FUR.

KEYNOTE: *The use of intelligence and mental subtlety as a protection against storms and trials.*

Coming just after the preceding symbols and as the fourth stage of a five-fold sequence, which is usually related to some kind of technique, this symbol may at first seem irrelevant. The key to its interpretation, missed by the commentators, is *fox* fur. In symbolism and mythology the fox is always a clever and subtle animal. It represents the intellect at its early stage of "cunning"; in a broader sense, it also refers to "intelligence," considered as the ability to adapt to any and all life situations. Spiritual will and the ability to stand in facing tests are necessary in any crucial or challenging situation that an individual meets within a power-oriented group. But the sword-like will often has to be shielded, and intelligence or acumen can be the most precious help in danger. It is a personal (i.e. "animal" or instinctual) shield, perhaps even a camouflage. It hides the central will, but it keeps the individual from unnecessary hardships.

What we see symbolized here is a self-protective way of meeting the inclemencies of weather, actual or psychic, which abound as one leads a life consecrated to a vaster Whole; for this very consecration arouses strong enmities. Unnecessary risks are forbidden to the initiate, for the security of the Brotherhood might be endangered. The need for PRO-TECTIVE SHIELDING is imperative, and glamor can be an effective shield.

PHASE 345 (PISCES 15°): AN OFFICER INSTRUCTING HIS MEN BEFORE A SIMULATED ASSAULT UNDER A BARRAGE OF LIVE SHELLS.

KEYNOTE: *The need for thorough rehearsing before any complex and inherently dangerous social ritual in which power is used or evoked.*

In this fifth symbol of a series dealing with the confrontation with superpersonal group or occult power we see a picture which once again synthesizes what the four preceding symbols have implied, rather than stated. In social life, as well as occultism, conflict is always to be expected; one must prepare for it. At the close of the great cycle—in the zodiac, the sign Pisces— a deep-seated struggle is inevitable at least to some extent. It can be a struggle against the ghosts of the unfulfilled past, the "unlived life," or a confrontation with accumulated and often-eluded karma. Indeed, Pisces refers to a period in the year during which many generals and admirals have been born. The rules of the game, at least in traditional forms of warfare, can be known. One may have to rehearse the dangerous play, just as our astronauts endlessly rehearsed every step in the moon landings. Individual rashness cannot be tolerated. Even a deliberate sacrifice must play a well-conceived part—like the sacrifice of an important piece in a game of chess.

This is the last symbol in Scene Twenty-three. The entire scene dealt in various ways with the process of integration of the individual into a social Whole, a community, an occult Brotherhood. A concluding Keyword could be VALORIZATION. The concept of group-value dominates the entire scene.

SCENE TWENTY-FOUR: *PERPETUATION*
(Pisces 16° to Pisces 30°)

FIRST LEVEL: ACTIONAL

PHASE 346 (PISCES 16°): IN THE QUIET OF HIS STUDY A CREATIVE INDIVIDUAL EXPERIENCES A FLOW OF INSPIRATION.

KEYNOTE: *Reliance upon one's inner source of inspiration or guidance.*

In this last scene of the great ritual of cyclic existence we are dealing with various aspects of the process that enables man to "con-firm," formulate and perpetuate the original creative impulse which has become self-actualized in a myriad of ways throughout the cycle, short or long as the cycle may be. This first symbol strikes the keynote of truly significant creative processes: their source is above, beyond, but also around the individual creator. The inspiration, original and individual though it may be, is given a form which is conditioned by the cultural, social and religious background of the creative person. In a sense, every genius merely records an answer to the needs of his time. The hands that write, play an instrument, or mold a plastic material are his own; the urge or drive back of the flow of inspiration has arisen in the vast collective mind of Man.

This is the first of the seventieth series of five symbols. The individual aspect of the creative process is emphasized as is the individual's need for concentration and at least inner quiet. He must have faith in his own SUBJECTIVE STRENGTH.

PHASE 347 (PISCES 17°): AN EASTER PARADE.

KEYNOTE: *The capacity inherent in all great sociocultural Images to unite the members of a community in a display of excellence.*

Here we see, by contrast, the unifying power of great myths and symbols in truly organic and self-perpetuating culture. The Image of the Resurrection spurs all men within the pale of Christendom to appear at their very best and to dynamize themselves in some kind of self-renewal in response to the Christ *mythos,* and to the call of nature's springtime as well. Wherever found, this symbol emphasizes the value of attuning one's life activities and moods to the ritualistic patterns of society or Earth-nature, rather than acting in complete independence from the group.

At this second stage of the five-fold subcycle the Collective dominates the Individual, Yin overpowers Yang. It is a time for conformity to what constitutes the highest ideals of one's culture and for PARTICIPATION IN COLLECTIVE PEAK EXPERIENCES.

PHASE 348 (PISCES 18°): IN A GIGANTIC TENT, VILLAGERS WITNESS A SPECTACULAR PERFORMANCE.

KEYNOTE: *The collective appeal of a well-staged and exciting display of skill and/or oratory.*

At first, Marc Jones interpreted the "gigantic tent" as the locale for a revivalist's meeting; later he suggested a circus tent instead. In a sense, the basic meaning is the same. Whether it is the traditional performance of skilled clowns, acrobats or animal trainers, or that of a religious fundamentalist dramatizing an old religious imagery, what takes place is the use of personal achievement and conviction to bring a crowd to a state of enthusiasm sufficient to make it forget its boredom with everyday routine or its familiar sins of commission or omission.

At this third stage of the seventieth five-fold sequence, the individual person and the collectivity are brought together in a significant performance which subtly strengthens the communal spirit directly or indirectly. The implication of the symbol, whenever it is found operating, is that the time has come for the individual to dare to present himself and his works to his community for applause, or for the purpose of attracting a following. What is suggested is PUBLIC SELF–DRAMATIZATION.

PHASE 349 (PISCES 19°): A MASTER INSTRUCTING HIS DISCIPLE.

KEYNOTE: *The transfer of power and knowledge which keeps the original spiritual and creative Impulse of the cycle active and undeviated.*

The Hindu ideal of the sacred relationship between guru and chela (disciple) has of late become familiar to a vast number of young and not-so-young people. The doctrine of "the Apostolic succession" in the Roman Catholic Church has a similar significance. The Power and archetypal knowledge released "in the beginning" of any cycle (or at "Creation") must be perpetuated until the very Last Day—the Omega state of which Teilhard de Chardin glowingly speaks. This Power is the "self" of the cyclic manifestation, the unchanging Tone (AUM) of all existences within this cycle. It can be transmitted from master to disciple at the latter's "Initiation." It *must* be so transmitted for when the line of transmission (in Sanskrit, *guruampara*) is discontinued, the cyclic process begins to collapse in futility and spiritual darkness.

This fourth stage symbol gives us a clue to the supreme technique necessary for the continuation of all manifestations of power and spiritual understanding. The transmission is from person to person; it follows a general, unchanging pattern, yet it operates in terms of particular and individual circumstances. Keyword: INVESTITURE.

PHASE 350 (PISCES 20°): A TABLE SET FOR AN EVENING MEAL.

KEYNOTE: *An indication that in the end and at the appointed time the individual's needs will be met among those to whom he is linked by a spiritual (or biological) web of energies.*

The significant element in this scene is not only the meal, but the fact that it is an "evening" meal. To use traditional symbolism, after a long chain of personal existences the Soul returns to its spiritual home at the close of the day-of-manifestation. There it finds that which renews and amply sustains; the happiness of the "beyond of existence" is experienced—if all has gone well.

This last symbol of the seventeenth five-fold sequence promises a satisfying or fulfilling end to whatever one has been undertaking. As the life closes, the Soul-consciousness finds NOURISHMENT in the harvest of whatever, during the whole life, has been relevant to the archetypal purpose and destiny of the Soul—one of the myriad of aspects of the divine creative word which began the cycle.

SECOND LEVEL: EMOTIONAL–CULTURAL

PHASE 351 (PISCES 21°): UNDER THE WATCHFUL AND KIND EYE OF A CHINESE SERVANT, A GIRL FONDLES A LITTLE WHITE LAMB.

KEYNOTE: *Growth in consciousness in its earliest tactile awareness of the wonders of unsophisticated living.*

This symbol recalls the one for Phase 174 (Virgo 24°)—"Mary and her little lamb"—but it occupies a different position in the five-fold sequence and a new factor is added: the "Chinese servant." According to the occult tradition, the original Chinese race was an extension of the humanity (or "Root Race") preceding ours—thus the stress upon the biological factors of family and ancestors, and also on the dualism of the Yang and Yin interplay. The "Chinese servant" represents the past as a servant of the new evolution. (The "white lamb" suggests the sign of all beginnings, Aries.) This new evolution is just about to begin during the late Pisces phase of the year cycle. It is as yet an ideal, a white loveliness. The girl discovers the new feeling of the touch of wool and of animal warmth. The preceding five-fold sequence began with a symbol suggesting the inspiring revelation of new truths or facts which the creative person is seeking to formulate. Now we witness another kind of discovery —a sensuously emotional discovery, perhaps a presentiment of the mother-feeling.

This is the first symbol of the seventy-first sequence. It brings together past and future, an overlapping of levels. The Chinese kindly watching the white girl; the girl fondling the white lamb. There is charm and ingenuousness in the scene— a vision of WHITE HOPE, a hope for a future that can only be felt, almost naïvely.

PHASE 352 (PISCES 22°): A PROPHET CARRYING TABLETS OF THE NEW LAW IS WALKING DOWN THE SLOPES OF MOUNT SINAI.

KEYNOTE: *The need to bring down to the level of everyday existence the clear realizations made manifest in a great "peak experience."*

The symbol obviously refers to Moses after he received from the God of his people the basic principles upon which a new religion, and even more a new ritual of living, should be founded. This basic "Law" has to be "brought down." It represents a descent of formative and structuring power, a divine Revelation. This type of revealed knowledge contrasts with the kind of knowing born out of the experience of touch, of feeling, of warmth of contact.

This second stage symbol pictures a process to which a religious God-given character has been attributed in the past, but which today is being investigated at the personal and psychological level. The important point here is: what do you do *after* you have a peak experience, an inner revelation? The Keyword MANDATE is appropriate; but the basic problem is how to fulfill it in the right spirit.

PHASE 353 (PISCES 23°): A "MATERIALIZING" MEDIUM GIVING A SEANCE.

KEYNOTE: *The ability to give of one's own vital energy to substantiate one's conscious ideals or unconscious desires.*

The person who believes he or she has a mission or mandate, or any special gift that can be of value to his community, must substantiate this belief. He has to produce results. Sometimes this involves difficulties and special conditions or circumstances; it always demands to some extent the gift of some power of value which is deeply one's own. The thought of sacrifice was suggested by the "white lamb" in the first symbol of this five-fold series. Something precious involved in a deeply personal experience has to be surrendered, offered to others. The medium's psychic substance provides the materials made visible in the phenomena, if the latter are genuine. After the seance, the medium is usually exhausted. The performer gives of his very life to the performance.

This refers to the third stage in the seventy-first five-fold process. The display of psychic power that the symbol depicts can be interpreted positively or negatively according to the motives that induced the "medium" to give the seance. In its most constructive aspect it suggests the Keyword: SUBSTANTIATION. The shadowy aspect of the process is "deception."

PHASE 354 (PISCES 24°): ON A SMALL ISLAND SURROUNDED BY THE VAST EXPANSE OF THE SEA, PEOPLE ARE SEEN LIVING IN CLOSE INTERACTION.

KEYNOTE: *The need to consciously accept one's own personal limitations in order to concentrate one's energies and to live a centered and fulfilled life.*

Every individualized person is a small island in the vast ocean of mankind. The ego fulfills a necessary function, as it sets boundaries and gives a specific character to the consciousness. Within these boundaries a complex interplay linking and integrating the various aspects of the personal life can operate constructively. In time, these ego-boundaries can not only expand, but can become a zone of intense interchange between the inner and the outer, between the individual and the community, between man and the universe.

This fourth stage symbol tells us that the first duty of any man or woman is to be truly what he or she is as an individual. But this individual has a particular dharma, i.e. a place and function in a vaster whole. The island's inhabitants get subsistence from the sea, and in time learn to navigate this sea and interact with other islanders—and all eventually will come to realize their oneness within the whole Earth, which includes everything. An appropriate Keyword would be CENTRALIZATION.

PHASE 355 (PISCES 25°): A RELIGIOUS ORGANIZATION SUCCEEDS IN OVERCOMING THE CORRUPTING INFLUENCE OF PERVERTED PRACTICES AND MATERIALIZED IDEALS.

KEYNOTE: *The power of the Soul to intervene in the personal life and to induce necessary catharses.*

The necessary centralization of the conscious attention and will symbolized by the preceding picture most often bring negative results—exclusivism, pride, jealousy, greed for power and wealth. Every man is a Church that has the Soul as its god, but most men forget the Soul and live according to dogmatic rules and habits which not only have become empty of inner meaning, but very often have been perverted by the demands of the senses and the emotional nature, and by the ego with its rationalizing intellect. A purging or catharsis is needed to restore not only fresh and creative spontaneity, but even more the contact with the Soul and the God-ordained dharma.

This is the last stage in the seventy-first subcycle. It leads significantly to the series of five symbols which concludes the vast cycle, because the final consummation of the process of actualization of the potency inherent in the original Creative Act requires moments of crisis and PURIFICATION.

THIRD LEVEL: INDIVIDUAL–MENTAL

PHASE 356 (PISCES 26°): WATCHING THE VERY THIN MOON CRESCENT APPEARING AT SUNSET, DIFFERENT PEOPLE REALIZE THAT THE TIME HAS COME TO GO AHEAD WITH THEIR DIFFERENT PROJECTS.

KEYNOTE: *A keen appreciation of the value of individualized responses to any challenge of life.*

The rather obscure original notation for this zodiacal degree, "A new moon that divides its influences," when translated into practical terms refers to the fact that, confronted with the opportunity to expand their energy along new lines, modern individuals will react according to their own personal characters. One basic cosmic-spiritual impulse will lead these varied personalities to take equally varied steps. In any society that glorifies individualism, everyone should therefore accept this fact and not try to compel other individuals to conform to a single pattern of response.

This first symbol of the seventy-second and last series of five stresses the essential nature of the cyclic process of actualization of human potential, i.e. the emergence of the individual (cf. symbol for Phase 1). This should lead to a realization of THE FALLACY OF TOTALITARIAN-

ISM; at times we can all act like despots, demanding that others react to any situation exactly as we do.

PHASE 357 (PISCES 27°): THE HARVEST MOON ILLUMINES A CLEAR AUTUMNAL SKY.

KEYNOTE: *The light of fulfillment that blesses work well done.*

For astronomical reasons the full moon of early autumn, the harvest moon, appears slightly larger than all other full moons. In our temperate Northern Hemisphere, these are the days when the green of summer fields and woods has turned gold and warm brown—days for the reaping of the good harvest, if all has gone well. This symbol brings us the message that the time has come to reap what we have not only sown, but also cultivated —or failed to cultivate.

This second stage symbol once more stands in opposition to the one for the preceding stage—new moon having now become full moon, indeed the fullest of all full moons. The Keyword is CONSUMMATION. But in this consummation—this "karmic" moment—the seed of the new cyclic manifestation is already latent.

PHASE 358 (PISCES 28°): A FERTILE GARDEN UNDER THE FULL MOON REVEALS A VARIETY OF FULL-GROWN VEGETABLES.

KEYNOTE: *The full satisfaction of the individual's basic needs.*

This symbol would seem a duplication of the preceding one, but if it is related to the first of this five-fold series (Phase 356) its meaning becomes clear. What is stressed now is not the full moon itself or its light, but the moon's *power* to call forth the instinctive urge for growth; many things respond in many different ways. The symbol refers to a typical garden, not to a field.

Such a garden contains a variety of plants, herbs and vegetables grown specifically to fill an equal variety of human needs and tastes.

In this sense the third symbol of this seventy-second sequence combines the meanings of the first two. It is a symbol of ABUNDANCE, an abundance fitted to individualized requirements and wants.

PHASE 359 (PISCES 29°): LIGHT BREAKING INTO MANY COLORS AS IT PASSES THROUGH A PRISM.

KEYNOTE: *The analytical power of the mind necessary for the formulation of life processes in their many aspects.*

Cycles of existence begin in unity and end in what I have called "multi-unity." At the stage of consummation the many individual differences are totaled; they constitute a sum. Within that sum—a unified total—the inevitability of the future process of differentiation is implied, because every cycle leaves a mass of waste products slowly returning to the unconscious state of chemical matter, of "humus." What the symbol tells us is that unity will always break again into multiplicity. The "prism" is always there. There is no abolsute unity; if anything could be called "absolute" it is *the relationship* between the One and the Many.

This fourth stage symbol of the concluding five-fold sequence of phases points to the fundamental type of operation in all modes of existence. The most beautiful and seemingly everlasting experience of unity will in time be superseded by the need to attend to a multiplicity of details. Existence implies DIFFERENTIATION.

PHASE 360 (PISCES 30°): A MAJESTIC ROCK FORMATION RESEMBLING A FACE IS IDEALIZED BY A BOY WHO TAKES IT AS HIS IDEAL OF GREATNESS, AND AS HE GROWS UP, BEGINS TO LOOK LIKE IT.

KEYNOTE: *The power of clearly visualized ideals to mold the life of the visualizer.*

Nathaniel Hawthorne's story "The Great Stone Face" is used here in an allegorical sense to show the capacity for self-transformation latent in man. This power can be developed through visualization, when the emotions and the will are poured into the visualized mental image. At the highest spiritual-cosmic level this is the power used by the God-like Beings at the close of a cosmic cycle in projecting the basic Formula (the Word) which will start a new universe. In a biological sense, it is the power latent in all seeds—the power to produce and guide the growth of the future plant. A most fitting symbol for the last phase of the cyclic process. Within the end of the cycle the seed of a new beginning exists in potency—unless the entire cycle has proven to be a failure.

This is the last stage of the last scene of the great ritual play of cyclic transformations. It brings to us a realization of the power of archetypes as factors conditioning life processes. Thus we could use as a final Keyword: ARCHETYPALIZATION.

Part Three
THE NUMERICAL STRUCTURE OF THE ZODIACAL SERIES

1. Binary Relationships Between Zodiacal Signs

◉

NOW THAT I HAVE REFORMULATED AND INTERPRETED SIN-
gly and in terms of sequential order, the 360 symbols produced
by the remarkable revelation in which Marc Edmund Jones and
Elsie Wheeler participated in 1925, I shall devote my attention
to the various ways in which these symbols are geometrically
interrelated. First, however, let me remind the reader that the
symbols were visualized by the clairvoyant in a completely aleatory manner and at extraordinary speed, with no knowledge of
what zodiacal degree the clairvoyantly visualized pictures referred to—a point discussed at length in the second chapter of
Part One.

Because these symbols actually represent 360 phases of a
complete and self-fulfilling process, they are interrelated and
their sequence has an essentially functional character. This may
not be obvious at first sight, and often it has not been understood. In order to become aware of this functional character it
is necessary first to accept the idea that the entire set of 360
symbols is a whole, with a complete geometrical structure as
well as a specific rhythm of unfoldment—and that the cyclic

process which the set pictorializes has a basic purpose.

This purpose is at least suggested by the primary symbols, which are a holistic key to the meaning of the process. These symbols refer to the three essential moments in all cyclic processes: the beginning, the middle and the end. These moments are often represented by the Greek letters alpha, mu and omega. They correspond to Phase I (Aries 1°), Phase 180 (Libra 1°) and Phase 360 (Pisces 30°).

The symbol for Aries 1° states two things: (1) Every new cycle of activity implies an emergence from the infinite Ocean of potentiality—the "great Waters of Space," according to occult terminology; (2) Every new beginning finds itself surrounded by the at least relative failures of past cycles; it therefore has to overcome the backward, or "seaward," pull (or karma) of the past. The overcoming is made possible by the use of an objective, detached outlook (symbol for Aries 2°), and thereafter by the realization that every individual whole is not only part of a "greater Whole," but a microcosm of this macrocosm (Aries 3°). A polarization of energy (Aries 4°) is required to actualize this realization. Out of this polarization a "capacity for self-transcending" should be developed which will enable one eventually to reach a higher level of consciousness (Aries 5°).

This five-fold sequence of symbols constitutes the alpha statement at the origin of cycles, at least of those pertaining to the development of man's consciousness and his potential of being, first as an individual, and presumably also in terms of the entire evolution of mankind. What is potential should be actualized at the omega stage of the cycle. This stage is symbolized in various ways by the pictures relating to the last degrees of Pisces. The entire Scene Twenty-four should be carefully studied, but the symbol for Phase 360, under the cover of an allegory taken from Hawthorne's story "The Great Stone Face," is quite explicit. What emerged instinctively and subjectively in Phase 1 has reached the point at which it becomes completely identified with the very purpose of the emergence. Potentiality becomes actuality, the creative Impulse (the Logos, the Word-in-the-beginning) is embodied in an individual person who has been transformed into the likeness of his ideal.

How can such a *transformation* be accomplished? Once they are clearly interpreted the symbols that stand at the midpoint of the cycle tell the story in a very significant manner. The symbol for Virgo 30° (Phase 180) tells us that as a person reaches the midpoint of his evolution—which in a human life may be the age of thirty-five or forty-two, depending on one's level of evolution—he must be "totally intent upon completing an immediate task" and "deaf to any allurement." This concentrated attention can lead to "Initiation." Having surrendered the fleeting and unessential pursuits of human existence, the individual becomes fully aware of what he archetypally *is*—therefore, of the place he occupies, or could occupy, in *the permanent record* of Man.

The symbols that follow (Libra 2°, 3°, 4°, 5°) bring more light to the somewhat mysterious symbol for Libra 1°. The metamorphosis which leads to the revelation of one's permanent seed-archetype (butterfly) demands a "repolarization of inner energies." This repolarization throws a transforming light upon everything that has so far been seen only in the relative darkness of the mind-consciousness. Moreover, the light should be sustained not only by the efforts of the individual alone, but by a group of companions; their joint dedication inevitably brings the Teacher-Exemplar who transmits to them knowledge and power.

Of course in considering these symbols, one can get only a glimpse of what is at stake in the cyclic process of transformation. The internal structure of the cycle—and therefore the character of time itself, at least in terms of human experience—becomes apparent when the annual sequence of seasonal changes is used as a model. This model reveals that all life processes—at least on this Earth—imply the existence of two opposite and complementary forces, called Yang and Yin by Chinese philosophers. In relation to man's seasonal experience of light and darkness I have spoken of them as the Day-force and the Night-force.* The hemicycle in which the Day-force is dominant (spring and summer) witnesses the actualization of the potential of individualization, the formation and growth of

*Cf. *The Pulse of Life.*

specific forms and individual responses to life situations. The hemicycle in which the Night-force is dominant (fall and winter) emphasizes collective values and ideals in order that single units may coalesce and become integrated into larger wholes.

In the interplay of Day-force and Night-force, four characteristic moments are observed: the equinoxes and the solstices. In the zodiacal sequence they correspond to Aries 1°, Cancer 1°, Libra 1° and Capricorn 1°. They constitute critical phases of adjustment, and ancient astrologer-philosophers symbolized these four critical states of consciousness and modes of substantial existence as Fire, Water, Air and Earth. In studying the basic structure of cyclic time we are therefore dealing with a quaternary pattern that reveals the constant interaction of two polarizing principles of activity. When the astrologer refers to Fire and Water, he should have in mind the operation of two types of activity and consciousness required for the full process of individualization. This process operates at several levels: biological, psycho-mental and spiritual—the latter being, with a very few exceptions, beyond the comprehension of mankind in its present state.

At the biological level, Fire refers to all that makes possible the growth of organisms from the germinal state (alpha state); Water refers to whatever makes possible the steady, rhythmic maintenance and propagation of the organism. At this same level, Air refers to processes of interaction between single organisms living within a particular environment—an interaction of whose purpose living organisms are unconscious until a particular state in human evolution is reached. This state at first exists at a local-regional level; this leads to the formation of a variety of cultures upholding a few characteristic archetypes or paradigms. Then mankind slowly and often tragically evolves toward—and eventually will reach—the level of global-planetary interaction. The fourth "element," Earth, refers to the process of *consolidation* of the patterns produced by the interactions which have proven most adequate for the purpose of life.

The attribution of the characteristics of Fire, Water, Air and Earth to the noncritical zodiacal signs (i.e. the fixed and mutable signs) has only a secondary meaning when we consider the process in terms of a succession of cyclically repeated steps. But the cycle as a whole can be studied as well in terms of the *space-relationship* between its many phases; it is this approach that has been emphasized in the teaching of astrology. What is done, therefore, is to consider the cyclic process as a circle divided into 12 sections—the zodiacal signs. These sections— and their subsections, the decanates and the degrees of the zodiac—can be related to one another *geometrically*. These relationships are called "aspects." By analyzing the aspects we study the internal structure of the whole. This is an "archetypal" structure. In actual existence every phase follows another in *time-relationship*. Yet a consciousness that can embrace an entire time cycle at once—earlier I called this an eonic consciousness—can "geometrize" the existential process. It can operate at the level of archetypes.

The distinction between archetypal (also called structural) knowledge and existential (or empirical) knowledge has often been obscured by semantic and epistemological discussions among philosophers. There is nothing mysterious about it; the mystery arises only when it is spoken of as the distinction between Being and Becoming, and emotionally metaphysical meanings are given to those terms which glorify the former (permanence) and downgrade the latter (change).

It is not possible here to discuss the complexities introduced into what should be a simple concept by warring ideologies, but I mention this because it is essential for us to understand how all forms of symbolism, and astrology more than any other, make use of two opposite, yet complementary approaches—the time-approach (existential) and the space-approach (archetypal). We shall see at once what this involves when we refer to the concept of polarity in astrology.

When an astrologer speaks of Aries being a "masculine" sign, and Taurus a "feminine" sign, he applies the concept of polarization (or in general of dualism and binary relationship) to two signs mainly, if not exclusively, in terms of *sequence in time:* Taurus follows Aries. But when the astrologer speaks of Aries and Libra as "polarities," he refers to the division of a circle into two semicircles—a *geometrical space-fact.*

The two approaches are equally valid, but they refer to different levels of experience or to two kinds of concepts. If one considers astrology an empirical science based on traditional rules to be memorized and applied—rules the relative value of which could be determined by statistical research—the difference between the geometrical and the sequential points of view is of no great significance. On the other hand, anyone thinking of astrology as a symbolical language whose purpose is to reveal the essential meaning of life situations of all kinds should try to understand the philosophy behind the symbolism. An understanding of the distinction between time-values and space-values, between the existential and the archetypal approaches to knowledge, is most important here. The conceptual ambiguity found in practically every field of astrology is very often due to a lack of differentiation between these two approaches.

The type of geometrical polarization resulting from an opposition aspect—as between Aries and Libra—is not a matter of immediate experience in natural living. Mental objectivity and some degree of abstract thinking are required. The two factors in opposition (i.e. 180 degrees apart) *complement* one another within the larger scheme of the cyclic process, in the same way that Yang and Yin complement each other. But while every moment of life and every cyclic phase witness the interaction of these two cosmic factors, the relative victory of Yang over Yin during springtime is not *experienced* at the same time as—nor can it be immediately related to—the autumnal ascendancy of Yin over Yang.

On the other hand, Aries *needs* Taurus (the following sign) to "confirm"—i.e. to give substantial firmness to—its "fiery" impulse toward individualized existence in a clearly bounded and well-defined field of activity. Aries needs Taurus as a male needs a female—as a highly projective type of activity requires a bending of its straightforward expansiveness along a circular path which establishes the boundaries of personalized living and experiencing. In the same way, Gemini needs Cancer just as the multidirectional curiosity for knowledge and varied experiences demands the eventual establishment of a center and the conscious acceptance of limits; and without the sobering critical factors related to Virgo, the emotionally creative ego, strong in Leo, would be lost in empty dramatics.

The "masculine" signs need to be *confirmed* by the "feminine" ones that immediatley follow them. In any experience the future acts upon the present, just as the regressive or karmic pull of the past affects the fleeting now. The two signs in sequence therefore constitute *an operative coupling*. Aries and Libra, and all opposite signs, do not: they refer to activities that can be seen to be complementary only in terms of the harmony of the zodiacal Whole.

IF THESE BASIC CONCEPTS ARE WELL UNDERSTOOD IT IS EASY to see how the Sabian symbols for the first degrees of all twelve zodiacal signs fit into the pattern. *Each first-degree symbol* establishes a keynote (or potential of meaningful development) for the entire 30-degree span of the sign. I call the symbols for the six so-called masculine signs (Aries, Gemini, Leo, Libra, Sagittarius, Aquarius) "root symbols"; those for the six feminine signs "symbols of confirmation."

The Aries 1° root symbol *(A woman just risen from the sea. A seal is embracing her.)* is confirmed by the symbol for Taurus 1° *(A clear mountain stream.)*. In the first symbolical scene we see a human being just emerging from the vast ocean of unconscious potentialities—the regressive pull toward a past of failure still surrounding the woman's emergence into the field of conscious and individualized activity, i.e. the dry land. Will this emergence succeed? Will the "trans-formation" represented in potentiality by the Aries 1° symbol actualize itself? Will the "land" support life, the foundation for individualized consciousness? The Taurus 1° symbol "con-firms" this possibility of success; the pure mountain stream will become the great river on whose banks will develop a rich vegetation, then a tribal culture, and later a city. The river is an individualized form of water. The water was drawn up from the sea into clouds, and fell as rain or snow upon the mountain. In time the river will return to the sea, its water charged with the impurities and waste products of the creatures of the biosphere—especially human beings whose consciousness today operates in terms of destruction of matter (which inevitably implies waste products) and of intellectual analysis (which produces an enormous amount of psychic waste).

Because the emerging human being needs the reassurance that on land there will be water to support life, the symbol for Taurus 1° confirms the operational chances of success for the process beginning with Aries 1°. In the same way, the symbol for Cancer 1° *(On a ship the sailors lower an old flag and raise a new one.)* "con-firms" what was only a potential beginning in Phase 61 of the cycle, Gemini 1° *(A glass-bottomed boat reveals under-sea wonders.)*. This Gemini 1° symbol refers to the first conscious realization of the existence of a world of hidden ("occult") forms and energies by the individualizing mind. At a more ordinary level, the youth born on a remote farm finds as he reaches college age that his mind is inspired (and possibly bewildered!) by the contents of thousands of books and unfamiliar experiences. Can he act constructively in terms of this vast and so far unsuspected knowledge? The Cancer 1° symbol confirms this possibility. He can choose to operate in terms of new ideals and a new sense of value. As a conscious individual he can transfer his allegiance to a more-than-local or more-than-biological type of activity.

This in turn can lead to results symbolized by the picture accompanying Leo 1° (Phase 121): *Blood rushes to a man's head as his vital energies are mobilized under the spur of ambition.* This symbol was noted on the original Sabian cards in a peculiarly negative manner; indeed the process of "mentalization" of the body's biological energies can be seen in a destructive light. It is a dangerous process, as is civilization itself! The transmutation of energies required for the development of an individually creative mind, even if centered in the true self, tends at first to disrupt the harmony of nature, both within the individual person and in his society. This has been responsible for the prevalence of heart disease, and the incapacity of the body to dispose of the toxins and waste materials produced by the tense activity of the ego seeking to control and use biological energies for its own purposes—which usually means self-aggrandizement. But the symbol for Virgo 1° *(In a portrait, the significant features of a man's head are artistically emphasized.)* confirms the possibility of success, because a portrait reveals the interior transformation produced by the will to individual self-expression, a transformation most characteristically seen in the features and the expression of the face.

If we now turn to Libra 1° and its enigmatic symbol *(In a collection of perfect specimens of many biological forms, a butterfly displays the beauty of its wings, its body impaled by a fine dart.)*, we enter the second hemicycle of the process of transformation. This hemicycle deals essentially with the trend to collectivization—i.e. the domination of the Yin principle, or Night-force. The Libra 1° symbol implies that if mankind is to become one organized global whole it has to act in accordance with the archetype of Man. In other words, group-action is needed to actualize the full potential of human nature—one might say the entire "Idea" God had of Man. Conversely, if a collectivity of human beings is to be successful, it has to model its structure and behavior upon the divine Idea. Divine Manifestations, or Avatars, come to reveal the character and implications of this Idea both to individuals, who become "initiated" through the sacrifice of their fleeting ego-life, and to "seed-groups," who, growing through many crises and purgings, bring forth a new culture and society.

The symbol for Scorpio 1° *(A crowded sightseeing bus on a city street.)* suggests that the transition from the narrow surroundings of an ego-consciousness ruled by earthly biological patterns of activity to the wider field of the group-life of "citizens" animated by a broader sense of interhuman relationship is possible. Our modern cities and their alienated, competitive citizens offer but a caricature of what the "Holy City" (the New Jerusalem or Shamballah) is to be; yet the process of expansion goes on, even though it may be through the glorification of negative reflections of the archetypal Idea.

With Sagittarius 1° we come to a picture of a more cohesive type of collectivity, one which is based upon the sharing of struggles and hardships *(Retired Army veterans gather to reawaken old memories.)*. The group-life has produced what *theoretically* could be an elite of men whose characters and wills have been tempered by the overcoming of collectively met dangers. But what is the use of the long struggle? The symbol for Capricorn 1° *(An Indian chief claims power from the assembled tribe.)* confirms the validity of this struggle and of the special training it entails. These efforts make it possible for man to demand and gain social power—a type of power which results from social interplay and organized activity at the "political" level *(Polis* is the Greek word for "city.").

The symbol for Aquarius 1° *(An old adobe mission in California.)* refers to the institutionalized results of efforts on the part of a collectivity of men driven by an ideal, or a national and religious goal. A society demonstrates its ability to expand significantly as it leaves a permanent social, religious and cultural impress upon a foreign land. But is it really worth the struggle? The symbol for Pisces 1° *(In a crowded marketplace farmers and middlemen display a great variety of products.)* confirms that it is, at least at the level of the community. Institutions may last or they may crumble away but the impulse from them has established a continuing commerce or commingling of human beings which makes life richer and more comfortable for a community of people. *The level of human consciousness* has been raised through the expansion of viewpoints and interests. A circulation of values is produced which is gradually building "the Universal Community of Man" (in the words of Thomas Jefferson).

Thus the cyclic process has gone from the insecure individual emerging from the unconscious expanse of being to the greater social organism of a culture inspired by ideals and transcendent goals. The implication for the individual person is a transformation of his consciousness and a development of his mind and its powers, for it is only through complex relationships —complex and varied, yet within a structured field of group activities—that the consciousness of man can expand and reach a higher level of understanding.

FROM THE FOREGOING IT IS EVIDENT THAT THE ZODIACAL cycle is to be divided into six pairs, rather than into twelve signs more or less independent of one another. The wholeness of the cycle differentiates itself naturally into a six-fold pattern; therefore the number 6 plays a basic role in life, at least at the level at which consciousness reaches *objectivity*. We speak of such a type of consciousness as "self-consciousness" (or as Teilhard de Chardin called it, "reflective consciousness") because the impressions that constitute the raw data of consciousness are, at this stage, referred to a "center"—i.e. to an experiencer able to say "I" and "I experience . . . therefore I am" (a more significant statement than Descartes' famous "I think, therefore I am.").

The I Ching sequence of 64 phases symbolizes the cyclic interactions of two Principles, Yang and Yin; but there is no evident center to the great Tai Chi symbol. The hexagrams themselves, as geometrical forms, have a rather square shape. On the other hand, where the six-fold nature of the differentiation process is emphasized, the circular geometrical figure already mentioned on page 32 naturally comes to mind: that is, one which shows 6 contiguous circles of equal sizes surrounding a central circle of the same size. The central circle refers to "self" in the word "self-consciousness." It is the individual person at the center of his birth chart—the individual and not the Earth-globe!—at least from the point of view of a person-centered and "humanistic" astrology.

This central self is the experiencer. The six surrounding circles in the geometrical symbol represent the basic powers of this experiencer, the six essential ways he can not only experience his environment at all levels, psychic and spiritual-mental as well as physical and biological, but can *respond* to the impacts made upon him by this environment.

The capacity *consciously* to respond to an impact, and not merely to *react* chemically and electrically to it, is the mark of the self-conscious man. Physiological reactions are automatic and instinctive, but strictly speaking, "responses" carry the stamp of the individual experiencer. "Reactions" in plants and animals—and many times indeed in ordinary human beings—are "programmed" by a power that is generic but not individualized. Real "responses" are self-directed; they reveal and express a person's individuality.

There is always a degree of uniqueness in the responses of

an individualized person, but even more important is the fact that the individual consciously uses *power* (in Sanskrit, *shakti*) rather than merely releasing *energy.* "Power" comes from a center; "energy" may be released from any place at which an impact has been registered by appropriate senses and nerve centers. This is a very important, yet rarely stressed, distinction.

Where there is a center, an experiencer, there also is the capacity *to use power,* and to use it meaningfully, for different purposes and, as evolution proceeds, at different levels. During the "vitalistic" Ages, early man used power mostly at the biological level. He was a cultivator and a breeder of cattle, occupied with controlling the power of multiplication in the vegetable and animal seed. He dealt with the energies of "life," and he worshiped all that related to this power of seed-multiplication, which is the basic characteristic of life. He enthroned the power of life in the sky, identifying or symbolizing it by "the Lights" —the Sun and the Moon. And because he realized that this power was fluctuating and operating cyclically according to a regular sequence of modes of activity, he correlated these seasonal *changes* with the positions of the Moon and the Sun plotted along the background of the apparently *changless patterns* made by what came to be known as "fixed stars"—and in some specific instances with the first appearance of a star at the horizon at a certain time of the year.

Archaic astrology, which no doubt preceded by thousands of years the great periods of the Egyptian and Chaldean societies, dealt with the use of life power for the purpose of group-survival and expansion. But as the early tribes increased in size and larger social units and cities developed, a new level of consciousness and activity was added to the purely biological aspect of life. Social power can be used as well as the power of organic life. Wealth and other social advantages can be multiplied as well as physical seed. The level of activity to which our word culture refers can parallel that of biological cultivation, but the former is far more susceptible to differentiation and expansion than the latter, even if sociocultural activities must to a large extent depend on the satisfactory operation of biological processes.

Yet while the bipolar life power, symbolized by the Lights, remains the foundation of power for man, the many overtones of the sociocultural life and their varied and ever-changing combinations present a new field for the development of the individual. This is the field of the mind and of the infinite complexity of patterns of feeling-response which arise in answer to ever more varied experiences resulting from interpersonal and intergroup relationships. This new field was related by the astrologers of old to the planets and their rhythmically interconnected cycles.

There is an important distinction between the primordial bipolar power of life (Sun-Moon) and the differentiated secondary powers born of interpersonal and group relationships at the sociocultural level (the planets). Unfortunately, this distinction has been largely forgotten or played down by modern astrologers. It is important in terms of this present study because we are confronted here with two kinds of differentiation of the central Power of the universe, and the difference can affect the interpretation of the Sabian symbols and their most significant application to varied types of situations.*

The "root symbols" discussed in preceding pages refer to six fundamental *modes of operation* of the one life power. Together with the "symbols of confirmation" they characterize broadly the pairs of signs (zyzygies) which divide the whole zodiacal process into six periods. That is to say, as the entire "cycle of transformation" proceeds, six great purposes are being worked out in sequence. There must be, first of all, EMERGENCE from the Unmanifest—the "great Waters of Space," or

*I cannot discuss here the manner in which the planets differentiate the central and undifferentiated power of the Sun. I have dealt with the matter in several ways in three earlier books, *The Practice of Astrology, New Mansions for New Men,* and *Triptych.* The planets up to and including Saturn refer to five basic centers of activity or levels of consciousness in the human being: Mercury, Venus, Mars, Jupiter, Saturn. The planets beyond Saturn do not essentially "belong" to the solar system per se. They symbolize the processes of transformation operating during the transition between the lesser cosmic whole (the solar system or "heliocosm") and the greater cosmic whole, the galaxy.

Chaos in the metaphysical sense. This refers to the Aries/Taurus pair. What has emerged has to pass through a period of UN-FOLDMENT of its original potential of being (Gemini/Cancer). Then follows a period of EXPRESSION of this potential in its most characteristic aspect (Leo/Virgo). Self-expression, both in its creative and its structural-technical aspects, leads to a new level of realization and experience, and we reach the stage of REORIENTATION in terms of the values and the basic facts of that new level (Libra/Scorpio). The next step implies a new type of operation or of mode of power, and COORDINATION is the Keyword of the zyzygy Sagittarius/Capricorn. Then comes the symbolic COMING TO SEED which refers to the Aquarius/-Pisces pair.

If one considers such a sequence, and perhaps meditates upon its meaning, it can be seen how the key words can be applied to many kinds of situations and cycles. We can state briefly how the Sabian symbols for the first degrees of the two signs fit in with the keynote of the period of the zodiacal process which they constitute.

1. ARIES symbolizes all beginnings *at the level of life power*. It represents the start of the process of individualization, which leads to the establishment of stable forms of existence. Every new birth constitutes an "emergence" from an enveloping ma-trix—also a germination process, with all the struggle that en-tails. The symbol for Aries 1° implies not only a rising from the sea, but entrance to the new field of existence, the dry land. The symbol for Taurus 1° reveals an opposite or polar direction of the life power. "The pure mountain stream" flows *down* to the plains. It vouches for the possibility of life on land. The two symbols taken together evoke the well-known cycle of water: ocean, clouds, rain, river, ocean.

In the occult philosophy of India, this mode of operation of the universal Life-power (the *shakti* of the Supreme Being and Consciousness) relates to *Parashakti*, which is defined by Subba Row as "the great or supreme force or power. It means and includes the power of light and heat."* It can be said that "light and heat" are the two primordial aspects of the cosmic power which is behind the will-to-be of any living organism. "To be" means also "to radiate"; the quality of any being is demonstrated by the character of its radiations.

2. With GEMINI we come to a phase of revelation of potentialities of existence previously hidden to the consciousness. Thus the sign represents an avidity for experiences and knowledge of all kinds. The symbol for Gemini 1° is relevant because the consciousness of an individual is like a boat floating upon the immense expanse of possible realizations. What is to be known is infinite. But a part of the boat is made transparent and many hidden things are revealed, especially if the pilot (theoretically, the Teacher) leads it over most significant areas of the as-yet-unknown-but-knowable. The individual consciousness which once emerged from the sea of the Unconscious is now able to discover objectively some of its oceanic mysteries.

This period of "unfoldment" corresponds to the power called *Gnanashakti* in Sanskrit. According to Subba Row, this power has two aspects:

1. When under the influence or control of material conditions, it manifests particularly as (a) the power of the mind in interpreting our sensations; (b) its power in recalling past ideas (memory) and raising future expectations; (c) its power as exhibited in what are called by modern psychologists "the laws of association" which enables it to form *persisting* connections between various groups of sensations and possibilities of sensations, and thus to generate the notion or idea of an external object; (d) its power in connecting our ideas together by the mysterious link of memory and in thus generating the notion of self or individuality.

2. When liberated from the bonds of matter, some of the manifestations of this *shakti* are real clairvoyance and psychometry.

*Subba Row, "The Twelve Signs of the Zodiac" (in *A Collection of Esoteric Writings of Subba Row*, Bombay, 1917). Quotations from this article are also included in H. P. Blavatsky's *Secret Doctrine*, original edition, Vol. I, pp. 292–93.

At man's average level of consciousness today, this Gemini power deals with the interpretation, association, and classification of sensations and, at a later stage, of concepts. Then comes the Cancer phase, the basic purpose of which is the establishment of persisting and permanent connection between sensations and between ideas. In the case of sensations these connections produce the notion of *objects;* in the case of ideas, the notion of a *permanent identity or self.* The symbol for Cancer 1° pictures sailors ready to hoist a new flag. This symbol reveals the progressive unfoldment of the potentialities of the human individual as he seeks periodically to re-form the standards upon which he has built his sense of self and his orientation toward life in general. A man is what he "thinks in his heart," says the Bible. Gemini "thinks," but Cancer establishes a certain category of thinking in the "heart," and makes it a "persisting" and "permanent" keystone for the personal life. There is no unfoldment of being except through these two phases of individual existence: the creation of thought categories and of personal standards. Knowledge and self-realization are forms that this power takes.

3. With LEO we come to man's characteristic capacity for self-expression. In terms of the six-fold differentiation of the one original Power, this is in Sanskrit *Ichchashakti,* "the power of will." According to Subba Row, "It's most ordinary manifestation is the generation of certain nerve currents which set in motion such muscles as are required for the accomplishment of the desired object."

"Ich-cha" is literally the energy of self *(Ich).* It is the conscious, deliberate will of the "I" in contradistinction to the mostly unconscious bio-cosmic or spiritual impulse which compels the would-be child to emerge out of the womb, or any new beginning to occur out of the closing of a cycle. Aries is essentially life-expression, or God-expression (through new Ideas or creative Impulses), while Leo is self-expression. Thus the symbol for Leo 1° reveals the result of the will-full and determined

concentration of the individual upon reaching the level of the creative mind.

The symbol for Virgo 1° complements this picture by stressing the idealized features of a man in a portrait drawn by means of the artist's skill. Human evolution requires not only the exercise of the power of self-expression (Leo), but of the power of *selective* self-expression (Virgo). It requires, once more, a "standard." But while the Cancer symbol spoke of a "flag" raised on a ship—a *social* declaration of allegiance and purpose (of "nationality")—the Virgo symbol depicts an artist's "portrait"—thus an idealized expression born of creative vision and of an *individualized* piercing through appearances. Virgo deals with the establishment of a conscious and individual *standard of values*—thus with the discriminatory faculty. Self-expression (Leo) must always be united with discrimination (Virgo) if the individual is to fulfill the basic meaning of Man.

4. With the zyzygy of LIBRA and Scorpio we reach a period of reorientation. This literally means to find a new Orient, a new East, a new Source of Power; the rising Sun in the east always symbolizes the source of power and vitality. This new power is the power generated by permanent patterns of interpersonal sociocultural relationships. But as I have already stated, in order to be of permament value and to carry a more-than-personal meaning, any communal enterprise must be the "incorporation" of an archetype, i.e. of an idea and ideal that is part of the evolutionary structure and purpose of the cycle in which it takes form. Thus the basic need is to *visualize* the archetype. There are many ways this process of visualization can take place—for instance, the semi-unconscious and inspirational way of the great creative artist, or the more consciously directed way of some occult meditations. (This refers to the Libra 1° symbol of the butterfly.)

The Sanskrit term for this power is *Kriyashakti:* "The mysterious power of thought which enables it to produce external, perceptible, phenomenal results by its own inherent energy."

And Subba Row adds: "The ancients held that any idea will manifest itself *externally* if one's attention is deeply concentrated upon it . . . A yogi generally performs his wonders by means of *Ichchashakti* and *Kriyashakti.*" And this is also what New Thought practitioners claim to be able to achieve.

The effective visualization of an archetype (Libra) requires not only concentrated attention, but a deep *feeling-urge.* This is where the Scorpio phase of the process comes in. The symbol for Scorpio 1° may not at first glance seem adequate, but in a deeper sense it is significant. The new step must be *experienced* in the depth of one's being, physically and emotionally. One may think of the ideal of "civilization" in all its complexity of interpersonal relations, or at a higher level of the ideal of the true occult Brotherhood and the "White Lodge," but one *has to be there* in some deeply personal experience—perhaps a very vivid, unforgettable dream—if the ideal is to become an irrefutable reality for the consciousness and a steady, indestructible commitment.

5. SAGITTARIUS, with its operative polarity, Capricorn, reveals to us the need to achieve a stable and organic coordination of all the elements of the personality, starting with the most basic. In order to build an at least relatively permanent whole, the interactions between all the interdependent parts of this whole—whether they are cells and nerve centers in a human body, or individuals in a national State—must operate on a harmonious and steady basis. The symbol for Sagittarius 1° *(a gathering of Army veterans)* may not seem adequate, but again if we look at what is implied in it we can see how it refers to the results of a strongly "coordinated" relationship between social units—a coordination which in most cases acquired its crucial experiential strength in a stark struggle for survival.

This symbol is confirmed by the Capricorn 1° symbol, for coordination has to lead to a centralization of power through some form of leadership. The occult power related to this period is the much talked about and not too often understood *Kundalinishakti.* Subba Row speaks of it as

[The] power or force which moves in a serpentine or curved path. It is the universal life-principle which everywhere manifests itself in nature. This force includes in itself the two great forces of attraction and repulsion. Electricity and magnetism are but manifestations of it. This is the power or force which brings about the continuous adjustment of internal relations to external relations which is the essence of life according to Herbert Spencer, and that continuous adjustment of *external relations to internal relations* which is the basis of the reincarnation of souls according to the doctrine of the ancient Hindu philosophers.*

At the social level we can see how this definition of *Kundalinishakti* has a significant reference to the army of a nation, for the power of an army is the basis on which a nation relates effectively to other nations in terms of power, at least at the present stage of human evolution. Sagittarius refers to an innate yearning for expansion through an ever-wider "living space." It is a "Jupiterian" sign related to the lumbar region of the spine and the muscles and nerves controlling the pelvis and the legs. However, Saturn "rules" over the very root of the spine and the pelvic bones, and Capricorn over the knees, on which the function of the legs depends. Thus the two signs, Sagittarius and Capricorn, and their planetary rulers are involved.

In Yoga, *Kundalini* is referred to as a force coiled at the base of the spine within the Root chakra (center) named *Muladhara* and controlled by Saturn. This means that "the *universal* life-principle" (Subba Row), after having expressed a *particular* aspect of itself in a human body, exists in this chakra still in its universal nature, but "asleep." When it is fully reawakened it is said to rise along the central channel of the spine *(sushumna)*, drawing to itself the vital energies of every cell and organ of the body, which then appears to be lifeless. The rising of life currents to the head center *(Ajna)* polarizes the descent of a spiritual Force; Shiva unites with Shakti and the individualized consciousness is said to become universalized, at least to some degree. This "divine marriage" within the head releases a mys-

Op.cit., p. 7, footnote.

terious "ambrosia" which in flowing down through the cerebrospinal fluid is said to regenerate the whole organism.

6. We finally reach AQUARIUS. In a more mundane sense, the "ambrosia" can be related to the cultural products that are created during the great period of a society whose collective rhythms of existence and ideals have become stabilized, and that give concrete expression to the archetypes of that society. Works of art and literature immortalize the culture which produced them, thus establishing its meaning and function within "the Universal Community of Man." A society experiences its "coming to seed."

The symbol for Aquarius 1° *(a California mission)* needs no further explanation. We can easily visualize in it the seed of a society and a religion sown in a new land, perpetuating itself and its ideals. The symbol for Pisces 1° brings the process of coming to seed or harvesting to the level of vivid and vitalizing socioeconomic interchange. "A "public market" is a place for the exchange of "seed values," whether actual produce or money.

The power related to this phase of activity is *Matrikashakti.* In the words of Subba Row, this means "literally the force or power of letters or speech, or music. The whole of the ancient Mantra Shastra has this force or power in all its manifestations for its subject matter. The power of the Word which Jesus Christ speaks of is a manifestation of this *shakti.* The influence of music is one of its ordinary manifestations. The power of the mirific ineffable Name is the crown of this Shakti."

The Word-in-the-beginning (Gospel of St. John) is the germinating seed—a seed which was the product of the previous cosmic cycle and which is sown in a new field of Space, creating the *matrix* for a new universe (thus *Matrika-shakti*). A creative word or tone, a mantra, produces, as it were, a new field of Space in which a new spiritual Impulse can have its germinal beginning. At the sociocultural level, this power of the creative word refers to the symbol-releasing utterances and acts of "seed-men" in whom a cycle reaches its own omega state.

THE COMPLEMENTARY CHARACTER OF OPPOSITE SIGNS AND
degrees of the zodiac which I spoke of early in this chapter—
the second form of a binary relationships—has been stressed by
Marc Jones in his book, *The Sabian Symbols in Astrology*. Jones
states that "the degrees which lie face to face across the circle
will be found to complement each other in a fashion that is
mutually illuminating, and this fact has been of the greatest
assistance in working out the detailed symbolism." Personally I
find it difficult to recognize the validity of a great many of the
very abstract correlations worked out by this eminent pioneer
in the reformulation of astrology. This no doubt comes from the
fact that he and I approach symbols and the problem of interpretation from very different points of departure and with different types of mind. As he himself wrote: "There are unlimited
ways in which these Sabian symbols can be interpreted; and the
practiced student or professional astrologer need not confine
himself to any one mode of approach."*

My approach is not only holistic, but mostly in terms of the
potentiality of concrete experience. The zodiac, with its signs
and symbols, is a symbolic expression of a cyclic sequence of
archetypal types of experiences. It is existentially lived at all
times by human persons who have feelings, doubts, social problems, aspirations, and yearnings for transcendence. The symbols
themselves deal with very concrete scenes, usually everyday
experiences of Americans. I have attempted to extract from *all*
the elements of these scenes or images their vital significance
in terms of the transformation of seemingly haphazard events
into significant and purposeful phases of a process. We live this
process constantly, in small cycles or in larger ones. But it is a
whole process. It has direction. Real time is one-directional, and
I see it as purposeful. A great occultist and a healer with a most
compassionate heart, Dr. D. J. Bussell, once said that "Time is
the working out of God's Plan." Symbols are units of cyclic time.
They flow in an experience of duration toward a conclusion,

The Sabian Symbols in Astrology, p. 37.

which is also the seed of a new beginning. It is the living that is significant, and the direction in which this living is moving.

For these reasons, in relating Aries to Libra, for example, I seek to evoke the dynamic meaning that Libra should have to the "woman just risen from the sea"—the meaning of a goal establishing a direction. When using the term "goal," I do not mean what it might suggest to the life-insurance salesman or to the man ambitious to become his company's executive—i.e. not a rigidly set and particular, therefore limiting, achievement. I mean the fulfilling consummation of a central life ideal, which essentially implies the actualization of one's individual potential of being, *of what one has been born for.*

If one assumes such an attitude when interpreting the relationship between opposite zodiacal symbols, the interpretation takes on a teleological (i.e. purposive) character. We ask the symbol what the matter we are investigating is for. This immediately brings to mind a further question: What will it lead to? Thus the meaning of what occurs in the Aries 1° symbol becomes elucidated by considering the symbol for Libra 1°. Libra is already potentially present in Aries 1°—and as we saw at the beginning of this chapter, Pisces 30°, the end of the cycle, is potentially present in Aries 1°.

But two more basic questions are bound to arise: How can one best reach that end? and What is the essential meaning of the whole process? In other words, we are dealing with four fundamental issues the very moment a process begins; these can be most simply expressed by four little words: what, whereto, how and why.

It is on this basis that I understand the term complementary. It is not only a matter of two polar opposites, but rather of four elements of significance. This four-foldness brings us to the concept of the *mandala,* which has recently become quite popular. Indeed the usual mandala is the hieroglyphic expression of the four-fold character of the life cycles. It is clear that an astrological birth chart is a mandala—the mandala of the incarnation of a particular individual revealing the archetypal character of the human potential having emerged from the womb at a particular moment and in a particular place, and for a particular purpose.

The primary structure of a birth chart is defined by two axes perpendicular to each other, the horizon and the meridian. Here also we have a duality. I have spoken of it as the duality of consciousness and power.* Each of the two factors has two essential aspects. Thus we have the four Angles of the chart. The entire zodiac of 360 degrees is also a mandala whose four "Angles" (or critical phases) are the equinoxes and the solstices. By using this concept of four-foldness we can establish significant interconnections between Sabian symbols. This will prove particularly fruitful when, in Part Four, we will deal with the practical application of the symbols.

*Cf. my most recent book *The Astrological Houses: The Spectrum of Individual Experience* (Doubleday, 1972).

2. The Cross and the Star

THE CROSS FORMED BY THE HORIZON AND THE MERIDIAN—
the axes of consciousness and power—has given rise to varied
interpretations at several levels of meaning. When we are dealing with the Sabian symbols and their interpretation in terms
of cyclic process, we have to give a somewhat special but highly
significant meaning to the two ends of the axis of consciousness.
Consciousness results from activity, even if we have to realize
that the character of this activity, in its creative aspect, depends
upon a prior, but transcendent aspect of consciousness. Symbolically speaking, the process of germination that is the starting
point of activity in the vegetable kingdom brings out what is
latent in the seed. Every action can be said to come out of some
kind of seed; at the highest metaphysical level the universal
seed is Space.*

Universal space has often been symbolized by an ocean, an

*During periods of existential cosmic "manifestation," Space is extended
in many dimensions because there are a great many levels of cosmic activity.
But in terms of "non-manifestation," Space can be said to have withdrawn
inward in the dimensionless mathematical point.

infinite ocean of potentiality. In the Sabian set of symbols, the emergence of activity—and therefore of consciousness, as consciousness is implied in this activity—is represented by the Aries 1° symbol, because Aries 1° represents the beginning of a cycle of activity. A new *form of existence* is emerging, surrounded by the karma of the past *(the seal embracing the woman)*. In the subsequent symbols we see this activity gaining objectivity (2°), gaining a deep intuition of its wholeness (3°), achieving a feeling for the polarized energies on which it depends in order to operate (4°), and revealing a latent capacity to transcend its nature (5°, *the triangle with wings*). This emergence leads to a condition in which the creative impulse, after having passed through many maturing experiences, finds itself *essentialized* in the full revelation of the archetypal Seed-form that had called it into being for a particular purpose.

This archetypal form is symbolized by the perfect "butterfly" of the Libra 1° symbol. The form is perfect. The conscious mind, on the basis of the revelation of the archetype, is able to participate in a group as an equal among equals, *because* it has had the "vision" of its inherent archetypal perfection. For the American Indian, to have a vision of one's archetype (or totem) is an essential phase of the process at the end of which a boy is able to assume the responsibilities of manhood. As one medicine man stated: "A man who has not had his Vision does not know what his place in the world is. How can he live, then?" In the zodiac, Libra has little to do with "balance"—a most superficial interpretation of the symbol of the Scales—but it refers to the realization of one's *value* in terms of one's place and function in a larger community. Whether the community is small or large, it represents a "greater Whole" within which the conscious person can and indeed must operate. In Libra an individual learns the basis on which such an operation can significantly proceed.

Interpreted in this way, the relationship between the symbols for Aries 1° and Libra 1° can theoretically be applied to that between any two opposite symbols or phases of the cyclic process. In many instances, however, it is not easy to establish the meaning of such a relationship on this primary basis. The situation is usually elucidated by introducing the second axial relationship; that is, by studying the two symbols which are in square aspect with those being considered. In the cycle of the year the solstitial degrees, Cancer 1° and Capricorn 1°, are in cross-relationship to the equinoctial degrees, Aries 1° and Libra 1°.

The equinoctial phases of the year cycle represent the principle of *consciousness* because the two interacting energies (Yang-Yin, or Day-force and Night-force) being of equal strength, the *power* principle is neutralized. At the solstices of summer and winter one force, being *almost* totally dominant, normally makes a great show of power. The two primary types of power are (1) the power to be effectively what one is as a particular form of existence, and (2) the power to use what one is within a "greater whole" in which one is called upon to function. Thus, Cancer 1° *(sailors raising a new flag)* stabilizes with fully available Yang power and determination the form of life and consciousness that emerged at Aries 1°. On the other hand, Capricorn 1° pictures an "Indian chief" able to use *social* processes to make concrete and acceptable to his community the vision he had of his essential being. At this Capricorn stage we see public and official power in action.

The four-fold sequence linking the equinoctial and solstitial symbols is clear, and it stands as the prototype* of all similar quaternary or cruciform relationships between the 360 phases of the cyclic process and their symbols. The first degree symbols of the four "fixed" signs can be interpreted as follows: The "clear mountain stream" of Taurus 1° refers to the initial phase of the planetary cycle of water, seen from the level of life in the biosphere which depends on available water. When the mountain stream becomes the large river, men can build cities on its banks; today the rapid descent of the water to the plains can be used to produce electrical power. In the same way human beings are able to "dam" their life energies and transmute them

*A "prototype" is the first and basic concrete manifestation of an archetype. One might say it is a projection of the archetypal idea into earth substance as an "Exemplar."

into mind-power. That power is focused in the head (cf. the symbol for Leo 1°). The Scorpio 1° symbol shows people who perhaps have lived close to the land they have cultivated becoming fascinated by the big city. Clear at its source, life has become the ever-flowing interaction of men participating in the daily rhythm of city living, with its poisons as well as its cultural achievements. The stabilized and relatively permanent power of culture is then evoked by the symbol for Aquarius 1° *(a California mission).*

The four "mutable" signs of the zodiac can be seen related in a still more significant manner by the symbols for their first degrees, which strike the keynote of their respective periods in the cycle. Gemini 1° *(A glass-bottomed boat reveals undersea wonders.)* shows the nascent individual consciousness expanding through contact with the vast amount of knowledge gathered by mankind and now inherent in the collective Unconscious as well as embodied in millions of books. The symbol for Virgo 1° *(a portrait)* reveals, on the one hand, how mental activity leaves its mark upon and individualizes a face, and on the other, the creative power of a mind trained to discern and reproduce the salient characteristics of any living being or situation.

The contact with the accumulation of collective values which constitute the substratum of a culture (Gemini 1°) leads to the type of activity which in our world of conflicts is necessary to preserve and expand a "culture-whole"—a way of life and its great Images, a way implied in Sagittarius 1°. Lastly, society, which has been sustained by those who have risked their lives in upholding its standards, expresses its health and vitality through the complex rituals of the marketplace (Pisces 1°).

IF WE DIVIDE THE CIRCLE OF WHOLENESS GEOMETRICALLY by 4, we obtain the square, a figure whose symbolic meaning is stability, solidity and resistance to change. At the social level it is the bourgeois, the "square." Number 4 refers basically to the material world. In the universally emphasized seven-year cycle, the fourth year represents the bottom of the cycle. The first three years refer to the descent of spirit into matter (or of the Idea into concrete form) and the last three to the gradual evolution and refinement of the form and the spiritualization or dematerialization of the consciousness which at the beginning of the fourth year had become identified with the form and the energies of matter. The fourth year is therefore the turning point of the seven-year cycle. The consciousness now imbedded in a material form can either descend deeper into matter and lose altogether the spiritual momentum of the initial cyclic impulse, or it may progressively free itself from the pull of material energies and ascend to the "omega state" of *conscious and individualized* spiritual fulfillment.

Occult traditions everywhere refer to the present stage in the large cycle of our planet's existence and of mankind-as-a-whole as the fourth stage. It is the "fourth world," or according to theosophy, the "fourth Round." Numerologically speaking, the Vibration 4 dominates the collective consciousness of everything belonging strictly to the Earth's biosphere, the realm of life (using the term life in its strictest sense as the power that draws together, organizes, sustains and multiplies a collection of material units). From the point of view of the ascending process of development and the eventual spiritualization of human consciousness, the "Great Work"—to use an alchemical term—is *the raising of the Vibration 4 to the level of the 5.*

In its broadest sense this "raising" process is what is really meant by "civilization"—that is, civilization as a process of transformation of unconscious biological drives into the conscious and individualized structures of a mind pervaded by the "Light" of the spirit (the "Supermind," in Sri Aurobindo's terminology). When fully in control of a mind organized into a self-perpetuating system (a superphysical and superbiological organism), this spiritual *Light* takes the place that *Life* and its energies had occupied at the level of the biosphere, i.e. within physical bodies.

Such a Light has substance and power; it pervades the subtle and more spiritualized realm of mind-activity (Sri Aurobindo's "overmind"). The Light is esoterically symbolized by the Number 6, while Mind, as a form of activity which *can, yet need not*, become independent of biological impulses, answers to the Vibration 5. At the present stage of the evolution of mankind as a life-species, the Vibration 4 is dominant; yet the Vibration 5 of mental activity has been strongly developing for some 2500 years (since about 600 B.C.). Unfortunately, at this first stage of its development as a potentially autonomous mode of operation, the mind remains closely attached to, and influenced or controlled by, the biological needs and emotional drives of the body. It acts as what has been called the "lower mind," placing itself at the service of biological imperatives which, translated into psychic states (hunger, sex, aggressiveness, possessiveness, will to power, ambition, etc.), permeate most mental activities. The result is our present Western civilization with its monstrous cities, its holocausts and its ever-increasing perversions and psychoses.

Trying to separate himself from these bio-psychic emotional drives, Western man has glorified and overemphasized what he calls "Reason" and the intellectual and analytical power of the mind. He has idealized objectivity, at least in theory. But by trying to emphasize the mind *alone* no "vital" or "spiritual" results can be obtained that stand the test of time or avoid becoming the tool of forces operating in terms of material entropy.

The five-pointed star is the symbol of Mind as a mode of universal activity. The star can either point upward or downward. It is the symbol of Man; and a man can evolve his consciousness in the direction of Light (i.e. Spirit), or follow the path of "devolution" and be drawn eventually to the realm of unconscious absorption in undifferentiated matter, the "humus" which will feed the growth of seeds in a future cycle.

Symbolically stated, the issue is whether the emergent Number 5 will remain attached to the vibration (Number 4) of the biosphere and of generic mankind, or will become not only sensitive to, but eventually an operative agent for, the universal Love and Light represented by Number 6. This is the crucial issue. It is a cosmic issue which, one may assume, is to be met on every planet in which Man exists in one form or another as the focal point for Mind. The five-pointed star symbolizes this issue; it points to the character of the forces operating at the mental level. I must stress that the activity of Mind includes far more than what we today call "intellect"; neither should it be equated with intelligence per se—that is to say, the faculty inherent in *all* living organisms, but in a much more evolved form in human beings, which allows them to adapt to, make the best of, and eventually control the environment, whether natural or sociocultural.

Number 5 is a very special number, even from the point of view of arithmetic, a fact which has been discussed by several scientists. It is of particular interest to the biologist because five-fold structures appear in nature—at least on our planet—only when living forms have evolved. It is not found in crystals but it is featured in the growth of many plants, the disposition of leaves and the shape of flowers. Human anatomy also particularly displays this pentarhythmic type of structuring. It is as if the most advanced forms of life in nature were being prepared to become the foundations upon which the activity of mind could be developed.

We certainly cannot understand, and much less experience, what pentarhythmic patterns in the vegetable kingdom may support in terms of consciousness, but plants are essentially working with light; their chlorophyll captures the energy of the sun's rays and thus produces food for the animal kingdom and for man. At last in a symbolic sense, the man whose mind has become attuned to a supernal form of the Universal Light is also capturing Light-energy to feed the consciousness of men operating almost exclusively at the level of Vibration 4. All great, inspired works of philosophy, religion, art and literature can be considered instances of a transcendent type of photosynthesis. They bring down the 6 into the 5 of the mass-mentality of any culture.

If we return now to the Sabian symbols we will find that those which, beginning with Aries 1°, are singled out through a pentarhythmic process (the dividing of the whole zodiacal circle into five) form a five-fold sequence which is remarkably significant. These five symbols for degrees 72° apart are as follows:

ARIES 1°: *A woman just risen from the sea. A seal is embracing her.*
GEMINI 13°: *A famous pianist giving a concert performance.*
LEO 25°: *A large camel is seen crossing a vast and forbidding desert.*
SCORPIO 7°: *Deep-sea divers.*
CAPRICORN 19°: *A five-year-old child carrying a bag filled with gro-ceries.*

In order to understand how they refer to the mental proc-esses in their essential nature we must "pierce through" the superficialities of the allegorical scenes and uncover the sym-bols' archetypal implications. We are dealing here with a cyclic process, and with five characteristic phases of it; we might also say we are dealing with a type of activity that implies five types of operation.

The first (Aries 1°) is the emergence from the unconscious and compulsive tides of the biosphere. There had been previous and in a sense preliminary evolutionary emergences which led to regressive developments (the seal), but now with the human species we see outlined before our vision the Star of Victory, the magic Pentacle of the human mind.

The second step or principle of operation brings to us the picture of a man who has been individualized to the extent that he can successfully perform a social role—that is, he is able to help human beings to *feel intensely*, even though they might be leading routine or uninspired lives. He can help them to vibrate at a new speed of emotional response, and perhaps to become more sensitive to a more spiritual type of inspiration.

The third step or principle refers to the quality of self-reliance and independence from an always hostile and spiritu-ally barren environment. This correlates with the most important aspect of the process of individualization of con-sciousness, a process requiring a mind able to demonstrate self-sufficiency and endurance under all adverse circumstances.

The fourth step can be most significantly understood by relating it to the first. What the mind emerged from and left behind has to be courageously faced in terms of consciousness. The individualized mind must dare to return to the realm of compulsive life-tides and instinctual biological urges, and to extract from it an individual meaning. Without this, the conscious individualized mind, which is ruled by the ego, must always lack deep, vital and powerful foundations. Mind should emerge from the compulsions of life, but once formed and self-reliant it must return to objectively face and assimilate the contents of the depths of the Unconscious.

The fifth stage is symbolized by an apparently trivial scene. We are confronted with *a five-year-old* child, who is proving herself and asserting her innate potential of being by performing an act of *service*, and by assuming a role ahead of the normal evolution of the mass of human beings. This is a very good symbol for the often-mentioned "Path of discipleship." The person who can tread this path successfully must have reached stage 5 of his development as an individual—i.e. he or she must have developed a self-reliant and courageous mind. This person has become truly an "apprentice." He learns how to perform the alchemical Great Work, which in a sense means the transformation of the raw materials of the biosphere into the assimilatable stuff of knowledge. From this assimilated knowledge will rise wisdom, which in turn will become the foundation for a new emergence at a higher level of consciousness.

We should note that the second symbol (Gemini 13°) and the fifth (Capricorn 19°) refer to what one might call social roles. The first of these means that once the individual mind has emerged from the collective mentality of its culture it has *to prove itself* by demonstrating its capacity to move and inspire others. It does this, however, in terms of the ego (as a "virtuoso," often dramatizing himself on a public stage). Moreover, the cultural material he uses (i.e. the compositions he performs) is not his own. The performance often implies or suggests an act of ego-glorification.

This is a necessary phase, but sooner or later it leads to a period of spiritual barrenness which is a test of both self-reliance and the determination to persist, using only whatever one possesses within oneself *(the camel crossing the desert)*. Another kind of test follows. Deep-sea diving originally demanded that the diver develop a masterful control of the breath; this degree symbol might be related to certain forms of yoga practice, or to the Tantric approach to the process of spiritualization of basic forms of human bondage, such as sex and hunger.

The fifth and last principle is that of utterly dedicated and efficient service—the service of one's spiritual family, group or guru. The ego-dramatics of the "virtuoso performance" are left behind. The ego has been cleansed by harsh trials and tempered by the fire and heat of the desert sun; it is now filled with the assimilated contents of the psychic and biospheric depths. It has begun to vibrate to the 5 (i.e. *a five-year-old child*). The individual may experience the Star of Victory within his heart.

It is popular today to speak of "creativity" and of having a creative mind. What this means is the capacity to give form to raw and undifferentiated materials or to transform what has already been given a particular shape or structure. It is this capacity that operates in terms of five different types of activity. Above, by relating the symbols of a five-pointed star pattern beginning with the first degree of Aries, I presented the basic *prototype* of all such processes—just as the relationship between the four cardinal points of the zodiac establishes a prototype theoretically applicable to all similar quaternary relationships between zodiacal degrees and their symbols. The Cross and the Star are geometric archetypes that can give a general meaning to all existential processes operating according to the Vibrations 4 and 5. Any degree of the zodiac can thus become the head of a Cross, or the upper point of a Star—and, I might add, of the Star's negative reversed form.

This concept can be applied to the interpretation of every basic astrological factor in a birth chart, and theoretically to any complex cyclic activity. In practice, however, such applications are often more confusing than revealing, for they demand the skill to interpret symbols in terms of their innermost essence of meaning. The Sabian symbols are certainly not totally adequate for some refined types of analysis. Nevertheless, there is a way in which the pentarhythmic pattern can be very significantly applied in interpreting these symbols, and I have made use of it in Part Two when dividing the symbols into seventy-two sections, each containing five degrees.

This procedure was originally used by Marc Jones, but I do

not believe he saw certain features common to all these five-degree sequences. Moreover, I cannot quite agree with his characterization of *physical, social* and *spiritual* for the succession of three five-degree sequences; the examples he gives on page 146 of *Sabian Symbols in Astrology* do not seem to me at all convincing. The characterizations I have used are: *actional, emotional-cultural* and *individual-mental.* The difference in terms is not essential. Besides it is not always easy to find convincing reasons why a symbol refers more to the actional than to the emotional-cultural or the individual-mental. Indeed, I have had some doubt as to the validity of establishing these three levels of activity, but in a great many instances the practice seems significant.

What, however, is very evident is the five-fold rhythm revealed in every one of the seventy-two sequences. Particularly significant are the contrast between the first and the second beat of the rhythm, and the character of the fourth beat. The third and fifth symbols are often more difficult to fit into a general category. Nevertheless, each of the five steps of the process can be made to correspond to a phase of development related to a fundamental principle operating in every sequence. Moreover, it should always be kept in mind that the whole set of symbols deals with the universal Principle of Transformation, and that in these seventy-two five-degree sequences we deal primarily with the operation of such a principle at the three levels of the human personality. The process is directional and teleological. It goes somewhere—or if negative it falls away from the dimly envisioned goal.

1. The symbol for the first degree of the five-fold sequence suggests an evolutionary purpose or the essential character of a new phase of activity. I will discuss here the sequence which begins with Cancer 16° (cf. p. 120) because it is one that is not easy to interpret. In Cancer 1° we saw the individual opting for a change of allegiance, which implied a new set of values. At the second half of the zodiacal sign such a decision requires implementation. "Decision" (seventh scene) requires the "Consolidation" (eighth scene) of the position taken. Fundamentally all reliable forms of consolidation are internal: the individual

himself must become stable and well integrated—thus the mandala symbol of Cancer 16°.

2. Then the "God-seed" within (the mandala of individual selfhood) germinates. Action follows meditation. The energy that was inwardly oriented in the first step is now directed outward. This is the Principle of Contrast. The second degree of all five-fold sequences presents in some way a contrast with the first. This is not, however, to say that it expresses the "antithesis" to a stated "thesis," as we find in the usual dialectical process, which contain three stages. We are here dealing with a different type of dialectic, which operates in five stages—a type which, according to Count von Durkheim, has a definite place in Zen Buddhism.*

3. The symbol for the third degree of the sequence refers to the need to "feed" any germinal activity. In a sense it means relating what has been started to its environment, or to some larger frame of reference. For instance, the Aries 3° symbol relates the emergent individual (Aries 1°) to a wider field which he visualizes in his own image—a micro- to macrocosm relationship, or the imaging of God in man's image. In another sense, it suggests a kind of reconciliation between the two contrasting phases that came before. The subjective factor is now becoming involved in the objective world, and this leads to specific results, which of course take different forms in every sequence. One could speak here of the Principle of Sustainment, which implies some sort of interaction between the new development and what can support it in the greater Whole of which it has become a part.

4. The fourth stage always defines or at least evokes a certain type of method, procedure or technique which can be used to make the process work effectively. In this sequence the symbol for Cancer 19° pictures *A priest performing a marriage ceremony*. Meditating on a mandala should reveal the possibility of

*I outlined the concept of a pentarhythmic type of process in terms of socio-political organization in a memorandum sent in 1926 to Colonel Wetherill, then president of the Philadelphia Art Alliance. While in Paris in 1962, I heard Durkheim give a splendid lecture on Zen, in which he mentioned "la dialectique à cinq temps."

integrating two polarized forces; in the mandala of the year (the zodiac), the Day-force and Night-force are constantly active, one waxing in strength as the other wanes. The consciousness seeking integration and the consolidation of its individualized character must be ready to perform a mystic marriage which will provide a field for the relatively permanent interpenetration of the polarized life energies. We see the beginning of such a process in the symbol for Aries 4°. In Taurus 4° the rainbow symbolizes a way of uniting the sky and the Earth. In the Cancer 4° symbol we find another way of dealing with the outcome of one's acts—the method of "rationalization." The Cancer 9° symbol presents a variation on the theme of union between the self and some other attractive element of experience (i.e. the desire to possess and assimilate knowledge). Cancer 14° introduces a more transcendent approach: the consciousness seeks, beyond the relativity of ever-elusive truths, the absoluteness of a wisdom that has forgotten what it knew, as it faces the ever-hidden Source of all knowing.

What is at work at this fourth stage of the five-fold sequence is the Principle of Effective Self-expression—but here "self" can mean any form of integration, from the most possessive ego to the universal Self. In many instances a technique is suggested that will enable the mind to deal constructively with the new issues implied in the first stage.

5. Theoretically this phase brings to a new dimension, potency or level of consciousness the developments related to the four preceding stages. It usually suggests the workings of a Principle of Transformation, and here we witness the prelude to a new cycle or level of activity. In the symbol for Cancer 20°, *the serenading gondoliers* represent the ritualization of a social process of integration of two human polarities. The pattern of a particular culture—and Venice, built on the sea, is quite significant—brings social solidity and effectiveness to the search for integrating action. We shall see the same type of symbol, but more socialized and ritualized, as we reach the "emotional-cultural" level (Cancer 21°)—the *operatic prima donna*. In some instances, transformation requires the exaggeration of certain

traits, which by compensation leads to a new level of experience.

EVERY FIVE-FOLD SEQUENCE OF DEGREE SYMBOLS COULD BE analyzed in a similar manner. Some of them, like the sequences for the sign Pisces, outline a clear and at times dramatic story; others require a more penetrating interpretation. It should be evident that when a symbol is interpreted in terms of the place it occupies in several types of relationships with other symbols, each type will demand a slight change of emphasis in the interpretation. This should not affect the fundamental meaning of the symbol.

3. The Four Elements in Zodiacal Symbolism

◉

ONE OF THE FIRST THINGS A STUDENT OF ASTROLOGY LEARNS is that each sign of the zodiac is related to one of the four Elements: Fire, Water, Air and Earth. I have already spoken briefly of these, referring them to the four cardinal or "critical" moments of the year cycle: spring equinox (Aries 1°), summer solstice (Cancer 1°), fall equinox (Libra 1°) and winter solstice (Capricorn 1°).

When we speak of "Elements" we tend to think of material substances, or at least states of matter—solid, liquid, airy and fiery—and thus of different ways in which various types of particles are related to each other and in which they affect our senses—the solidity of a rock, the liquidity of water, the ubiquity and elusiveness and invisibility of the atmosphere, the dynamism and ever-changing aspect of flames. In a deeper sense these four Elements constitute different modes of operation of the One Power which, for us inhabitants of the solar system, has its primary source in the Sun. This One Power becomes bipolar the moment it is activated. Its two polarities (Day-force and Night-force, or Yang and Yin) constantly interact, alternatively waxing in strength and waning. Thus four phases in the cyclic activity of the One Power, the equinoxes and the solstices, stand out as moments of special significance. The One Power differentiates itself into four "cardinal" types of energies. Each type of energy has its own characteristic rhythm, and as any steady rhythm develops a form which appears to our senses as "matter," we can speak of four basic states of matter.

We should think of the Elements as modalities of power when we refer them to the zodiac because the zodiac symbolizes the cyclically changing relationship of the Earth to the Sun. Each Element is thus to be conceived of *primarily* as a mode of power release (that is, a certain type of energy), and only secondarily as a state of matter. The Chinese astrologer gives different names to the Elements, relating them to different kinds of substances, but they too refer to modalities of power. In my early book, *The Astrology of Personality*, I spoke of Fire-power, Water-power, Air-power and Earth-power,* and I added that three basic operations dealing with the manifestation and use of power should be considered: the generation, the concentration and the distribution of power.

Power is *generated* in "cardinal" signs of the zodiac (Aries, Cancer, Libra, Capricorn). It is *concentrated* in "fixed" signs (Taurus, Leo, Scorpio, Aquarius) and *distributed* in "mutable" signs (Gemini, Virgo, Sagittarius, Pisces). Thus each of the four Elements appears in the zodiacal cycle under three forms and a triangular or trinitarian relationship can be established between the three signs that express the three aspects of the same Element. Such a relationship constitutes the astrological "aspect" called *trine*.

The trine is considered the most "benefic" or "fortunate" type of relationship just because it brings out the full manifestation of one of the four modalities of power. It is thus an aspect of completion. Symbolically speaking, repeating an action three times finalizes it. All mythologies and occult traditions agree on this point, which is the basis of the divine trinities found in most cultures. If three planets form what is called a "grand trine"

*See original edition, p. 261.

they activate an Element in three different ways: the activation is total, and the character of the planets indicates the three paths along which the process of activation should (or will naturally tend to) proceed.

To call a trine "good" has meaning only in terms of what to us, normally and in most circumstances, is estimated to be favorable and productive of happiness or comfort. It is thus a matter of ethical or value judgment. The real fact is simply that the Element animated by this trine relationship between two or more planets is being stressed—it can be for better or for worse depending on the circumstances. There are many circumstances in which a combination of several modalities of power is required for effective action.

THEORETICALLY, THE SYMBOLS OF THE DEGREES OR CYCLIC phases that are in trine relationship (i.e. 120 degrees distant) should tell a consistent symbolical story. In actual practice, this presents difficulties. It is evident that if the same symbol has to be interpreted in relation to a two-fold, three-fold, four-fold, five-fold and six-fold relationship with other symbols, one has to extract from all these scenes or images a very general and abstract kind of significance. Nevertheless, the attempt is often very revealing, and it is an excellent exercise in the training of the interpretative faculty, i.e. the capacity to see *through* ordinary facts and to reach their essential meaning. This is "clair-thinking," if not clairvoyance.

Let us consider each sign's first degree and its symbol. The usual role of the first-degree symbol is as prototype of the entire sign's characteristics.

FIRE SIGNS: These signs deal with the three aspects of the basic power released at the start of all cyclocosmic processes—that is, the power to induce a structured series of transformations. Occult tradition in India speaks of three fires: electric fire, solar fire and fire by friction. These correspond respectively to Aries, Leo and Sagittarius.

Electricity in its multiplicity of aspects is primary, and seems to be found wherever there is motion and the beginning of new life. Broadly interpreted, the symbol of Aries 1° refers to the emergence of new potentialities of existence. This emergence takes place at the level of biogenesis, i.e. under the compulsion of "Life." All living processes require electrical energy.

Solar power is related to the solar sign Leo. What had emerged biologically and instinctually in Aries, driven by the desire-to-be, is now ready for a "second birth": birth in individuality. This implies a transmutation of life energies into mental processes which at first express the ego's will-to-power. Leo *personalizes* the pure, unconditioned desire-to-be of Aries fire. It stresses the "I am" and the ego-will. Suns are great autocrats of the universe—glorious and radiant in the assertion of a new type of power, but also essentially ambitious and desirous to show this power, *their own,* to all their planets. Sunlight is an individualized form of galactic energy. The symbol for Leo 1° lets us witness the rushing of the blood to the head, a throne for the ego and his intellectual processes of rationalization. Yet a Sun is also a star, one of billions within the immense galaxy, which symbolizes the spiritual realm.

Fire by friction is related to Sagittarius, for here we find at work the power that builds up, sustains and expands civilization, and that energizes all social processes. These processes are implied in the union of man and woman, once human beings develop a conscious sense of responsibility for their progeny— that is, the lasting realization that they are parents and educators whose primary task is to teach the child what they have inherited from the past, as well as to attempt to make for him a safer and happier future. As I have already stated, in our era, the root process of social survival and expansion is *warfare,* in the broadest sense of the term (which includes competition in all its forms). The symbol for Sagittarius 1° refers to the development of human fellowship and particularly of a comradeship based on the experience of total group-dedication to a social Cause.

WATER SIGNS: These deal with the power required to sustain, and to integrate through the stabilization of basic life rhythms, whatever has emerged as an organized system of activity. "Water"-power is the capacity *to feel and to respond as an organic whole.*

In the symbol for Cancer 1° we see "sailors lowering an old flag and raising a new one." The Day-force (Yang), which in Aries began to overpower the Night-force, here reaches its maximum strength. Cancer refers not only to the home, but also to the concretely established and stabilized person. In a deeper sense it suggests the realization by the microcosm—the person —that it is a cosmos, that it is analogous to the whole universe. Without the Water element there would be no circulatory processes and no feeling of wholeness; this feeling is at the very root of the ego-consciousness. What emerged rather passively and hesitantly in Aries 1° is now definitely "above the sea" (the ship) and able to display its own determination-to-be, its course of action and the direction it will follow.

The symbol for Scorpio 1° suggests that this second aspect of Water-energy now operates in the linking of the individual to a larger social whole, the modern city. This individual can feel and respond to a wider sphere of relationship. In a sense he is proclaiming his new allegiance to a wider and more dynamic state of group-consciousness.

The symbol for Pisces 1° *(a crowded marketplace)* reveals the individual's total and effective participation in an organized society and its complex rhythm of production and distribution. Thus from the personal realm of feeling-response to new possibilities (Cancer 1°) we have come to the sphere of all-absorbing social interchange (Pisces 1°), through the transition process evoked by the symbol for Scorpio 1° *(A crowded sightseeing bus on a city street.)*

AIR SIGNS: The Element Air refers to all pervasive and stimulating means of communication. It brings separate individuals together in group-activity. Indeed, the air that fills the lungs and cells of the most proud isolationist or racist inevitably links him, whether he is aware of it or not, with those he may refuse to befriend or the existence of whom he may not even acknowledge. In a few days the winds carry the same air all around the globe, as if to mock our national sovereignties and exclusivenesses. We all breathe it and throw the wastes of our bodies into it. It circulates as oxygen within the depths of all human beings, and without it there could be no life. It is a dynamic force—archetypally, an equinoctial Element, Libra—but unlike Fire, it does not transform. Instead, it gives human individuals a new spiritual-social dimension. In many languages the words which at first referred to "air" or "breath" later on lose their earlier meaning and take on the meaning of spirit *(pneuma, atma)*.

The sign Libra is popularly connected with the concept of "balance" because of the symbol of "the Scales" used to characterize the whole sign, but this is a very superficial interpretation; people in whose charts Libra plays an important role are no more psychologically balanced than any other human beings. At the fall equinox the Day-force and the Night-force are of equal strength, balancing each other but the same situation exists at the spring equinox in Aries. The difference is that Aries begins the hemicycle of "Individualization," while Libra begins that of "Collectivization." The first process depends on Fire-power, the second on Air-power.

The symbol for Libra 1° *(the impaled butterfly)* at first does not seem to fit the concepts associated with the Element Air, but we can give profound meaning to the relationship if we realize that an archetype is the *unity-aspect* of all the particular and diverse existential forms that can be referred to it. Thus the archetype Man relates all human beings to each other. Religiously speaking, the Element Air (which in its highest sense becomes the Holy Spirit) makes all men Brothers, and thus Sons of the archetypal Father. The perfect butterfly is the archetype Man. Every man can identify himself with it, not only when his spiritual metamorphosis is completed, but when he is totally willing to surrender all that he is as an individual to the perfecting (i.e. archetypalizing) of mankind-as-a-whole.

Every organized society has its own cultures based on a few archetypes or "prime Symbols" (Spengler). It is the archetype that, spiritually speaking, brings the group together at a time and in a locality where the vital *need* to which the archetype is a cosmic, superpersonal answer is a dominant feature of human existence—or we might say of the group's collective karma. In the second Air sign, Aquarius, we see the image of the archetype concretized and made relatively permanent in the collectivity. Thus the symbol for Aquarius 1°: *An old adobe mission in California*, or any ancient Temple or Medieval Cathedral that embodies not only a religious but a social and protective function.

The symbol for Gemini 1° pictures man operating at a relatively sophisticated cultural level and able to build "glass-bottomed boats" which allow him to come into contact with occult powers and transcendent forms of existence. Libra-Air *generates* collectively acceptable archetypal values. Aquarius-Air *concentrates* these values within cultural institutions. Gemini-Air *distributes* as knowledge what such institutions have produced.

EARTH SIGNS: Thanks to atomic physics we know that matter in the solid state is not really a mass of heavy materials, but mostly empty space within which atoms and their constituents whirl at terrific speed, separated by distances that are enormous in relation to the atom's incredibly small size. Powerful forces hold these swirling atomic and subatomic entities within definite patterns of organization. The strong cohesive links between billions of electrical particles present our senses with the feeling of solidity. At another level solidity becomes *solidarity*, the foundation upon which lasting socio-political and cultural institutions are built.

The physicist speaks of a "binding force" within the atom, or of gravitation. The psychologist, if his vision were penetrating enough, would see similar forces operating at the level of the psyche and leading to the formation of the ego—the stabilizer of what we call "character." Some egos are massive and resist splitting or disintegration; others can only loosely relate the different drives and conscious interests of the psyche and the mind, thus making possible personality splits or possession by elemental-astral forces.

The symbol for Capricorn 1° *(An Indian chief claims power from the assembled tribe.)* emphasizes the will to integration under a centralized control, i.e. the demand for a power that can hold the group together, especially in critical circumstances. The symbol for Taurus 1° *(a clear mountain stream)* refers to the descent of a power which will enable man and all living organisms to participate healthfully in an ecological whole, in which every participant has a more or less definite biological role. The symbol for Virgo 1° *(a portrait)* reveals the intellectual and creative capacity to extract from a biological and psychic type of integration (the face of a person who has become individualized within a particular culture) what is most characteristic and significant in the person, and thus most revealing. We see the Earth Element at work in the social (Capricorn), the biological (Taurus) and the individual-personal (Virgo) realms of activity.*

By relating the four Elements to the equinoctial and solsticial points we obtain holistic and *archetypal* sequences showing the relation of the Elements under three aspects within the whole zodiacal cycle. But the more ordinary way of interpreting the sequence of these Elements is to study it at the *existential* level—that is, as one sign follows another in time. Then Aries-Fire is followed by Taurus-Earth, Gemini-Air and Cancer-Water and the four-beat series of Fire, Earth, Air and Water repeats

*There is much rather negative talk in astrological circles today about people having no planet in signs related to one of the four Elements. Where a planet is located, there the person's attention normally will tend to, and *should*, be focused. But this does *not* mean that the qualities (or the mode of operation) symbolized by an Element, if not stressed by a planet, necessarily will be lacking in the person's nature. It may mean that these qualities need not be stressed, because they are innately well developed, or only of secondary importance in the present life cycle. They might have been too strongly relied upon in a past life, or they may be dominant in the family or culture within which the person is born. Other qualities now must be emphasized. In late life there may be a reversal, just as men in old age tend to become more feminine and women more masculine. Also, the type of activity represented by a nonemphasized Element may take place at a transcendent level. In popular practice, too much is made of the four Elements. The interrelationships of the planets, wherever they are located in the zodiac, and the positions in the Houses are far more important. (See my book, *The Astrological Houses: The Spectrum of Individual Experience.*) Astrology does *not* depend primarily on the signs of the zodiac, important and basic as the concept of the zodiac is as a symbol of *operative wholeness and cyclic activity.*

itself, beginning with Leo, and then later with Sagittarius.

From such a point of view the entire cycle is divided into three periods, each beginning with an "emergence." Each emergence takes place at a specific level of activity and consciousness: the bio-psychic level, the personal-individual ego level, the social-collective level. We see then the possibility for a human being to experience a birth in the body, a birth in individuality, a social (and in some instances, truly spiritual-occult) birth. These three periods, referring to the cycle of the year when the zodiac is considered, can be studied as well in the cycle of an archetypal human life, once man has reached the stage at which it is possible for him to become truly an "individual," independent of his racial-cultural matrices, and self-reliant. These are the three 28-year periods in a life span of 84 years —the cycle of Uranus. An individualized life is infused with the Uranian power of self-transformation, while man in the tribal state (which many human beings today have not yet transcended!) remains an example of racial-cultural pattern, a "specimen" only superficially characterized by personal reactions to a particular set of circumstances, and the archetypal life span for him is 70 years.*

From the existential point of view of succession in time, the element Fire is polarized by Earth, within the pairs (or zyzygies) discussed in the first chapter of this section. In the same way Air is polarized by Water. We are dealing thus with pairs of opposites and actually with a six-fold division of the cycle. We witness the differentiation of the One Power into the six great creative-transforming energies, or *shakti*. In Sanskrit this One Power is called *Daiviprakriti*, and in some other Hindu systems, *Vach*— the Voice of the Creative God. It corresponds broadly to the Holy Ghost of the Christian Trinity, in which the Son has the astrological Sun as his counterpart.

A seven-fold division of the circle of wholeness leads us to the "irrational," because dividing 7 into 360 does not produce a whole or rational number. *Geometrically*, and therefore ar-

*These three 28-year periods have been discussed in both my books, *The Astrology of Personality* (1936) and *The Astrological Houses* (1972).

chetypally, speaking, 7 refers to the fact that six circles completely surround a seventh circle—all circles being of the same size. *Existentially,* we constantly deal with cycles divided into seven periods (and four times 7 equals 28); but what the geometrical fact tells us (if we are ready to listen) is that "the seventh" occupies a special place in the existential sequence. It is the "seed" of the six-fold life development. This seed synthesizes the 6, and at the same time leads to a new cyclic process, hopefully at a higher level of growth.

The discussion of further divisions of the circle would lead to unnecessary complexities, though significant relationships could be established between the first and the sixteenth degree symbols of each sign, and the eight-fold division is no doubt a very significant one if we refer it to the actual release of power in electromagnetic fields (45-degree angle). It may also be that the 40-degree angle will receive more attention in the future. It refers to a nine-fold scheme, and the number 40 has great significance in occult symbolism.

What I sought mainly to show in this part of the book is the very remarkable manner in which the Sabian symbols can be related to one another according to several structural schemes, geometrical and sequential—schemes which have meaning in terms of number and the release of basic life energies. The structural interconnections of the Sabian symbols according to various modes of division of the whole cycle is, I believe, unique in the field of symbolism—especially considering the aleatory manner in which the symbols were obtained. It gives them a kind of validity which is until now unparalleled. This does not mean that a more perfect set of symbols cannot be produced, but it establishes a very important criterion of validity.

Part Four

THE ORACULAR
AND ASTROLOGICAL
USE OF THE SYMBOLS

Why Modern Individuals Seek Answers from "Oracles"

◉

A PERSON SEEKS ADVICE FROM A CLAIRVOYANT CONCERNING whom he or she has heard glowing reports; another person attends a spiritualist meeting in the hope of receiving a message which might solve an emotional problem or give a clue to a disturbing mystery; still another consults an astrologer or learns to erect and interpret horary charts; and thousands of young and not-so-young individuals throw Chinese coins or yarrow sticks to seek from the I Ching answers pointing to a way out of their difficulties or revealing what is the best way to face their anxieties and decide between alternative courses of action. All these people are eager and ready to consult one kind of "oracle" or another. They have problems they feel unable to solve rationally and intellectually on the basis of what they know, and their traditional religious leaders seem unable to provide them with satisfactory answers.

Why do these people not go to scientific experts—to psychologists or psychiatrists, to doctors, to college-trained and officially certified men and women who have studied many new techniques? Many do go to these specialists; but just as many do not believe that they can rely on the type of modern intellectual and empirical knowledge taught in our universities—a knowledge based on a multitude of data and completely lacking in an all-embracing philosophy of life. Moreover, because a great many persons today—especially if quite young—tend to look with disfavor upon any and all *personal* intermediaries between themselves and whatever they may call God, Life or the universe, they may not completely trust the many self-proclaimed spiritual Teachers whose personalities often reflect some of the unpleasant features of our competitive way of life. Neither do they completely trust themselves as they face the often-bewildering complexities of modern life.

What then can they do? Hardly any alternative is left except to learn how to use *impersonal* intermediaries. This means learning a "language" which transcends the analytical and rational level of knowledge at which our scientists operate. Scientific knowledge has brought an immense increase in comfort and in power. But in a great variety of circumstances, it cannot tell us which one, of many, is the most significant course of action; it cannot tell us what will make us more fully what we deeply, yet dimly, feel we are, but find ourselves unable to actually become.

There is a great difference between knowledge and understanding. We may know an immense number of facts and recipes, equations and formulas that enable us to perform acts which will have important results. But we may not understand the value of these results. Do we understand where modern technology is leading mankind? Can we understand, by the use of mere factual and rational knowledge, *why* we should choose between two or more courses of action, when the possible results of these actions obviously depend upon many unknown and *to us* unknowable factors?

Modern scientists may proudly feel that they have immensely reduced the number of such unknowns, and they seem to have done this spectacularly within certain well-defined fields. Yet our science-based civilization has produced new and more complex problems for every one it has solved. It has left the basic problem more acute and anxiety-producing than ever

—the problem of the meaning of human existence, and particularly the meaning and purpose of each individual person: the meaning and purpose of *my* life, or *your* life.

How can this meaning be discovered when, as is the case in all but a very few instances, it is neither clear nor unquestionably valid to the individual? How can we be sure that the alternative we choose is the one that will help us live more purposefully, more significantly? How can we be sure that the attitude we take in meeting a difficult situation involving an interpersonal relationship or a career opportunity is the most valid, the most fruitful one? How frustrating and anxiety-producing it is not to know!

For these reasons, men and women are consulting oracles today more than they ever have in the past (except perhaps during the slow decadence of the Greco-Roman society). And to consult an oracle means either to implicitly trust an intermediary, or to learn an oracular language—a language of symbols.

IN THE FIRST CHAPTER OF THIS BOOK I TRIED TO EXPLAIN what symbols are. I shall now attempt to restate in a somewhat different way what I said there, for not only does it bear repetition, but it can be stated in many ways.

Any language is a coherent, consistent and traditional set of symbols. What we ordinarily call "language" is made up of words. Religion, art and mathematics are also complex and systematized organizations of symbols. Astrology, when properly understood and freed from either superstition or the scientific approach of many recent researchers and statisticians, is also a language that uses symbols to communicate basic facts related to the organization of any living organism, and particularly of human individuals.

All languages communicate not only facts, but at least intimations of the meaning of these facts. These facts can refer to various levels of existence; their meanings may be related to several frames of reference, depending on the scope and quality of the consciousness seeking understanding and the solution of personal or social problems.

A very simple example may help to clarify the preceding statements. I see something moving across the street and I exclaim, "A dog!" I am using a symbol. This symbol—the word-sound "dog"—was created by my distant ancestors and has been used by billions of human beings to communicate to other human beings the knowledge they had acquired concerning billions of animals of a certain kind with which they had intimate dealings. As I say the word "dog," I tell my friend, who has not seen the dog, that a kind of animal is approaching from which we may expect a very general, but characteristic, kind of experience. The word "dog" *signifies* the possibility of such an experience.

If I say, "A mad dog!" this general possibility becomes limited to a smaller set of experiences with which the sense of danger and the emotion of fear are associated. As I add more words to the original—for instance, "A black police dog whose mouth is foaming!"—I limit the field of possibilities even more, and I define more precisely the knowledge I am imparting to my friend. The symbol becomes not merely a vague picture of a four-legged animal with very general dog-like characteristics, but a clear-cut *scene* with dramatic, actional implications, in which the main actor presents us with a definite challenge to act in a definite manner.

If my friend or I have been bitten by a dog before, and a serious illness resulted, the challenge becomes very vivid; it calls up memories of past experiences and stimulates glandular activity in our bodies, arousing direct emotions. But even if we have not had such a personal experience, the word-symbol will be sufficient to evoke for us a condensed form of the essential experiences of our ancestors. Thus the symbol will make us *feel;* it will also give us some knowledge of how best to *act.* We will meet the particular situation confronting us, not as surprising, isolated and unrelated to anything that has ever happened, but as something already experienced by countless men.

The situation, then, acquires a "meaning," one which is commonly accepted by millions of people who have gained knowledge from the experience. Because I can identify the experience with a symbol, and can give it a name, there is much less chance of my becoming overwhelmed by it. I know that there is an effective way to meet it, a traditional way. I am no longer facing the difficulty or danger alone. The strength of multitudes of men is behind me. What they done with it, I can do—and better. Because of them, I know more about the meaning and purpose of the event or challenge confronting me.

Symbols integrate the separate experiences of a vast number of men. They take events, from the realm of the fortuitous, the unprecedented and the incomprehensible, and put them into the realm of "universals." The logical sequence of symbols which one finds in all languages, in all scientific theories, in all traditional art forms and in all religious rituals makes the myriads of seemingly chaotic, unpredictable and senseless facts of life fall into patterns of order and meaning. A thousand events or personal situations come to be seen as mere variations on a central theme. The symbol depicts this one significant theme. And the theme is part of a coherent sequence of similar challenges, which acquire purpose through their relationship. Expressed through symbols, life becomes condensed into a relatively few, *inter-related* units of experience. Each unit is a concentrate of the experiences of millions of people.

While these symbols filled with meaning are the "seed-harvest" of the past experiences of a whole collectivity, they are also powerful in molding the feelings, thoughts and behavior of future generations. All children absorb these symbols, emotionally and mentally, throughout their formative years. From them the child learns to give definite meaning to whatever confronts him, and to feel "one with" all the people who accept these meanings as valid.

If instead of saying the words, "A mad dog approaching your house where your children are playing," I was able to project into the mind of my distant friend a picture showing the dog entering her garden and attacking her children, I would also be communicating the meaning of an approaching event. In this case the projection of the image would refer to a clear-cut concrete event that my friend could identify at once. But if such a literal and precise image could not be projected I might still perhaps send a danger signal, something that might suggest that the children were in danger and quick action was needed. The suggestion could take the form of a more general symbol that might require some knowledge of how to interpret it.

If a person feels himself faced with a confusing and potentially dangerous situation, he might attempt to gain a deeper understanding of *what is involved in it* by throwing Chinese coins. The I Ching hexagram he obtains might imply some danger and the best way to face it. This person is actually receiving a communication that increases his understanding and might save him serious trouble, just as in the preceding case the woman with children in danger received a communication from a friend or perhaps from a police officer warning people in a city block about a mad dog. Now, however, it is the I Ching that gives the warning. But what is the I Ching, or the Tarot cards, or the set of Sabian symbols? This is the puzzling question; and it so puzzles the mind trained in the intellectual and rational procedures of our classical Western mentality that it usually dismisses the whole matter as nonsensical. Yet oracles work! The problem is that they require interpretation. They also usually require certain procedures to ensure the validity of their answers, and above all they demand of the inquirer a certain *frame of mind*, an open attitude and even more a *real need* for an answer. *This need exists when the person seeking a communication from the oracle has already earnestly tried to find a way to meet his baffling problem and has been unable to come to any logical or rational solution, perhaps because so many unknowns were involved.*

In periods during which a particular society and its culture and religion flourished, the members of this society find in the traditional cultural structures basic answers that readily can be applied to most personal problems. A culture is founded upon archetypes or paradigms—that is, on great images and symbolically valid scenes of the life of greatly respected exemplars who constitute embodiments of values accepted by all the members of this particular society. There are men who, having been trained in the understanding of all that these values imply, are easily available for help and guidance. But today we are facing a world situation characterized by the near-breakdown of all traditions, and the great images of the past seem empty of meaning. Where can one find new images, or symbols which are valid beyond all cultural limitations—*"transcultural" symbols rooted in the common experience of all human beings?*

The search for such symbols inevitably leads to astrology, because astrology originated in the most basic, most primordial experience of mankind—the majestic pageant of the stars across the darkness of the night sky, and the experience of seasonal and biological rhythms so obviously synchronized with the cyclic motion of the Sun and the Moon. The dichotomy of celestial order and earth-surface chaos has been fundamental in all religions. The sky became the one great symbol of order and of the rhythmic unfoldment of biopsychological functions and activities. The sky was "the creative"; the earth, "the receptive"— *natura naturans* and *natura naturata*. The whole problem of the meaning of existence could be solved if there could be a way to interpret the ever-changing pictures made by the Creative on the background of celestial space.

Out of this need astrology was born. All great civilizations of the past used its symbols. An oracular language of symbols was gradually developed, in which planets and their interconnections became vowels and consonants, and charts were made which revealed meaning and purpose to those who had carefully learned the celestial language.

It is a complex language, and like all languages it can be used at different levels. Ordinary English can serve to make possible clear-cut and entirely factual business transactions— and now we have an even more concrete and bare form of it in computer language. But English words can also be used in poems to evoke complex feelings and spiritual insights. In the same way, dance music or military marches employ a language intended to move bodies and arouse biological emotions, while the great devotional music of old India and the music of Scriabin aimed at inducing mystical experiences.

Words can state facts, but in poetic combinations, they can also evoke images that act upon the deepest feeling and consciousness of the reader or listener. The astrology that deals simply with the planets (including the Sun and Moon) and the patterns they make in terms of this or that frame of reference (zodiacs, Houses) in most cases has been event-oriented— whether at the biological, social or psychological level. But there is also an astrology that attempts to go beyond, or through, concrete events, and to evoke a deeper, less particularized mode of consciousness. This more transcendent kind of consciousness deals with the *essence* of events and the *quality of being* which undertones the functional activity of the planets. It seeks to transcend the usual kind of astrology by dealing directly with the *phases of all cycles*—one might say, with "cyclicity" itself.

Somehow the old Chinese wise men realized this possibility and developed the mysterious, but extremely potent, patterns of the I Ching. The cyclic series of the 64 hexagrams no doubt developed against the background of the seasonal cycle of the year, but they transcend this frame of reference. They lead us to a world of archetypes, which subsumes or undertones seasonal changes and therefore can be applied, theoretically at least, to any cycle. Because of this they have universal validity —universal, yet referring essentially to the level of consciousness at which the Yin-Yang dualism controls every existential manifestation, and the unfoldment of cyclic activity can best be identified by a 64-fold rhythm.

As already stated in the first chapter of this book, it is logical to believe that our complex society with its involved patterns of interpersonal relationships calls for a greater number of archetypal phases. The archetypal sequence of 360 symbols is an attempt to meet this need—the number 360 refers cosmically to the *abstract* relationship between the period of rotation of the Earth around its axis and the period of its revolution around the Sun (cf. page 16).

The Sabian symbols, like the symbols of the I Ching, constitute a foundation for oracular pronouncements. But these symbols have to be adequately interpreted, and this *interpretation naturally has to vary with the level of consciousness of the interpreter.* Many commentaries have been written in the past about the I Ching; no doubt there already have been and there will continue to be many different interpretations of the Sabian symbols. I make no claim that the Sabian symbols are perfect or universally valid. The images and scenes they present are the products of a sensitive American mind operating shortly after World War I. But the symbols have a very real oracular potency —that is, they can communicate to the questioner valid answers to questions asked in great earnest about real personal or inter-personal *needs.*

Why they can do this will no doubt puzzle many people accustomed to find rational and "scientific" explanations for everything. Many will say that if valid answers are given by the oracle it is purely by chance. But what is "chance"? What kind of "scientific proof" could be produced in matters so personal and so susceptible of subjective interpretation, either by the inquirer himself or by some intermediary more skilled in the interpretation of the oracular language? Many Christians in moments of confusion or sorrow have turned to the Bible, opened it at random and with closed eyes have selected a line of the text which was interpreted by them as an answer to their inquiry or a solace to their grief. They established a communication with what they believed to be a divine source of wisdom, the very word of God.

But it seems obvious that, in any literal sense, "God" did not write the Bible, nor the Angel Gabriel, the Koran. At the time the Sabian symbols were visualized and recorded, some super-human or masterful intelligence may have been present, some-how inspiring (or *in-spiriting*) the process of formulation. But the actual images were obviously conditioned by the mind of the clairvoyant, and the wording of the brief statements by that of Marc Jones. Still, if on one hand we consider the aleatory and amazing speed of the process of formulation, and on the other the remarkable structural organization of the symbols when reduced to their essential meanings, we cannot avoid deducing that some transcendent intelligence must have been operating behind the scenes.

"God," too, operates behind the scenes of the universe and through the immensely varied complex, yet ordered and amaz-ingly organized and interdependent phenomena we observe and from which we forever learn. It has been said that the works of God prove His existence. This is a specious kind of proof. Nothing can be "proven" by the scientific mind except in the sense that a certain sequence of events is thoroughly consistent with some basic assumptions. No intellect can objectively prove the absolute validity of these assumptions or postulates. We cannot really *prove* the existence of God, and even less disprove it; we can only observe what the belief in God as a supreme Person with whom a dialogue can be pursued *does* psychologically to men and women who *need* the experience of contact with a divine Being. We can observe as well what the lack of such a belief can produce in many individuals who psychically require this kind of experience. The experiences are real to those who have them. Reality is that which satisfies the vital, essential need of a person or a collectivity. Any other definition of this much abused word results from the subjective illusion, and perhaps pride, of a mind which seeks self-glorification by asserting that its own values and concepts are "absolute"—i.e. true for all people at all times. But even such an assertion may meet the very real need of insecure minds, so it too is "reality"!

We may dismiss as "pure chance" the way the Chinese yarrow sticks fall, gradually determining the shape of the one I Ching hexagram that is relevant to the situation of the questioner. We can speak of "synchronicity," (a word that actually only adds to the mystery) or we can place the responsibility upon the "unconscious"—another word that is simply a modern and totally unclear substitute for the old concepts of a daemon within the soul, of the Higher Self or a guiding Angel. The simple fact is that when a person's need is real, some power or intelligence either within the person or intimately connected with him is able to use a language of symbols in order to communicate valuable information and directives for action. What this power and/or center of intelligence "is" can never be fully ascertained by our own conscious mind, simply because it must transcend the conscious mind if the oracle is to be at all effective in meeting the person's need. Perhaps it is simply *the polar aspect of this need,* as light polarizes shadow, and Yang polarizes Yin. The principle of universal Harmony requires that for every need there is a corresponding answer potentially neutralizing the need.*

I repeat that oracular communications may take a multitude of forms. They may be "dreams" remembered on awakening (a very special kind of dream), or words heard within the head, or "omens" one meets along the path to a goal. They may be Chinese hexagrams, or Sabian symbols, or Tarot cards if the person *has attuned himself to the reception of guidance through these specialized means.* The I Ching and the Sabian symbols are particularly significant as "specialized means" because, first, they constitute some guarantee against self-deceit and subjective giving in to biological or psychological complexes, and second, they reveal how the individual's problem relates to universal issues—or at least to issues that are significant to, and faced by, a vast number of people because they represent specific phases in the unfoldment of human consciousness at a particular level of evolution.

*Cf. "The Gifts of the Spirit" in my book, *Triptych*, pp. 19–20.

How to Use the Sabian Symbols as Oracles

THERE ARE MANY WAYS IN WHICH A PERSON SEEKING INFOR-
mation or guidance can discover the Sabian symbol that will
significantly meet his need. Perhaps the simplest method is to
use an ordinary deck of cards.

It will be apparent at once that the deck contains twelve
figure cards—that is, king, queen and jack in four suits. From
this it logically follows that the four kings can represent the four
cardinal signs of the astrological zodiac, the queens the fixed
signs, and the jacks the mutable signs. As I see it, *Hearts* stands
for the spring quarter, fountainhead of life-rhythms; *Diamonds*
for the summer quarter, the squaring of life, the "Diamond
Soul"; *Spades*, whose shape has a polar connection with the
Hearts, for the fall quarter, the darkening of the life force, and
the emergence of the the collective mind stressing the Night-
power; *Clubs* for the winter quarter, their three-fold shape
symbolizing the fulfillment of mind and all institutionalized
power.

All one need do to find the relevant degree of the sign is use
the number cards of three suits: *Hearts* can be used to corre-

spond to the numbers 1 through 10, *Diamonds* to refer to numbers 11 through 20, and *Clubs* to numbers 21 through 30.

The simplest procedure is first, to hold face down in one hand (normally the left hand) the twelve figure cards, and to select one of the cards at random with the other hand. This gives the relevant zodiacal sign. Then the same procedure is repeated with the pack containing the thirty number cards to give the degree numbers. The two packs, of course, should be thoroughly shuffled. If, for instance, the jack of clubs is taken out of the pack of twelve figure cards, and the seven of clubs is selected from the pack of number cards, the zodiacal symbol for the degree Pisces 27—or Phase 357 of the cycle—is the one to be read and interpreted.

Various procedures can be devised to help the inquirer to concentrate upon what he or she is doing. But simplicity makes involvement in ritualistic forms unnecessary. What is essential is: (1) that the problem should be clearly formulated in the inquirer's mind, and (2) that the intent of the inquiry should be sincere, and the gestures of card selection made in earnest. Any oracular procedure based on curiosity, or merely for fun, is doomed to failure—even though occasionally the intellectual curiosity may really hide a deep-seated need, and the oracular answer may prove startlingly revealing. A clear formulation of the problem is essential, for in this as in all kinds of problem-solving (including laboratory experiments in science), *the formulation conditions the answer one gets.* It has been said, "Ask and you shall receive," and we must be very careful of what we ask, for we must live with what is received. Moreover, we should never ask the same question repeatedly, even if the answer obtained seems irrelevant or a poor solution. In such cases the oracle often has very irritating ways of apparently mocking us or showing us our weakness.

There is another method, less concrete and very often less reliable, for obtaining a symbol which answers to a personal need for discovering the archetypal meaning of a complex or difficult situation. In a sense, this method is better suited to the mentality of individuals who are familiar with oracular procedures and have a deep faith in what can be called inner guidance. It may have definite drawbacks for people whose con-sciousness is not open to the validity of such practices, and it should therefore be used with care and common sense.

This method is simply to focus attention upon the problem whose meaning one seeks to understand better so as to be able to act wisely, while at the same time concentrating on whatever one feels to be the transcendent source of the desired guidance —whether it be God, one's higher Self, a more-than-human Being, or even "the unconscious." Then as the mind is kept still, one should ask that a number be revealed vividly to the con-sciousness. This number will be that of the phase of the cycle whose symbol constitutes the oracular answer to the clearly formulated question. If a number does not rise inside the mind almost at once, vividly and authoritatively, the issue should *never* be forced, and the card method of selection should be used.

Sometimes a number larger than 360 may come to mind. In such a case 360 should be subtracted from it until it is reduced to a figure below 360. But if this happens, the symbol most likely refers to a situation involving transcendent features which the questioner may not be ready as yet to understand, or to a trend which has not come yet to maturity.

IN ORDER TO CLARIFY ALL THIS, I SHALL MENTION ONE actual incident. Quite a few years ago, a man came to me be-cause he was unable to understand the meaning of a personal tragedy which was bringing confusing changes to his life. The testimony of the astrological charts which he knew well did not seem very clear-cut or convincing to him. There were many ways of interpreting Uranian transits and "difficult" progres-sions. The man kept asking, "But what does it mean? How am I to take it?"

After a while I asked him to be quiet for a moment, and with his mind at rest, to see if a number would intrude into his consciousness. He looked astonished, hesitated for a moment, closed his eyes, then suddenly said, "Yes, I quite definitely feel something in my head saying 342. What does it mean?"

I explained briefly the value and purpose of the Sabian

symbols, and we read the description of the symbol for Phase 342, or Pisces 12°. It is the second symbol in the five-degree sequence which begins with Pisces 11°. In this sequence, a person is making some sort of claim for a new spiritual-mental status.

If the reader refers to pages 274 through 278 he will find the symbols for this five-degree sequence, which begins with a picture of "Men traveling a narrow path, seeking illumination." The symbol for Phase 342 reads: *In the sanctuary of an occult Brotherhood, newly initiated members are being examined and their character tested.* This was the oracular pronouncement which reached my client's mind through the intermediary of the Sabian symbols. If he had been conversant with this symbolic language my presence as an interpreter would not have been necessary; yet the presence of an interpreter who has gained the special ability to see through and concretize the oracular statement can be of great value, just as a psychologist can be of immense importance to a person seeking to uncover all the implications of an evidently significant yet unusual dream.

The implication of the symbol referring to Phase 342 was that something had happened to this man which brought him in touch, at a deeper level of his being, with a totally new and demanding situation, probably involving a new type of relationship. He was being "tested" to reveal his reaction to this situation. Who or what it was that made the testing matters little. The words "sanctuary of an occult Brotherhood" need not be taken *literally*—as a general principle, no oracular statement or dream should be taken literally, even though in some instances it indeed may appear to apply in a most precise sense to a situation. The symbol nevertheless suggested that my client was entering a new phase of his *inner* development, though in some cases it could also refer to coming into new responsibilities at a strictly social or business level.

My client had asked what the meaning of a tragedy he had experienced was. The symbol answered by pointing out that the tragedy itself could be considered a test of character—a test made necessary because he had already taken a definite step in his individual development, even though he might not be aware of this in his everyday consciousness. He had been "seeking illumination" (Phase 341). He had "entered the Path," spiritually speaking. Now he was being tested—by life, God or "the Master"—to prove his worth, i.e. his "qualifications."

I repeat that the term "initiated" in the symbolic statement was not necessarily to be understood in a strictly occult sense. Initiation simply means entrance into a new field of activity, a field in which one is to act in the company of beings who have already mastered the requirements of that field, at least to some extent. A new kind of cooperation is therefore implied, and the group of which one has become a part demands a probationary period of testing. This is true at any level at which groups of men operate in an organized manner.

This was what the oracle told my client; if he were open to the "revelation" his entire approach to the tragedy he had experienced would be changed. Instead of feeling beaten down by an inscrutable fate and meaningless events, he would realize that these events indicated his having taken a major step in his life, a step necessary for further growth, as the grinding of the coarse material surrounding a diamond is necessary in order to allow the pure stone to reveal its beautiful translucency.

WHAT, WHERETO, HOW AND WHY

IN PART THREE I DISCUSSED THE STRUCTURAL RELATIONships between Sabian symbols that reveal how the entire set constitutes an organized and integral whole. In the chapter "The Cross and the Star" I showed that a basic—though sometimes not easily perceptible—pattern of meaning can be established between symbols opposed to each other and forming a perfect cross. The simplest manifestation of this type of structural patterning can be seen when relating the symbols referring to the four cardinal points of the year cycle, the solstitial and equinoctial points. I stated that when confronted with any important event and basic change, four questions should always arise in the mind: What is the nature and meaning of the event? To what is it leading (i.e., What is its potential outcome?)? How can I best handle the situation? and What is the ultimate purpose of this entire process of development?

In an astrological chart these four questions can be related to the four Angles: Ascendant (WHAT), Descendant (WHERETO), Nadir (HOW), Mid Heaven or Zenith (WHY). We will see in the next chapter that such an analytical approach in a great many cases can be significantly applied to a birth chart, the more validly perhaps the more the person is consciously in touch with the realm of archetypal meanings—even though one certainly cannot make this a general rule.

In the case of the person who drew to his mind the symbol related to the number 342, this symbol was to be taken as the WHAT of the situation. The oracle told *what* the situation meant in the total life span of the inquirer. But any such answer in turn poses many questions. The first is, "If this is so, then where will this lead me? What kind of result can I expect, or at least work for?"

The answer to the WHERETO of the situation is theoretically to be found in the symbol for the phase of the cycle in opposition to the first symbol. Astrologically speaking, if Pisces 12° is the basic symbol referring to the inquiry, then Virgo 12° will give the symbol answering the WHERETO question. This symbol is: *After the wedding, the groom snatches the veil away from his bride.* I have interpreted it as indicating penetrating beyond the "veil" of natural appearances to the essential reality of existence.

What we see, therefore, is that *if* the inquirer succeeds in passing through the testing process, and thus is accepted as a full-fledged participant in the type of group-relationship operating at the new and normally higher field of activity, he will develop the mental ability to tear away the "veil of Isis" and to come in contact with hidden realities. He may be able to deal forcefully and creatively with occult energies. Or if the inquirer operates only at the social or business level, he should be able to reach some "inner sanctum" of power and wealth.

I said *if* the inquirer succeeds in passing the tests. The next question inevitably follows: "HOW can I best act in order to succeed?" For an answer to this question we turn to the symbol for Gemini 12°, because this degree is 90 degrees ahead of Pisces 12°. In a "solar" chart, in which each House contains thirty degrees, if the Ascendant Pisces 12°, the Nadir point (Imum Coeli or cusp of the fourth House) is Gemini 12°, which means phase 72 of the cycle (342 plus 90 equals 432, which reduces to 72 when 360 is subtracted.)

The symbol is formulated thus: *"A Negro girl fights for her independence in the city."* The keynote is: "Liberation from the ghosts of the past."

This symbolic scene is elucidated by the preceding one, which refers to newly opened lands offering the pioneer new opportunities for experience. The man who has "entered the Path" leading to a new field of relationship and new powers is indeed a pioneer. But the tragedy of all pioneering ventures is that the pioneers too often bring to the new land or any new opportunity "the ghosts" of their past—their old habits and prejudices, their fears and insecurities. Pioneers along any new lines of social or group activity have to fight not only against whoever occupies established positions in the social environment, but against their own past. They often have to overcome a basic uncertainty and lack of faith in their own ability to succeed. The symbol therefore tells the inquirer that he must stand for what he knows is right against all opposition. And here we can note that according to occult traditions the testing of the aspirant to a new status includes the materialization of illusory shapes of frightening appearances and a sort of condensed precipitation of the candidate's basic weakness now confronting him and barring his way. He needs courage and a keen grasp of what is happening. He must claim what is his due. He must "liquidate" the past by strong, persistent and wise action.

The fourth question that calls for an oracular answer is, "WHY all this? What is the ultimate goal that I am to reach, the essential *purpose* of the struggle?" The answer is to be found in the symbol for Sagittarius 12°, which is the point opposite Gemini 12°, and thus completes the "cross" begun at Pisces 12°, the original symbol selected by the inquirer.

The symbol for Sagittarius 12° reads: *"A flag turns into an eagle; the eagle into a chanticleer saluting the dawn."* This peculiar symbol is susceptible of various interpretations, but in reference to the situation occupying our attention the most important meaning seems to be that the purpose of the events which had so disturbed the inquirer was to impel him to transform his ideals from the abstract (the flag) to the spiritually concrete (the eagle). His ideals had to become alive and able to withstand the intensity of a "solar" illumination at the highest level reachable by Earth-nature (the high-soaring eagle), so he could act as a herald of the New Day (the crowing chanticleer announcing the rising of the sun).

This was what was implied in the oracular appearance of the number 342 in the man's quieted consciousness. The four symbols which formed a crosslike constellation of meanings quite clearly gave the crisis which so confused him a positive, creative value. The test he was experiencing was real and dangerous, but it was a test, and if he could summon the courage and strength to face it and to overcome his karmic handicaps and the obstacles placed in his path, the results would be immensely valuable and would make him one of the pioneering spirits of the coming Age.

In short, what the oracle said in answer to my client's question was something like this: "You personal crisis means that you are being tested as a result of a deep interior phase of growth of which you may not have been aware. Provided you firmly and persistently demand your freedom from past conditioning, you can be given a new revelation of the power of life, a new sense of your own worth as a creative person. But do not just *think* of what you will be able to reach as being an abstract ideal. Do not either merely look at it or experience it ecstatically in high flights of imagination. Act it out among your people. Let your vision be known. Become a heralding agent of the creative Power of the universe."

IT SHOULD BE CLEAR FROM THIS EXAMPLE THAT THE ORACU-lar pronouncement did not refer to any particular future event.

The inquirer was seeking meaning, not fortunetelling. He might have asked whether or not he should sign a contract with a new firm, or marry someone with whom he had fallen in love. But any inquirer wise in the ways of the oracles would never ask; "*Should* I do this or that?" The only sensible way of phrasing a question to an oracle is: "What would be the meaning, or the results, of such an action?" What the oracle can tell the questioner refers essentially to the *quality* of the results of the action; it has to do with *the relationship* between the performer, the performance and the results of this performance. And we shall now see how this character of all oracular pronouncements applies to an interpretation of each of the basic factors in a birth chart; how one can use the symbols of the degrees on which the ten "planets" and the four Angles are located in order to reach a new dimension of astrological interpretation—the dimension of *qualitative meaning*.

The Use of Degree Symbols in the Interpretation of a Birth Chart

THE PLANETS IN A BIRTH CHART (ALWAYS INCLUDING SUN and Moon) represent the basic *functions* which can be seen operating in all *organized systems of activity*. Such systems may be galaxies, solar systems, cells and atoms as well as plants, animals and human beings. All these systems are organized wholes, and we may use the adjective "organic" (some writers have said *organated*) instead of organized, if we are willing to say that the universe and all its component wholes are "living" organisms. We may even extend the concept of organized whole, if not organism, to a nation or a more or less permanent and self-perpetuating institution.

Whether we use the term "life" in a universal or in a more restricted biological sense, the fact is that wherever there is a whole the constituting parts of which are definitely structured and in a relatively steady state of constant interaction, we can isolate a certain number of essential functions which operate interdependently. The particular genius of astrology is to be able to significantly refer *all* interrelated modes of operations within any organized whole to ten fundamental functions, each represented by a planet.

These functions have basically the same character in all organized systems, from atoms to men as well as from nations to galaxies, but they operate at many different levels; they deal with an infinite variety of substances (physical or superphysical) and produce an immense multiplicity of actual results. But as varied as these results may be, Jupiter always stands for the functional ability to expand, and Saturn for the capacity to define clearly and to maintain the original structure of the organism. The Sun will always refer to the fountainhead of power from which flow the energies used in the activities of all or most parts of the organism, and the Moon will always symbolize the organism's power to adjust to its environment and its capacity to distribute the "solar" energies to any part in need of them, whenever and in whatever form they are needed. Mars represents the ability to mobilize the organization's energies in order to achieve desired results, while Venus establishes the value of what is to be striven for, or feared and avoided—thus what attracts or repels. Mercury always stands for all means and methods of internal and external communication, everything that establishes links and patterns of association.

Then there are the three trans-Saturnian planets—Uranus, Neptune and Pluto—which refer to a more mysterious capacity inherent in life-species, particularly in man, but also perhaps in all forms of cosmic and microcosmic organizations—the capacity to transform oneself and to transcend one's limitations, a capacity which should almost certainly be considered a response to the challenge of the "greater Whole" within which the lesser whole operates as an organic part capable of responding to changes in the greater Whole. A living organism may experience a mutation in its seed because its species is either adjusting to new planetary conditions and some basic changes in the biosphere or taking a new and preordained step in its evolution. An individual man is even more able to transform his ancestral nature or animal background when aroused by the vision and example of an *Avatar* (divine Manifestation) heralding a new phase of human and planetary evolution. Uranus refers to the revelation of the new goal or archetype; Neptune refers to the dissolution of the old structures, personal and social; and Pluto stands for the chaotic stage which already contains the latent promise of future reorganization.

The ten planets represent functional activities, each of which has a definite character. Each symbolizes an essential and typical mode of operation, somewhat as each organ of the body (heart, lungs, stomach, sex organs, nervous system and brain, and so fort) performs definite biological operations. The astrological aspects between these planets in a birth chart tell us how these ten basic functions are related to one another in a particular person, at both the biological and the psychological levels; or alternatively from the standpoint of the "humanistic" type of astrology I have promoted, the aspects indicate what kinds of interplanetary relationships are most fruitful, so that the process of actualization of the individual's birth potential might be able to take place effectively and creatively.

But how can we gain at least intimations of the special *quality* of any one planet's operational activity? If Jupiter represents the function of expansion and the ability to increase the scope of a person's power and authority, what are the implications of this expansionistic or managerial drive which every living organism possesses to some extent?

The traditional astrologer will try to measure the *strength* of a planetary function according to the system of "dignities"— a system based on the old concept of rulership, exaltation, and strength or weakness due to position in a particular natal House. But strength is not quality! A type of activity may be strong in a coarse, heavy or self-defeating manner; it may display an exuberant, aggressive strength, or it may achieve its end in subtle, gentle, persuasive ways. What appears to be "weakness" in special circumstances may lead to success if it implies being sensitive and attuned to higher Powers.

When he uses the simpler traditional means, what the astrologer sees is in a sense two-dimensional; and much of astrology is based on either-or judgments. A third dimension of meaning is necessary once astrology ceases to be almost exclusively "events-oriented" and attempts to guide individuals in choosing the most significant way (it may not be the most "successful" in a conventional sense) of actualizing their innate potential. Some special techniques—for instance, the so-called Arabian Parts—have been used to uncover the subtler character of planetary activities in relation to a particular individual. But I personally feel that in many cases—though perhaps not in all—a consideration of the symbols of the degrees on which each planet is located adds a type of information which nothing else can quite give—*provided* one uses this kind of information wisely and understands its limitations.

There are undoubtedly limits to what can be learned in this way, and above all one should realize that such information should be used not so much as a means to know what a person *is*, but what *he is meant to be*. This is where humanistic astrology differs from the astrology that is so often only a glorified form of fortunetelling (which all predictive methods actually are, scientific or not). The humanistic astrologer is not trying to find out "how a person ticks," or to discover his strengths and weaknesses. He is not attempting to "analyze" a client or a friend, or his wife and children. Instead he seeks to act as an intermediary, a focusing agent and interpreter, whose only function is to help another person to realize himself more fully and to become a "whole person," an integrated and multifaceted individual able to fulfill the essential purpose of his having been born (his individual destiny) at a particular time and in a particular social-planetary environment.

Thus the symbol of the degree on which a natal planet is located should be used not so much to tell someone, "This is the special way in which your Mars function operates. You had better know it and perhaps do something about it." Instead, the humanistic astrologer will say, "This is the type of quality of consciousness and behavior you can best demonstrate when this particular function operates. It may of course already operate in this manner, if you let it work spontaneously. But perhaps this quality is only latent in your nature. It needs to become more mature, richer, more expressive, more conscious—provided that consciousness does not mean intellectualization or pride, or in a negative sense, fear and moral confusion."

In many instances the symbol points to a quality which the individual has not been able to apply in the exercise of the planetary function to which it refers; and if the reader refers to the beginning of Chapter Three, "The Positive and Negative Approaches to Individual Experiences," he will note the following statement (page 36): "To live is to consume energy. There are two basic ways in which this consumption of energy can be said to take place: the *purposeful use of* power, or the *automatic operation of forces.* In either case energy is consumed, but the meanings given to this consumption differ; that is, the type of consciousness arising from the living and experiencing of life is positive in the first instance and negative in the second."

Let us take as an example the symbols associated with the natal Sun of several personages whose birth charts were given in my booklet, "First Steps in the Study of Birth-Charts."* A rather typical case of negative approach is shown by the Sun's zodiacal degree in the chart of the unfortuante czar Nicholas II of Russia, who was killed by Bolsheviks at Ekaterinberg. The Sun is on the 28th degree (27°46') of Taurus in the ninth House, but practically conjunct the Mid Heaven. The formulation I have offered (page 87) is: *A woman, past her "change of life," experiences a new love,* and the commentary speaks of the need for the individual to "freely open his or her mind to the possibility of always new rebeginnings," to "rise above biological limitations," etcetera. The word "biological" should be replaced by "cultural" or "traditional," because here we have the chart of a man who was also the national symbol of the old aristocratic Russia. He represented an entire culture and its ruling class, a ruling class that, when confronted by the challenge to transform itself, was unable to revitalize its basic approach to life, to "rise above" obsolete tradition that held captive its capacity to use power in a spiritually positive manner.

The position of the retrograde Saturn in the fourth House, opposing Mercury in the tenth House (Mercury being the ruler of the Ascendant Virgo) may show why a negative approach was taken. Saturn stands alone in the chart's lower hemisphere, and

*This is now a section of the volume entitled: *Person-Centered Astrology: A New Approach to the Meaning and Use of Birth-Charts* (C.S.A. Press, Lakemont, Georgia, 1972).

there is also a tense square relationship between a Venus-Uranus conjunction in Cancer and a triple grouping of Jupiter, Moon and Neptune. Yet some man may have been born with the same or nearly the same chart who could have used the implied tensions to release the positive potentiality of this natal Sun's degree. We also find a ninth House Sun in Henry Ford's chart (Leo 7°6'), and the symbol is interesting because it shows how one must go beyond the literal statement and extract the essence of the symbolic scenes: *A communist activist spreading his revolutionary ideals.* Henry Ford assuredly was no communist, but he revolutionized the ways of mankind all over the globe by the introduction of cars which new techniques of mass production made available to a very large section of the population. The Keyword given at the end of the commentary, "catabolic action," is certainly not inappropriate, for the popular car has been responsible for much of the breakdown of the old way of life, of American mores and morality.

In Ford's chart the Moon on the 11th degree of Aquarius is just past its Full Moon phase and on a degree symbolized as follows: *During a silent hour a man receives a new inspiration which may change his life.* Whatever inspired Henry Ford certainly changed his life, and billions of other lives as well. Perhaps he experienced some kind of "overshadowing" (cf. page 255). The quintile aspect of the Sun to Jupiter at Libra 20° 26' was a good omen for social success. It could have told Ford he should expand socially in a creative manner and use the energy implied in the square between this Jupiter and a seventh House Uranus. Jupiter's symbol is very fitting for it pictures *A Sunday crowd enjoying the beach,* an enjoyment made possible by the family car.

In a totally different field of existence and consciousness we can appreciate the significance of the Sun's degree in Sri Aurobindo's birth chart. The great Hindu leader, yogi, poet and philosopher, whose centenary has very recently been celebrated all over the world, sought throughout forty years of intense and daring inner concentration to bring down into physical manifestation a new type of transforming spiritual energy. His Sun's symbol reads: *In a circus the bareback rider displays her dangerous skill,* a symbol of audacity and perseverance in controlling the powerful energies of what he called the "vital level in man's existence. [The Sun was about to rise in Sri Aurobindo's chart, with Jupiter (Leo 13½°) practically on the Ascendant's degree (Leo 12°27′. The Jupiter symbol tells of "The yearning for self-actualization" and of the attempt to let the spiritual Being fully manifest his power.] The Ascendant's degree (see page 139) may not seem so justified, yet there was a time when Aurobindo was a pioneer in the political movement which freed India from the English, and it took a crisis (a year in jail) to show to the uncompromising leader that his work of destiny was not in such a tempestuous field of activity but instead in the intense concentration of the room in which he passed the last forty years of his life, talking to only a handful of people. In other words, this solitary concentration on inner experiences was the way of destiny for him, and he had to learn this.

The Moon symbol in Aurobindo's chart is also significant: *An old bridge over a beautiful stream is still in constant use.* Aurobindo sought to go back to the sources of India's greatness and spirituality by reinterpreting the ancient Vedas, the sacred books of several thousand years ago. The ancient tradition had helped to bridge the chasm between the human and the divine. Aurobindo thus linked the future to the past, formulating a philosophy and a way of life which, above the stream of the ever-flowing spiritual life of India, established a direct approach to what man should become as he actualizes the full potential of his being. The Moon symbol evokes a certain quality of manifestation in Aurobindo's capacity to adjust to his environment and to distribute his "solar" audacity and courage.

In the chart of the great German occult philosopher, educator and creative artist, Rudolph Steiner, the Sun at Pisces 9°20′ is located on a degree symbolized by *An aviator flying through ground-obscuring clouds* (page 274). Implied here is a potential destiny of masterful control of energies which allows one to penetrate into a cloudy realm of existence and, relying on inner powers of direction, to go on toward a definite purpose. The opposition of this Sun to Saturn retrograde in square to Uranus suggests that much self-transforming strength and courage will be needed if the life goal is to be reached.

We have an interesting problem of symbolic interpretation in the chart of the promoter of Italian Fascism, Benito Mussolini. In his chart a conjunction of the Sun and Mercury occurs on the 6th degree of Leo. The symbol (page 135) pictures *A conservative old-fashioned lady confronted by a "hippie" girl.* What does this mean? Mussolini's Fascism was a return to the ancient archetype of the Roman Empire, which he dreamt to reconstitute. In a more general sense, the rise of Fascism was— and remains today, in one form or another—the result of a collective fear of the new political development, Communism. At first a highly neurotic young man, Mussolini overcame his inferiority complex by an overcompensative type of aggressiveness. In the symbol, the "old-fashioned lady" anchored in the glory of her past is both frightened and enraged by the ultramodern and aggressive young girl facing her. This is, alas, the normal reaction, the line of least resistance based on pride and insecurity. Mussolini followed that line, but the positive implication of the symbol is that in such a situation the old order and the new dream should reach some sort of understanding. This proved difficult; Mussolini adopted the negative way, and was destroyed.

This example shows that the commentary I have written for the symbol does not always exactly fit a particular situation. If Mussolini could have accepted the fact that all social fashions and ideologies have only a "relative value," he might not have indulged in his coarse and totalitarian use of power. He represented a return to an obsolete Image to which he gave an absolute value. The fact that his natal Saturn stood on a degree symbolized by *Aroused strikers surrounding a factory* points to the deep character of his (and many of his contemporaries') insecurity, for wherever Saturn is located in a birth chart we find the area of maximum weakness. Anything occurring at this point tends to make a person panic and resort to aggression or to a self-defeating retreat into traditional forms of security. Mussolini's Moon on the 9th degree of Gemini, very close to Saturn, further emphasizes the pressure exerted by this panicking Saturn. The Moon's symbol *(A quiver filled with arrows)* evokes a return to primitive forms of aggressivity; yet this image of "conquest" need not reveal a destructive use of power. It may refer to an ability to survive in the midst of natural predators and a constructive alertness to danger. It is a symbol of preparedness.

Another interesting case is that of the tragic philosopher, Friedrich Nietzsche, whose natal Sun was Libra 22°7', a degree symbolized by *Chanticleer's voice heralds sunrise.* In the once-famous play of the French poet, Edmond Rostand, the rooster who is the main personage not only salutes the dawn in ringing tones, but is possessed by the belief that it is he whose voice brings about the rise of the sun. Nietzsche was one of the first poet-seer-philosophers to dream of the rise of a type of human being who would bring forth a new civilization. His was a tragic life ending in what we call insanity, and his passionate, hammering words have aroused destructive forces in many people; yet through and beyond this destructiveness he nevertheless acted as a herald of much that has taken more positive form since his death near the turn of this century.

Nietzsche's natal Mars culminating in his tenth House and ruler of his Scorpio Ascendant is located on the 28th degree of Virgo. The symbol, *A baldheaded man who has seized power,* stresses the "Power of the Will" in times of crises. Interestingly enough, when I wrote those Keywords for the degree I was unaware that Nietzsche's ruling planet, Mars, was located at this place; and one of his most famous books is entitled *The Will to Power.*

ONE COULD GIVE COUNTLESS EXAMPLES. THOSE I HAVE DIS-cussed may be sufficient to show how the use of symbols requires that we go to the very root of the symbol's meaning and in many cases ignore the superficial features of the commentaries, mine or anyone else's. The most important symbols are those referring to the Sun, the Moon and the Ascendant, unless one has to focus one's attention upon definite problems related to a particular function within the total person of the inquirer. Moreover, I should state once more that what the symbols indicate is not so much what *is* as what should be developed in order that a person be fully able to actualize his birth potential.

Thus, if Nietzsche in youth had consulted an astrologer able to use the Sabian symbols, he should have been told that being a herald for a new type of social or personal development was inherent in his essential temperament and individual destiny. The opposition of Pluto (not yet discovered) to the Sun tells us in retrospect how deep-seated and relentless this "solar" commitment of Nietzsche's essential nature was, and how expectable its tragic or sacrificial implications. Yet this was Nietzsche's destiny, potentially schizophrenic as it may have been when seen from a commonplace and normative point of view. This was his dharma. The oppositions of Mars to Jupiter, Mercury to Uranus, and Pluto to the Sun posed a tough problem of what Jung called "personality integration"—one not made easier by the square of a ninth House Venus to a rising Sagittarian Moon (on the interesting 9th degree of Sagittarius—a degree of "social concern" and assistance to the less evolved). But these aspects generate power, and Nietzsche obviously needed a deep source of power within himself to hammer at prejudices and taken-for-granted social and intellectual values. The Hindu god Shiva is both destroyer and regenerator; he is said to absorb into his body the poisons released by his catabolic activities. This is the fate of the true pioneers in times of social crystallization and vulgarization, for such historical periods not only invite, but demand disintegration.

If one has the time to study a birth chart in depth, the consideration of the symbols of the degrees on which all the planets are located is certainly worthwhile. In many instances by looking attentively at all these symbols—to which should be added those of the four Angles and at least of the Part of Fortune—a total feeling may emerge, although it may be abstract and difficult to describe. This is not likely to be a picture of scenes or potential events, but something more like the total resonance of a complex chord, of which the qualities implied in all these symbols would be the separate notes. When one meets a person for the first time, one often gets a clear "feeling-intuition" of what this person stands for, vibrates to, and perhaps may mean in one's life in days or years to come. In the same

way, out of all the degree symbols in a chart an overall *quality
of being-ness* may impress itself upon our consciousness. This is
what I have called a "holistic" response to a situation. It may
come by simply looking at the chart as a whole with an "inner
eye," and without ever thinking of degree symbols; yet the
latter can add a new dimension to one's intuitive response—one
might almost speak of a particular "flavor."

I spoke in the preceding paragraph of the value of considering the symbols for the four Angles of the chart. The problem
here, of course, is that we are not always sure of the exact
moment of a person's first breath. The "rectification" of a birth
chart rarely leads to absolute certainty, for there are many ways
in which we may attempt such a rectification, and none is either
foolproof or acceptable to all reputable astrologers. Each Angle
characterizes in an essential or archetypal manner one of the
four basic psychic functions (or modes of being) of which Carl
Jung speaks, particularly in his book *Psychological Types:* that
is, intuition, sensation, feeling and thinking. I have related these
functions respectively to the Ascendant (intuition), the astrological Nadir (feeling), the Descendant (sensation), and the Zenith
or Mid Heaven (thinking).

In view of the uncertainty about the exact degrees of the
four Angles I shall use my own birth chart as an example, although in general I am strongly opposed to making public one's
birth chart, or at least the precise moment of one's first breath,
i.e. one's Ascendant. However, in my case these Angles have
been made public in several places in spite of my request that
the information be not publicized, and at my age and in my
situation the matter is of relatively little importance.

I was born with the 14th degree of Sagittarius rising, and the
12th degree of Libra at the Mid Heaven. (The Sun was on the
3rd degree of Aries and the Moon on the 25th of Aquarius.) The
reader should now turn to pages 51 and 264 where the symbols
are described and commented upon. What I shall attempt to do,
as an example of what can and (if possible) should be done, is to
interpret the interrelationships between the four symbols of the
Angles and the basic four-fold character of psychic activity (i.e.
intuition, feeling, sensation, thinking) in my own case. I shall try
to be as fully objective as one should be toward the close of an

already long and full life—a life lived in terms of the discovery of meaning.

There are two ways in which the interpretation can be approached. The first is simply to refer each of the four basic modes of psychic activity to a degree symbol. Thus my *intuitive processes* should be referred to the symbol of *The Great Pyramid and the Sphinx*. This suggests a rootedness in whatever these immensely old Egyptian monuments can mean to the interpreter. For me, it means an ancient wisdom which had been able to formulate its attunement to the cosmic order and incorporate it in massive and totally symbolic structures. It means having some sort of cryptic and therefore "occult" knowledge as an intuitive "background." But what the symbol really implies is not *the existence* of such a background as much as the indication that I should attempt to develop my intuition along lines that have at least a general reference to a type of wisdom in the possession of a group of men such as the builders of the Egyptian edifices.

The Ascendant, more than any other astrological factor, points to the *type of experiences* through which one may best realize one's individual uniqueness of being and destiny. Thus the symbol of my Ascendant gives me the message that, *if* I want to discover who I really am, my archetypal self, I should seek to gain experiences that are in some way related to a quality of knowledge, wisdom or power symbolizable by the Pyramid and the Sphinx. This is really *all* that the symbol suggests; no special glamor should be attached to it and it would be unwise to deduce from it a literal connection between my individuality and the Egyptian tradition or those who may still be its depository. It should be clear that this degree of the zodiac must be found in numerous birth charts, and many of the individuals with such an Ascendant very likely have (or have had in the past) no conscious relation to ancient wisdom or what now is called esotericism. Yet even in such cases today the symbol may be valid, and significantly points to a *direction*, should the person experience a deep-seated urge to reach beyond the superficialities of his social-cultural environment and its strictly normal and average responses to life.

The Nadir point (fourth House's cusp or I.C.) in my birth chart (Aries 12th degree) carries a symbol which I have explained at length on pages 57–58 because I believe that so far it has been inadequately interpreted. In the symbol *A flight of wild geese* the emphasis should not be on the wildness of the geese, but on the deeper factors to which such a flight refer, i.e. the regular seasonal nature of the flight attuned to planetary changes and the geometrical pattern outlined by the flight. The symbol of the "wild goose" is a very ancient one, and in old India the name *hamsa* referred not only to the wild goose but to the human soul as well. Interestingly enough, I chose this name, Hamsa, for a magazine I started in 1920–21 before I ever knew that it referred to the symbol of my fourth House cusp.

This cusp, the astrological Nadir, is the point of personal foundations. In a deeper sense it is also the center of the globe on the surface of which we live. It is at this point and through the fourth House that an individual can best experience his rootedness in whatever to him represents solidity and security —his land, his home and all that contributes to the concrete integration and strength of his personality. What therefore does this "flight of wild geese" symbol have to say about my *feeling-processes* and my sense of personality integration?

The rather obvious implication is that whatever can give me a concrete experience of rootedness and security does not relate to—and should not be sought in terms of—a particular land, soul or home. Instead, it should be found in a kind of earth-transcending instinct attuned to the rhythm of planetary or seasonal factors. The feeling-processes should also be controlled by some sort of "group formation" rather than operating on a strictly individualistic basis. They should perhaps operate in a way symbolized by a triangular wedgelike shape and on the background of an impersonal celestial order. In my commentaries, I wrote: "The symbol therefore refers to the Soul-consciousness, as visualized by the heaven-oriented mind"; but in this particular birth chart what is especially at stake are the feeling-processes. What most people call "soul"—at least without a capital letter—is based on the feeling-nature; this is accurate because the feelings are the direct, more or less spontaneous expressions of *the whole person's spontaneous evaluation of his experiences.* Thus the soul refers to the wholeness of the person, to his consciousness of being a whole, an "I."

The symbol quite evidently fits me well, for I never had the sense of being rooted in a particular land or home. I left all that referred to my ancestral tradition, culture, and language as soon as the opportunity arose at the age of twenty-one, and afterward I moved a great deal across America following what often were seasonal rhythms. Any sense of security I have ever experienced has been a feeling of "center" and of being an organic part of a group operating in terms of an ineluctable superpersonal or "cosmic" necessity—a spiritual instinct which could not be disobeyed.

The symbol for my Descendant (Gemini 14°) is formulated as follows: *Bridging physical space and social distinctions, two men communicate telepathically.* The basic interpretation is given as a reference to the capacity to transcend the limitations of bodily existence.

How this symbol can throw light upon the aspect of psychic activity usually called "sensation" in my life may not seem clear at first. But here again we have a symbol that fits well in the total picture already begun by the symbols of the Ascendant and the Nadir. Sensations result from contacts between one's body and various other *physical* objects, or at least the emanations from them. On the other hand, the symbol of telepathic communication pictures what is essentially a *nonphysical* contact. Of course no one as yet knows precisely how telepathy operates, but in terms of symbolic meaning, it should be evident that what is at stake is a transcendent type of interaction between minds rather than bodies. Therefore, what is implied here seems to be that a process of mentalization of physical relationships is, and should be, at work—a process giving more importance to mental communication than to the data provided by physical senses. One could even say that there is a suggestion that the development of subtle senses and mind-rapport with individuals I may never have physically seen is something for me to work on.

The symbol of course does *not* say whether I have been

successful in the attempt! The fact that Neptune is located on that same degree stresses the transcendental potentialities implied in this Descendant symbol. It also suggests other elements concerning the close associations I have made and maintained which need not be discussed here, but which could give added significance to the "flight of wild geese" symbol. It may relate to the emphasis I have placed on the need for "nonpossessiveness" in human relationships if a new order of society is to be built. It may also explain my attraction for music and for astrology, for it seems obvious to me in spite of a carelessly transmitted nineteenth-century tradition, that astrology (with all its so often imprecise and confusing symbolism, and its universal mystical appeal so unlike the sharp-illuminating and revolutionary character of Uranus) is "ruled" by Neptune and not by Uranus.

The symbol for the Mid Heaven (Libra 12°) is also significant: *Miners are surfacing from a deep coal mine.* Coal has been the main source of energy and heat in our Western society for a long time, at least before oil came into wide use. Both coal and oil are products of the remains of what was once a multitude of living organisms. The coal miner symbolically descends into the depths of the collective Unconscious and releases from its dark and potentially dangerous passageways what will produce warmth, power, and electric light for his fellow-men.

This symbol stands in polar opposition to the one for Aries 12°—but the "public life" (tenth House) is also in polar opposition to the "private life" (fourth House). The *personal* feelings of transcendence and instinctive reliance upon cosmic order have to be polarized by a *sociocultural* commitment to the task of un-earthing from the depth of an ancient human past materials suitable for the generation of collective power and an enlightened mentality. The Mid Heaven refers to an individual's "achievement"—i.e. to the coming to a head (*caput* means head, and from it the word "chief" is derived) of a whole cycle of personalized activity.

A definite picture should emerge from this consideration of the four symbols of the Angles in my birth chart. Again let me say that it is a picture of the *way of destiny* which has been mine to follow, i.e. the way to the actualization of my birth potential.

No astrologer could definitely state from a study of my birth chart whether or not, or to what degree, I have been successful in achieving these innate potentialities—at least not on strictly astrological grounds. But the determination of success or failure is not the business of any truly wise astrologer. All that he should be asked to do is to help his clients—and himself, of course—to be more aware, more certain, more objective (and thus "impersonal") in their approach to the ever-renascent problems they face. The most important and most crucial problem, which always seems to take new forms, is that of realizing—intuitively, feelingly, concretely through personal relationships, and within a lucid and unafraid mind—*who* you are, and what life, destiny, God *expects* of you.

IN CONSIDERING THE SYMBOLS FOR THE FOUR ANGLES OF A birth chart, one can also use the four-fold type of questioning discussed in the preceding chapter: WHAT, WHERETO, HOW, WHY. In this case it seems best to go first from the Ascendant (WHAT) to the Descendant (WHERETO), for the very first question that comes to mind—at least to most minds—when a situation begins to take on clearer features is: WHERE will this lead?

A birth chart refers to a "situation," because it is conditioned by a particular birth time and birthplace, and it occurs within a social-cultural-national organism—in my case, France. Somehow there must have been a meaning to this birth situation—the first breath of a physical organism which was to develop individual features. In a very real sense, *I am this meaning*. If there is no awareness of this meaning in the consciousness that says "I," then there is no *concrete working knowledge* of who or what "I" *is*. There is consciousness, of course, but no consciousness of who is being conscious, because the essential character of any human "who" is that it is potentially conscious of being conscious—and secondarily of being conscious of why it is what it is. The innate urge to search for this "why" in all circumstances is what makes a living organism "human"; otherwise it remains only a specimen of an animal species with unused potentialities.

Returning now to my birth chart: the answer to the WHAT question is the symbol of *The Great Pyramid and the Sphinx*. It is not too clear an answer perhaps to most people, yet it implies a great deal that can become explicit if the proper type of individualizing experiences occur. And I must emphasize here that it is not the astrologer's task to do *all* the interpreting for his client, for this would rob him of the opportunity to discover, in a vivid intuitive flash of awareness, what the meaning of the Ascendant symbol is—the meaning *to him,* the client, at a particular time of his life and in a particular situation.

Everyone may give his own meaning to the symbol for the 14th degree of Sagittarius, and the meaning will likely change as one grows in understanding and interpretative skill. For some people the Pyramid is still thought of as the tomb of a proud Pharaoh; for most occultly-inclined persons it stands as a witness to an ancient system of "Initiation." The Sphinx hid the entrance to the symbolic "Path" (of trials and tests) which led to a great experience of psychic transformation and repotential-ization while lying in trance in the Sarcophagus at the center of the King's Chamber.

But here again the WHAT symbolized is only the potentiality of a certain type of life unfoldment. It does *not* say: "You are that," but instead: "This is the way that is divinely or cosmically determined; this is the birth situation the potentiality of which may or may not unfold and be fulfilled." It also may be partially fulfilled. Above all, no glamor is implied. No "is-ness"; only potentiality. If there is fulfillment, then to the extent that there is, it will lead to what the Descendant's symbol indicates: i.e. the capacity to communicate at a superphysical level, to establish conscious contacts with other minds. Nothing is told about what the other minds may be, or how adequate the communication. There can be many disturbing factors! What matters is that some kind of end results are suggested which give added meaning to the "Pyramid and Sphinx" situation.

The next question is a very crucial one: HOW can these results be achieved? Here, the "wild geese" symbol may not seem too helpful, yet it contains a basic key and an implied directive: "Follow the cosmic order of your own nature. Keep in close formation with your companions. Trust your own spiritual instinct—and be careful if you come to rest on a lake on the earth's surface. Watch for hunters!"

Then comes the final question: WHY have I to struggle through life? Of what use would my achievements be if I should be successful? In other words, what part or role am I supposed to play in the great drama of human existence? The Mid Heaven symbol clearly implies the answer: "Be like a coal miner descending in the depth of the Unconscious to bring back to your society, or to generations to come, that which may warm and illumine their lives."

When these four answers of the oracle given by the birth sky are related to each other, the picture of an individual destiny should emerge. The meaning one gives to it will naturally depend on the level and the quality of the interpretative consciousness. Symbols deal with the quality of living, not with events. They focus universal meanings upon particular situations. It has been said that life should be lived *sub specie aeternitatis*, which may be translated as "in the consciousness of eternity." But our Western thinkers have misunderstood the word eternity. *Eternity means the wholeness of a cycle*. What I have called, according to the Gnostic tradition, the Eon is the cycle in its essential unity—which includes a vast series of phases, symbolized in this book by the 360 symbols of the Sabian set. He who does not really "transcend" time, but rather includes in his greatly extended perceptions the whole of the cycle of his living as a person—and ultimately, as a spiritual Buddha-like being, as the Soul-source of a long series of personalities—has developed *eonic* consciousness. He understands the meanings of and the unfolding interconnections between all the phases of his evolution as a center of consciousness and of power. He is truly "awakened," truly wise.

Concentration on symbols and the living of a symbolic life constitute a way—but not the only way—to the attainment of at least some degree of eonic consciousness.

The Symbolic Life

◉

THE LIVES OF GREAT SPIRITUAL PERSONAGES—AND THERE may be some in fields not commonly associated with "spirituality," including statesmanship—are truly rituals. Every major event in these lives should be understood as a ritualistic act whose archetypal character can be revealed to the consciousness able to see through the existential facts and perceive the place these facts occupy within the life of the person considered as a significant whole. The life is significant because it brings the individual person and his sociocultural environment into a relationship which clearly fulfills an evolutionary or historical need of mankind, or of some portion of mankind. The more basic this need and the more important the function of the great personage, the more perceptible the archetypal character of the events of his life.

In the lives of human beings who have rightfully been called Avatars or Divine Manifestations—men like Gautama the Buddha, Jesus Christ, Baha'u'llah, or even St. Francis of Assisi— every event has a symbolical meaning in terms of the special character of these persons who fecundated the collective mind and aroused the Will-to-Transformation-and-Transcendence in millions of people. Their lives were rituals in the sense that whatever the superficial biographical facts may have been, all major events had a "transpersonal" significance as specific phases of a process unfolding according to structural, cosmic and eonic principles.

We can believe that every move in such ritual lives was preordained—as Jesus is reported to have said, "in order to fulfill the Scriptures." But we have to be careful in defining the meaning we give to the term preordained. The "order" is not an imposition from the outside, a pattern forced upon an *individual* person—thus, what is usually understood as "fate." The Avatar is *not* an individual in the ordinary ego-sense of the word. He *is* the order that ritualistically gives structure to the life span of his body and determines the function and meaning of his responses to the actions and the "thinking-feeling" of his community. He is the embodiment or incarnation of a principle of activity, a quality of being, impersonally—or rather transpersonally—determined by the needs of his time. In a still broader sense, what he is and does is the spontaneous, superinstinctive answer to the fundamental requirements of human nature when the time has come for it to surrender to the transforming power of cyclic evolution—or some would say, to the Will of God.

In lesser men a conflict is nearly always in evidence between the transpersonal order—their "destiny"—and the reactions of a personal ego-will still responsive to biological and psychic urges. However, in the great spiritual personage whatever is left of this conflict—the Temptations of Jesus, for instance, or Buddha's initial unwillingness to teach others what he had experienced—takes on forms which in themselves are archetypal; i.e. they are characteristic manifestations of the very nature of generic man, *Homo sapiens,* when faced with the possibility of consciously becoming more than he is as a species in the earth's biosphere. The events that can be related to these inner conflicts or temptations are "symbolic." Every human being can experience them in analogous circumstances.

At the beginning of this book I discussed the difference

between facts and symbols. We must always deal with facts, with elements of actual experience, personal and collective. But we should not stop at perceiving, registering, associating and classifying these facts. We can go *through* them to a level of perception and understanding at which a multidude of facts can be *directly* (not merely intellectually) referred to a relatively small number of archetypes.

This "transfactual" process of the intuition and, at a more perfect stage, of the illumined mind enables the consciousness to grasp the essential meaning of all facts, and particularly the events of a human life dedicated to the process of transformation. Such a self-dedicated life is especially transparent to meaning. The events that fill the years of that life are "translucent"; they allow the light of meaning to go through them. The life is a symbolic life.

Essentially, all lives are to some extent symbolic. Outer events reveal their purpose and function to the mind able to pierce through appearances and to intuit the underlying order and meaning of the whole. If the whole universe is a "theophany"—a manifestation of divine Harmony and Power—then every human being potentially is a manifestation of one particular aspect of the Soul that sought embodiment at a particular moment of our universe in order *to establish a specific relationship* with conditions prevailing then and there. He is or can be a "hierophany"—literally, a "sacred" manifestation.

Much has been written concerning the realm of the sacred in contrast to that of the profane. Mircea Eliade's book *The Sacred and the Profane* is particularly well known but its analysis of time suffers from the Western thinkers' inability to differentiate adequately between the archetypal structure of a cycle, and the existential events that fill the life span of that cycle. The genetic structure of, let us say, *the* Lilac, and the meaningful place it occupies in the biosphere are revitalized every spring, but a particular lilac bloom of this year is not actually the same flower that appeared last year or may appear next year. There is archetypal identity, but there are existential differences. The essential structure may return cyclically, but the actual events are never the same. There is an infinite possibility of solutions to the fundamental problems of existence.

To live a symbolic life is to live a transpersonal life, a life in which every event can be referred to an archetype, thereby acquiring a "sacred" character. What we call a *mythos** is a sequence of events clearly embodying an archetypal series of phases referring to a fundamental life process, including the process of metamorphosis involving a radical change of level or mutation. The life of a Gautama or of a Jesus is a *mythos*. *Through* the actual events which tradition records—and these need not be exactly "true," existentially speaking—the sacred character of the *mythos* is clearly perceptible. When the great Persian Baha'u'llah, who his followers consider a divine Manifestation, indeed the Avatar for the new era of man's evolution, was thrown into a deep, nearly airless and filthy cistern, with heavy iron chains around his neck and feet, in the midst of some one hundred and fifty criminals, that event had a deep symbolic meaning. That this underground dungeon was reached by *three* steep stairs, and that it was while in this dreadful state for four months that this son of a minister in the Persian government received the inner revelation of his world mission in the form of a Maiden who brought to his consciousness "the remembrance of the name of my Lord" (his own words) are all full of symbolic significance. These were sacred "events," as was Jesus' crucifixion, because they bring to the mind able to pierce through the tragic facts a realization of what these facts will mean for mankind during the historical cycle to which they were a prelude.†

Historians today claim that it is often impossible to know where "real facts" end and "the myth" begins. But the existen-

*I use the Greek word *mythos* in order to guard against the popular meaning of the word myth: "This is only a myth!"

†Baha'u'llah was born in Teheran at sunrise on November 12, 1817. When his father died, twenty-two years later, he refused to assume his governmental position. He espoused the Cause of the Bab, in his twenty-eighth year, which led to his imprisonment. The Bab was a Persian youth (a descendant of Mohammed) who in 1844 proclaimed the end of the cycle of Islam and the coming of a great personage who would open a new era. The Bab was executed and thousands of his followers were tortured and killed.

tial facts of the past have meaning for us today only insofar as we may discover that archetypal principles of operation are embodied in their interrelationships. Jesus' crucifixion, seen as a sacred event or *mythos,* throws a revelatory light on the meaning of this entire "Piscean Age" now about to close. The life of the Buddha illumines the development of the civilization of most of Asia since 600 B.C.—even where Buddhism was repudiated and India's old religious attitudes were capped by an upsurge of intense devotional fervor (*bhakti* cults) compensating for the overobjective impersonality of many of the followers of the Buddha. And today, 2,500 years later, at the start of one of four "seasons" in the vast 10,000-year cycle which seems related to Buddha's appearance, many American and European youths are being re-sensitivized to the still-vibrant call of the great Meditator, the Awakened One.

The kind of history that is now being taught mostly in our universities is a fundamentally meaningless pursuit. It deals with the minutiae of strictly profane events and refuses to admit the existence of structural and cyclic patterns in the collective "organic" growth and decay of societies. Because, as Arnold Toynbee points out in his monumental *Study of History,* human societies and their cultures are organic and cyclic, studying them should imply an attempt to reveal the *mythos* which they embody. Any significant *mythos* should certainly be founded on existential facts, but facts are only the raw material from which meaning should emerge. Without such an emergence of the archetype out of the existential, life is meaningless and empty, if not "absurd"—to use a term dear to so-called existentialist thinkers whose minds are prisoners of the chaotic and the profane.

The significance of astrology is that it can transform the profane into the sacred, the facts of astronomy into the revelation of a cosmic order manifest in the cell and the human person as well as in the solar system and the galaxy. To try to make astrology a "science" based on empirical facts and statistics is to deny its essential and ancient nature. Astrology deals with the *mythos* of the Sky. The elements it uses are archetypes. Therefore, to live one's life in terms of the revelatory message symbolically implied in one's birth chart is to live a life in terms of the "sacred" character of existence. It does *not* mean to feel oppressed by "bad" aspects or elated by "good" ones. It does *not* mean to avoid confrontation with existential facts and to escape into fanciful dreams of pseudo-occult transcendence. It demands instead that life be lived strictly on the basis of *non-escapism*—that is, an attitude of acceptance of what is, but an "is" that remains transparent to the "eternal."

Alas, the words "eternity" and "eternal" have been made to refer to an escape from minds haunted by a desperate urge to transcend biological and intellectual compulsions, just as nirvana in its popular sense has been equated with a concept of negation and annihilation. These perversions are at the root of the deepest tragedies that mankind is now experiencing. An eternity is a complete cycle of time. The consciousness which can perceive things and events in their eternal nature is one which sees every happening as definitely related to a particular phase of some more or less vast cycle of existence.

It is on the basis of such an attitude of life that this study of the Sabian symbols and of their possible use really makes sense. I do not claim that this cyclic series of 360 symbols is a completely adequate expression of universal archetypal principles. I simply say that under the conditions in which these symbols were obtained and at the time they were obtained, the set is of unusual and indeed quite startling significance. Its study and application may well lead to a revelation of values filled with transforming potency. It leads to such a revelation when a person approaches it in an adequate philosophical spirit and with a keen sensitivity to the ever-present possibility of discovering the "eternal" at the core of the particular, and the sacred under the fleeting shapes of the profane.

Our Western society, witnessing the disintegration of the great Images which once gave archetypal value to its so often tragic enterprises and its fanatic crusades and revolutions, finds itself hypnotized today by the chaotic contingencies of an almost totally profane collective living. References to archetypal values are mocked by our middle-aged and so often obsolescent intelligentsia. Yet during the last years a remarkable surge of interest in at least what passes for "eternal" values, and in many techniques of personal or transpersonal transformation, has occurred. A growing number of individuals are seeking, often desperately, to restructure lives disjointed and disconnected from the now-profaned sanctuaries of man's inner life. They attempt an often naïve "return to source"—a return to what they hope will resemble the original creative spirit of our society, or of still more ancient societies, before perversions set in.

This is wonderful, even if chaotic and confused. But archetypal principles are not to be discovered by returning to a mythical, sacred past. The "eternal" is now; the cycle—the Eon—surrounds us. We live in it, just as the space of the galaxy pervades every cell of our bodies. It is not to be sought in glamorous Aboves or Elsewheres. There is no essential difference between the sacred and the profane, the symbolic and the real, nirvana and samsara. What differs are our attitudes to events, inner or outer. What we must change is our frame of reference—and to avoid accepting or refusing to believe in *any* frame of reference is still to have a negative one. The atheist who denies God merely affirms in reverse. It is all a question of inner attitude. To the consciousness that has realized the existence of cycles and is able to shift gears from the profane to the sacred, the whole of living becomes imbued with the magic of eternity. Every event is accepted as a necessary phase in the ritual process of existence radiating at every moment the significance and inner peace that wells out from the security of knowing oneself to be an essential and operative part of a vast cyclic whole.

This is the symbolic life. It is also the life of wisdom, for to be wise is to know with unimpeachable knowing that the Whole is fulfilling itself at every moment *through* and *within* every act of life, once this life, illumined by nonpossessive love, is rooted in the certainty that order, beauty, rhythmic interplay and the harmony of ever-balanced opposites are here and now, indestructibly.

Appendix

AN EXCHANGE OF LETTERS WITH
MARC EDMUND JONES

In the September 1944 issue of the magazine *American Astrology*, in the section "Many Things," pp. 27–29, the following exchange of letters appeared: a letter I had written to the editor-founder, Paul Clancy, then his comments, and then a letter sent to Clancy by Marc Edmund Jones, presumably in answer to one which Clancy had written to him. These letters are reprinted here because of their historical significance. I might add that a copy of this September 1944 issue was very kindly sent to me by Joanne S. Clancy, now editor of the magazine, after I had ascertained it contained Marc Jones's letter.

Los Angeles, California

I have been thinking for some time about the possibility of a series of studies dealing with the Sabian Symbols, as I have found these symbols of the zodiacal degrees, in the main, amazingly significant and accurate. Not only have they proven of great practical value, but I am very much interested in the general structure of the sequence of meanings and images they display. Here is a *whole of meanings* with definite structural characteristics, and as such this series of symbols is quite a remarkable phenomenon in Western thinking—one which could be compared, for instance, with some ancient Chinese equivalent. I understand that the *Yi King* translation by Wilhelm (translated by Baynes, with a commentary by C. G. Jung) will be at last published very soon in New York. And therefore a study of these Sabian Symbols would seem particularly well-timed this year.

I would not discuss every symbol, or follow them in their sequence, but I would rather study the general structure of the series as a whole—starting with the symbols for the equinox degrees, establishing relationships between the symbols, etc. I have mentioned the idea to Marc Jones and his reaction to my project was very favorable. I feel that it is the kind of study which definitely belongs to *American Astrology* as it represents a really new departure and you have been the great pioneer in all these new fields. Thus I am asking you whether you would like me to go ahead and prepare the first installment of such a series of studies—to start preferably with the October issue (Fall Equinox).

RUDHYAR

COMMENT: This new series on the Sabian Symbols will commence in our next (October) issue of *American Astrology* Magazine. The Sabian Symbols were compiled and interpreted by Marc Edmund Jones and published by him under the title "Symbolical Astrology." Mr. Jones furnishes the following information on the origin of the Sabian Symbols, the details of which have never before been released:

During many years in experimenting with horoscopic interpretation, I had found that the symbolical degrees worked out by John Thomas, the Welsh seer, and published under his pen name of Charubel, were remarkably suggestive as far as their ideas were concerned, but that they suffered from the fact that they had been moralized; in other words, some were put down as bad, some as good, and so on. On the assumption that good and bad are relative terms and assuming that the meaning of each degree has as much a constructive as a destructive function, I found that these degrees were exceedingly valuable. My first idea was to obtain permission to re-interpret them, describing them in such a fashion that both good and bad points could be brought out.

At this time, I had a student who was a rather highly gifted psychic, making her living as a professional medium. She was greatly distressed by the idea that so much spiritualistic work was dishonest and cheap, and had wanted for a long time to do something of enduring worth. She is deceased, and for the record her name was Miss Elsie Wheeler, of San Diego, California, a woman of rather brilliant mind and very interesting to me because she was hopelessly crippled with arthritis, living in a wheel chair, and remarkable for her indomitable determination to make her own way and be dependent upon no one. When I first met her she accomplished this purpose by dressing dolls of a rather unusual sort and I perhaps am somewhat responsible for encouraging her in facing the world professionally as a medium, which was her deepest desire, and at which she was very successful up to the time of her death. I asked her if she would be interested in participating in an attempt at gaining 360 fresh symbols for the degrees on the pattern of the work of John Thomas.

Two factors were responsible for my making this suggestion. The first of these was the fact that during investigation quite a number of years before in New York, I had experimented with the idea of a series of 52 symbols for the playing cards, in the construction of a special form of the Tarot which I then used and still use as a psychological training device for students under occult discipline. A New York woman of high psychic gifts had insisted upon attempting this and so I had tried it with rather striking results. For the record, this woman, who never did any professional psychic work, was Miss Zoe Wells, who passed on quite a number of years ago. At the time of working with Miss Wells, she made reference to a certifying symbol which she saw at the beginning and end of the project. I paid no attention to this at the time and do not know its nature. I was not interested in what gave her assurance as to the worth of what she was doing because to me, the test was how well the symbols worked, and I didn't expect them to work very well, although they proved quite remarkable.

The second factor in these symbols is something which carries out the boundary of knowing to thresholds where any assurance of truth is impossible and the investigation is beyond any kind of control as yet evolved by science. Many of the basic factors leading to the work I had done in the clarification of Astrology were gained by me out at and beyond this threshold, but I have only given serious attention to the results based upon such a foundation which have proved themselves in practice. I had never given out or passed on any of these suggestive things of themselves, but have checked carefully and shared the results when the results proved their value by the fact that they work. If the symbolical degrees were possible, they would have to rely for their origin upon these same materials. I decided that what had been done in a smaller way with Miss Wells might be done in a larger way with Miss Wheeler. I gave myself the task of watching or checking these factors of suggestiveness, using Miss Wheeler's mind for the visualization of an acceptable picture. I have no way of knowing the truth of the matter, but I am inclined to believe that I have been tapping in on a mine of old Sumerian culture or establishing some sort of psychological rapport with that forgotten civilization which first perfected Astrology. What I was trying to do was to re-create the same basic matrix used by John Thomas.

I knew from a considerable amount of research work done in Spiritualism, almost as much as I have done in Astrology, that certain physical factors were necessary. I took Miss Wheeler out in my car, arranging to keep her alone with me all day. We worked in four sections, doing a quarter of the degrees each time. We parked the car at a place in Balboa Park, San Diego, where we were cloistered as far as any chance of being spoken to or interrupted was concerned and at the same time were within a stone's throw of a very busy intersection of city streets and life. I used a series of blank cards of a size permitting them to be shuffled constantly, each of which was marked on the back with a sign and degree, and with 360 to cover the zodiac. Neither Miss Wheeler nor myself ever knew what degree was dealt with when she described the pictures she saw which I wrote down hurriedly as I selected the picture. At times, I would reject and sometimes she would correct. The cards were shuffled constantly so that a law of random selection in statistics could work, and I gave continual attention to checks of an occult sort. After an approximate quarter of the cards were done we rested, driving around the park and then returning to the location, where another quarter were done. Then I drove her well out of town to a place where we could have lunch with little chance of meeting anyone we knew. We finally returned for the last two quarters, which were done in the same fashion.

With this much accomplished, I put the cards away in a trunk carefully, deciding that this was stepping too far afield from the kind of scientific work in which I was interested, and thinking that I would keep in the realm of spiritualistic investigation. One day someone asked me if it were true that if the cards were lost it would be impossible to repeat the feat, granting it had any merit, and so I had the symbols that were roughly penciled on the cards copied in a typed script, giving the carbons to several of my students who did considerable astrological work and asking them as a matter of interest to check the pictures and see how they worked. Their reports were on the enthusiastic side so that I was encouraged to take the next step in putting down the mathematical structure of the whole and issued them for the research group in mimeograph form along with the other astrological mimeograph series.

The next step in the story was that Dane Rudhyar, with whom I shared all this mimeographed material at the time he was beginning his public astrological work in writing, became so interested in these symbols that he asked permission to incorporate them in an abridged form in his *The Astrology of Personality*. He was really instrumental in awakening a countrywide interest in these degrees. I am starting at the present time to prepare them for book publication and I am trying to find enough validated charts so that if possible, an example can be given of every planet in every degree in the horoscopes of well-known people. I figure that I have at least a two- or three-year task and I am afraid I may not be able to get enough charts to give the amount of illustrated application I would like. I may issue a general appeal for help in getting charts for this purpose.

MARC EDMUND JONES

ABOUT THE AUTHOR

Dane Rudhyar is probably the most widely respected astrologer today, but he is also a philosopher poet, novelist, composer, painter and aesthetic theoretician. Born in Paris in 1895, he came to America late in 1916. The next year his musical compositions were performed in New York along with works by Erik Satie and other French composers in the first performance of dissonant polytonal music in America. He became interested in astrology in 1920 and combined this interest with studies of Oriental philosophies and, after 1930, the psychology of Carl Jung. His widely acclaimed book *The Astrology of Personality* was originally published in 1936 and reissued in paperback in 1970. Since 1933 Rudhyar has written extensively for astrological publications and has published more than a dozen books in which he has developed a "humanistic" approach to the ancient science. In March 1972, radio station KPFA in San Francisco celebrated Rudhyar's seventy-seventh birthday with a retrospective of his work. His piano compositions have recently been performed from coast to coast and are now available in records. He is a popular lecturer and maintains an energetic schedule of appearances throughout the country.

VINTAGE FICTION, POETRY, AND PLAYS